Law Questions & Answers

EC LAW

Questions and Answers Series

Titles in the Series

'A' Level Law
Company Law
Constitutional and Administrative Law
Conveyancing
Criminal Law
EC Law
English Legal System
Equity and Trusts
Family Law
Land Law
Landlord and Tenant
Law of Contract
Law of Evidence
Law of Torts
Wills, Probate and Administration

Other titles in preparation

Law Questions & Answers

EC LAW

Third Edition

NIGEL G. FOSTER
BA, LLM, Dip German
Senior Lecturer in Law, University of Wales, Cardiff
Director, Law and German Degree

BLACKSTONE
PRESS LIMITED

Published by
Blackstone Press Limited
Aldine Place
London W12 8AA
United Kingdom

Sales enquiries and orders
Telephone +44-(0)-20-8740-2277
Facsimile +44-(0)-20-8743-2292
e-mail: sales@blackstone.demon.co.uk
website: www.blackstonepress.com

ISBN 1-84174-103-5
© Nigel G. Foster, 2001
© Second Edition Revisions Nigel G. Foster and Jackie M. Jones, 1998
First published 1994
Second edition 1998
Third edition 2001

British Library Cataloguing in Publication Data
A catalogue record for this book is available from the British Library

Typeset in 10/12pt Times by Style Photosetting Limited, Mayfield, East Sussex
Printed and bound in Great Britain by M & A Thomson Litho Limited, East Kilbride

Contents

Preface   vii

Table of Cases   ix

Table of Primary Legislation   xix

Table of European Community Secondary Legislation   xxiii

Abbreviations   xxv

1   Introduction   1

2   The Origins, Institutions and Development of the Communities,
    the Legislative Process and Budgetary Process   5

3   The Sources and Forms of Community Law   32

4   The Supremacy of Community Law and its Reception
    in the Member States   52

5   The Jurisdiction of the Court of Justice   75

6   The Free Movement of Goods   118

7   The Free Movement of Persons   141

Contents

8   Competition amd Merger Law   164

9   Sex Discrimination   191

10 Mixed Subject Questions   212

Bibliography   236

Index   239

Preface

This third edition of *Q & A EC Law* takes account of the developments which have occurred in EC law since the publication of the second edition in 1998. The most far-reaching change is the renumbering of the EC and European Union Treaties by the Treaty of Amsterdam, which has been taken account of throughout the text (see the further comments on this in Chapter One). Unfortunately, further treaty revision will take place following the Nice 2000 IGC and again following the next IGC proposed for 2004. Otherwise, the existing text has been updated to reflect changes in the law which have taken place and the opportunity has also been taken to make additional changes by replacing some questions where it was considered this assisted the presentation of topics. In the first edition, I wrote:

> Whilst, in some quarters, questions and answers books are not regarded too highly and they are fraught with danger in the wrong hands, they do fill an increasing gap in legal education as we struggle to keep up standards in the face of ever higher numbers. Consequently, there is not as much time today to see individual students and provide them with exam coaching or to go through or mark model questions which they have prepared. Hence, a book such as this, if used intelligently, can make up for less personal tuition and assist the student, not only in identifying the correct material and structure to provide in an answer but also to provide a method to test knowledge for exam revision and preparation and hopefully then to boost confidence before the exam itself. I hope therefore the comments and answers provided will succeed in these aims. I would be grateful to receive from any readers, comments on the range of topics, the contents of the answers and the style and presentation of the material in the book.

If not more so today, the above stands.

For errors and omissions in this material I am responsible. My continued thanks go to my colleagues; to Robin Churchill and Phil Fennell of Cardiff Law School for permission to use a number of questions formulated jointly and severally for tutorial, essay and exam questions used on the courses on European Community law over the last seventeen years; to the staff of Blackstone Press; and to the now c. 3,000 + students who have helped develop my approach to EC law teaching. Thanks again to research staff and secretarial staff who assisted on the previous editions and whose contribution survives in this edition. Thanks also to my secretary, Linda Mackleworth, for both general and specific support in helping me to get on with this and thanks to Jackie Jones with whom I made the revisions to the second edition. Thanks also to Dawn, Lynsey and Alexander at home who have understood, or at least said they have, my self-imposed isolation in my study whilst working on this third edition.

Nigel Foster
Cardiff
November 2000

Table of Cases

9/56 Meroni & Co. v High Authority [1957-58] ECR 133   117
7/61 Commission v Italy (Italian Pigmeat) [1961] ECR 317, [1962] CMLR 39   83
2 & 3/62 Commission v Luxembourg & Belgium (Gingerbread) [1962] ECR 425,
    [1963] CMLR 199   125
16 & 17/62 Confédération Nationale des Producteurs de Fruits et
    Légumes v Commission [1962] ECR 471, [1963] CMLR 160   88, 93
24/62 Germany v Commission (Re: Tariff Quotas on Wine) [1963] ECR 63,
    [1963] CMLR 347   94
25/62 Plaumann & Co. v Commission [1963] ECR 95, [1964] CMLR 29   89, 94
26/62 NV Algemene Transport en Expeditie Onderneming Van Gend en
    Loos v Nederlandse Administratie der Belastingen [1963] ECR 1, [1963] CMLR 105
        30, 35, 38, 42, 43, 44, 49, 50, 53, 54, 56, 58, 60, 62, 80,
        84, 108, 110, 120, 213, 214, 215, 216, 218, 220, 223
28-30/62 Da Costa en Schaake NV v Nederlandse Belastingadministratie
    [1963] ECR 31, [1963] CMLR 224   104, 106, 110
31 & 33/62 Milchwerke Heinz Wöhrmann v Commission [1962] ECR 501,
    [1963] CMLR 152   116, 227
75/63 Hoekstra v Bestuur der Bedrijfsvereniging voor Detailhandel en Ambachten
    [1964] ECR 177, [1964] CMLR 319   29
90 & 91/63 Commission v Belgium and Luxembourg [1964] ECR 625,
    [1965] CMLR 58   83
106 & 107/63 Alfred Toepfer KG v Commission [1965] ECR 405, [1966] CMLR 1   94
110/63 Willame v Euratom Commission [1965] ECR 649, [1966] CMLR 231   99
6/64 Costa v Ent Nazionale per l'Energia Elettrica (ENEL) [1964] ECR 585,
    [1964] CMLR 425   30, 53, 54, 56, 58, 60, 62, 64, 67, 73, 106, 213, 214, 215
56 & 58/64 Éstablissements Consten SA v Commission [1966] ECR 299,
    [1966] CMLR 418   171, 172, 174, 180
10/65 Deutschmann v Germany [1965] ECR 469, [1965] CMLR 259   126
32/65 Italy v Council [1966] ECR 389, [1969] CMLR 39   116
48/65 Alfons Lütticke GmbH v Commission [1966] ECR 19, [1966] CMLR 378   113, 227
61/65 Vaassen Göbbels v Beambtenfonds voor het Mijnbedrijf [1966] ECR 261,
    [1966] CMLR 508   108
5, 7 & 13-24/66 Firma E. Kampffmeyer v Commission [1967] ECR 245   97, 98, 99, 101
8-11/66 Cimenteries CBR Cementsbedrijven NV v Commission (Noordwijks
    Cement Accord) [1967] ECR 75, [1967] CMLR 77   88, 227

28/67 Molkerei-Zentrale Westfalen/Lippe GmbH v Hauptzollamt Paderborn
[1968] ECR 143, [1968] CMLR 187   126
7/68 Commission v Italy (Art Treasures) [1968] ECR 423, [1969] CMLR 1   79, 83, 120
10 & 18/68 Edridania v Commission [1969] ECR 459   113
24/68 Commission v Italy (Statistical Levy) [1969] ECR 193, [1971] CMLR 611   130
4/69 Alfons Lütticke GmbH v Commission [1971] ECR 325   96, 99
48/69 Imperial Chemical Industries Ltd v Commission (Dyestuffs) [1972] ECR 619,
[1972] CMLR 557   174, 176, 179
69/69 SA Alcan Aluminium Raeren v Commission [1970] ECR 385,
[1970] CMLR 337   89, 94
77/69 Commission v Belgium (Belgium Wood Case) [1970] ECR 243,
[1974] 1 CMLR 203   83
9/70 Grad v Finanzamt Traunstein [1970] ECR 825, [1971] CMLR 1   39, 42, 60
11/70 Internationale Handelsgesellschaft mbH v Einfuhr-und Vorratsstelle für
Getreide und Futtermittel [1970] ECR 1125, [1972] CMLR 255   55
15/70 Chevalley v Commission (1975) ECR 975   111, 112
22/70 Commission v Council (Re ERTA) [1971] ECR 263, [1971] CMLR 335   88
41-44/70 NV International Fruit Co. v. Commission [1971] ECR 411,
[1975] 2 CMLR 515   93
80/70 Defrenne v Belgium (No. 1) [1971] ECR 445, [1971] 1 CMLR 494
                                                                           195, 197, 209
5/71 Aktien-Zuckerfabrik Schöppenstedt v Council [1971] ECR 975
                                                      89, 96, 97, 98, 101, 102, 228
8/71 Deutscher Komponistenverband eV v Commission [1971] ECR 705,
[1973] CMLR 902   113
15/71 Firma C. Mackprang Jr v Commission [1971] ECR 797, [1972] CMLR 52   227
42/71 Nordgetreide GmbH & Co. KG v Commission [1972] ECR 105,
[1973] CMLR 177   112
48/71 Commission v Italy (Second Art Treasures) [1972] ECR 527 [1972] CMLR 699   79, 232
6/72 Europemballage Corporation v Commission [1973] ECR 215,
[1973] CMLR 199   181, 189
8/72 Cement Association (Vereeniging van Cementhandelaren) v Commission
[1972] ECR 977, [1973] CMLR 7   174, 180
21 & 22/72 International Fruit Company v Produktschap voor Groenten en Fruit (No. 3)
[1972] ECR 27, [1975] 2 CMLR 1   35
29/72 Marimex SpA v Minstero delle Finanze [1972] ECR 425,
[1973] CMLR 486   127, 131
39/72 Commission v Italy (Slaughtered Cows) [1973] ECR 101,
[1973] CMLR 439   37, 41, 83
76/72 S v Fonds National de Reclassement Sociales des Handicapés
[1973] ECR 457   150
2/73 Riseria Luigi Geddo v Ente Nazionale Risi [1973] ECR 865,
[1974] 1 CMLR 13   123, 136
6 & 7/73 Instituto Chemioterapico Italiano SpA v Commission, [1974] ECR 223,
[1974] 1 CMLR 309   167, 175, 181
40-48/73 Coöperativ e Vereniging 'Suiker Unie' (Sugar Union) v Commission
[1975] ECR 1663, [1976] 1 CMLR 295   175, 179, 185
134/73 Holtz & Willemsen GmbH v Council [1974] ECR 1   227
152/73 Sotgiu v Deutsche Bundespost [1974] ECR 153   144, 153
167/73 Commission v France (Re: French Maritime Code) [1974] ECR 359,
[1974] 2 CMLR 216   83, 133
169/73 Compagnie Continental France v Council [1975] ECR 117,
[1975] 1 CMLR 578   99
181/73 R. & V. Haegemann Sprl v Belgium [1974] ECR 449, [1975] 1 CMLR 515   35, 101

2/74 Reyners v Belgian State [1974] ECR 631, [1974] 2 CMLR 305   145, 161
8/74 Procureur du Roi v Dassonville [1974] ECR 837, [1974] 2 CMLR 436
                                    121, 122, 124, 129, 133, 134, 136, 138
17/74 Transocean Marine Paint Association v Commission, [1974] ECR 1063,
    [1974] 2 CMLR 459   28, 35
33/74 Van Binsbergen v Bestuur van de Bedrijfsvereniging voor de Metaalnijverheid
    [1974] ECR 1299, [1975] 1 CMLR 298   145, 150, 161, 162
41/74 Van Duyn v Home Office [1974] ECR 1337, [1975] 1 CMLR 1
                                        42, 50, 60, 149, 150, 159, 233
74/74 Comptoir National Technique Agricole (CNTA) SA v Commission
    [1975] ECR 533, [1977] 1 CMLR 171   97, 101
100/74 CAM SA v Commission [1975] ECR 1393   89
32/75 Fiorini aka Christini v SNCF [1975] ECR 1085, [1975] 1 CMLR 573   145
43/75 Defrenne v Sabena (No. 2) [1976] ECR 455, [1976] 2 CMLR 98
                                    44, 50, 194, 195, 197, 202, 207
87/75 Conceria Daniele Bresciani v Amministrazione delle Finanze [1976] ECR 129,
    [1976] 2 CMLR 62   35
26/76 Metro-SB-Grossmärkte GmbH & Co. KG v Commission [1977] ECR 1875,
    [1978] 2 CMLR 1   167, 171
27/76 United Brands Co. v Commission [1978] ECR 207, [1978] 1 CMLR 429   175, 180, 181
51/76 Verbond van Nederlandse Ondernemingen v Inspecteur der Invoerrechten
    en Accijnzen [1977] ECR 113, [1977] 1 CMLR 413   39, 49
64 & 113/76 P. Dumortier Frères SA v Council (Gritz and Quellmehl cases)
    [1979] ECR 3091   97, 98, 99, 101, 102, 103, 228
74/76 Ianelli & Volpi SpA v Meroni [1977] ECR 557, [1977] 2 CMLR 688   123, 127
83/76 Bayerische HNL Vermehrungsbetriebe GmbH & Co. KG v Council
    [1978] ECR 1209, [1978] 3 CMLR 566   98, 101, 102, 228, 229
101/76 Koninklijke Scholten-Honig NV (KSH) v Council [1977] ECR 797,
    [1980] 2 CMLR 669   88, 93
30/77 R v Bouchereau [1977] ECR 1999, [1977] 2 CMLR 800   149, 154
103 & 145/77 Royal Scholten-Honig (RSH) v Intervention Board for Agricultural
    Produce [1978] ECR 2037, [1979] 1 CMLR 675   101
106/77 Amministrazione delle Finanze dello Stato v Simmenthal SpA [1978] ECR 629,
    [1978] 3 CMLR 263   54, 55, 56, 58, 59, 60, 214, 215
113, 118-121/77 NTN Toyo Bearing Co. Ltd v Council (Japanese Ball-Bearings companies)
    [1979] ECR 1185, [1979] 2 CMLR 257   93
123/77 Unione Nazionale Importatori e Commercianti Motoveidoli Esteri (UNICME)
    v Commission [1978] ECR 845   89
143/77 Koninklijke Scholten-Honig NV (KSH) v Council (Isoglucose) [1979] ECR 3583,
    [1980] 2 CMLR 590   98, 101, 102, 228, 229
149/77 Defrenne v SABENA [1978] ECR 1365, [1978] 3 CMLR 312   195, 197
156/77 Commission v Belgium (Art 184) [1978] ECR 1881   117
22/78 Hugin Kassaregister AB v Commission [1979] ECR 1869 [1979] 3 CMLR 345   181
92/78 Simmenthal SpA v Commission [1979] ECR 777, [1980] 1 CMLR 25   73, 116, 117
93/78 Mattheus v Doego Fruchtimport und Tiefkühlkost eG [1978] ECR 2203,
    [1979] 1 CMLR 551   104
110-111/78 Ministere Public v Van Wesemael [1979] ECR 35, [1979] 3 CMLR 87   161
120/78 Rewe-Zentral AG v Bundesmonopolverwaltung für Branntwein (Cassis de Dijon)
    [1978] ECR 649, [1979] 3 CMLR 494
                118, 119, 122, 128, 129, 132, 134, 135, 136, 137, 138, 139, 140
125/78 Gesellschaft für Musikalische Aufführungs-und Mechanische Verfältigungsrechte
    (GEMA) v Commission [1979] ECR 3173, [1980] 2 CMLR 177   113
128/78 Commission v UK (Tachographs) [1979] ECR 419, [1979] 2 CMLR 45   37, 41
132/78 Denkavit Loire Sàrl v France [1979] ECR 1928, [1979] 3 CMLR 605   130

148/78 Pubblico Ministero v Ratti [1979] ECR 1629, [1980] 1 CMLR 96   49, 220, 223
152/78 Commission v France (Advertising of Alcoholic Beverages) [1980] ECR 2299,
     [1981] 2 CMLR 743   84
209-215 & 218/78 Van Landewyck Sàrl v Commission [1980] ECR 3125,
     [1981] 3 CMLR 134   186
230/78 Eridania Zuccherifici Nazionali SpA v Ministry of Agriculture and Forestry
     [1979] ECR 2749   39
231/78 Commission v UK (Import of Potatoes) [1979] ECR 1447,
     [1979] 2 CMLR 427   124
232/78 Commission v France (Import of Lamb) [1979] ECR 2729,
     [1980] 1 CMLR 418   83, 124
253/78 & 1–3/79 Procureur de la République v Giry, Guerlain SA, Rochas SA,
     Lanvin SA and Nina Ricci SA [1980] ECR 2327, [1981] 2 CMLR 99   171
34/79 R v Henn & Darby [1979] ECR 3795, [1980] 1 CMLR 246   122
44/79 Hauer v Land Rheinland-Pfalz, [1979] ECR 3727, [1980] 3 CMLR 42   34
90/79 Commission v France (Re: Reprographic Machines) [1981] ECR 283,
     [1981] 3 CMLR 1   126
98/79 Pecastaing v Belgium [1980] ECR 691, [1980] 3 CMLR 685   148, 153, 156
104/79 Foglia v Novello [1980] ECR 745, [1981] 1 CMLR 45   105, 106
129/79 Macarthy's Ltd v Smith [1980] ECR 1275, [1980] 2 CMLR 205   61
136/79 National Panasonic (UK) Ltd v Commission [1980] ECR 2033,
     [1980] 3 CMLR 169   184
138 & 139/79 SA Roquette Frères (Isoglucose cases) v Council
     [1980] ECR 3333 and 3393   18, 93, 101
149/79 Commission v Belgium (Re: Public Employees) [1980] ECR 3881,
     [1981] 2 CMLR   144
155/79 AM & S Europe Ltd v Commission [1982] ECR 1575, [1982] 2 CMLR 264   185
159/79 R v Pieck [1980] ECR 2171, [1980] 3 CMLR 220   154
66/80 International Chemical Corporation (ICC) SpA v Amministrazione delle
     Finanze dello Stato [1981] ECR 1191, [1983] 2 CMLR 593   107, 117
69/80 Worringham v Lloyds Bank Ltd [1981] ECR 767, [1981] 2 CMLR 1   50, 209
96/80 Jenkins v Kingsgate (Clothing Productions) Ltd [1981] ECR 911,
     [1981] 2 CMLR 241   196, 200, 204
113/80 Commission v Ireland (Metal Objects) [1981] ECR 1625,
     [1982] 1 CMLR 706   121
138/80 Borker [1980] ECR 1975, [1980] 3 CMLR 638   109
244/80 Foglia v Novello (No. 2) [1982] ECR 3045, [1982] 1 CMLR 585   105
246/80 Broekmeulen v HRC [1981] ECR 2311, [1982] 1 CMLR 92   109
12/81 Garland v British Rail Engineering Ltd [1982] ECR 359,
     [1982] 1 CMLR 696   50, 61, 196, 197
61/81 Commission v UK (Re: Equal Pay for Equal Work) [1982] ECR 2601,
     [1982] CMLR 284   200
102/81 Nordsee Deutsche Hochseefischerei GmbH v Reederei Mond Hochseefischerei
     Nordstern AG & Co. KG [1982] ECR 1095   109
104/81 Hauptzollamt Mainz v C.A. Kupferberg & Cie KG [1982] ECR 3641,
     [1983] 1 CMLR 1   35
115-116/81 Adoui v Belgium State [1982] ECR 1665, [1982] 3 CMLR 631   148, 153, 156
124/81 Commission v UK (Re: UHT Milk) [1983] ECR 203, [1983] 2 CMLR 1
     125, 129, 130, 133, 137
246/81 Lord Bethell v Commission [1982] ECR 2277, [1982] 3 CMLR 300   112, 227
249/81 Commission v Ireland (Re: Buy Irish campaign) [1982] ECR 4005,
     [1983] 2 CMLR 104   124
261/81 Walter Rau Lebensmittelwerke v De Smedt PVBA [1982] ECR 3961,
     [1983] 2 CMLR 496   103

283/81 CILFIT Srl v Ministro della Sanità [1982] ECR 3415, [1983] 1 CMLR 472
                                                                          28, 29, 106, 110
314-16/81 Procureur de la République v Waterkeyn [1982] ECR 4337,
    [1983] 2 CMLR 145   84
40/82 Commission v UK (Re: turkeys) [1982] ECR 2793, [1982] 3 CMLR 497   85, 133
42/82 Commission v France (Re: Italian Table Wines) [1983] ECR 1013,
    [1984] 1 CMLR 160   125, 130
286/82 Luisi v Ministero del Tesoro [1984] ECR 377, [1985] 3 CMLR 52   145
314/82 & 189/83 Commission v Belgium (Re: packaging of margarine)
    [1984] ECR 1543, [1985] 1 CMLR 120   124, 127, 131
13/83 European Parliament v Council (Re: Transport Policy) [1985] ECR 1513,
    [1986] 1 CMLR 138   112, 113, 114
14/83 von Colson v Land Nordrhein-Westfalen [1984] ECR 1891, [1986] 2 CMLR 430
                                        46, 47, 51, 68, 191, 196, 202, 207, 224, 233
16/83 Prantl [1984] ECR 1299, [1985] 2 CMLR 238   121
22/83 Liefting v University of Amsterdam [1984] ECR 3225,
    [1984] 3 CMLR 702   209, 210
63/83 R v Kirk [1984] ECR 2689, [1984] 3 CMLR 522   34
72/83 Campus Oil Ltd v Minister for Industry and Energy [1984] ECR 2727,
    [1984] 3 CMLR 544   121, 122
79/83 Harz v Deutsche Tradax GmbH [1984] ECR 1921, [1986] 2 CMLR 430   46
107/83 Ordre des Avocats au Barreau de Paris v Klopp [1984] ECR 2971,
    [1985], 1 CMLR 99   150
145/83 Adams v Commission [1986] 1 CMLR 506, [1986] 1 CMLR 506   186
249/83 Hoeckx v Openbaar Centrum voor Maatschappelijk Welzijn, Kalmthout
    [1985] ECR 973, [1987] 3 CMLR 633   153
261/83 Castelli v Office National des Pensions pour Travailleurs Salariés (ONPTS)
    [1984] ECR 3199, [1987] 1 CMLR 465   150
267/83 Diatta v Land Berlin [1985] ECR 567, [1986] 2 CMLR 674   145, 154
274/83 Commission v Italy (Public Works) [1985] ECR 1077 [1987] 1 CMLR 345   78
293/83 Gravier v City of Liège [1985] ECR 593, [1985] 3 CMLR 1   145
294/83 Partie Ecologiste 'Les Verts' v European Parliament [1986] ECR 1339,
    [1987] 2 CMLR 343   29
25 & 26/84 Ford Werke AG v Commission [1985] ECR 2725, [1985] 3 CMLR 528   188
75/84 Metro SB-Großmärkte GmbH & Co. KG v Commission [1986] ECR 3021,
    [1987] 1 CMLR 118   171
94/84 Office National d'Emploi (ONE) v Deak [1985] ECR 1873   145, 158
142 & 156/84 British American Tobacco Co. Ltd v Commission [1987] ECR 4487,
    [1988] 4 CMLR 24   188
152/84 Marshall v Southampton and South West Hampshire Area Health Authority
    (Teaching) [1986] ECR 725, [1986] 1 CMLR 688
                    40, 42, 43, 44, 45, 47, 49, 51, 68, 80, 191, 195, 196, 202, 207, 224
161/84 Pronuptia de Paris GmbH v Pronuptia de Paris Irmgard Schillgalis
    [1986] ECR 353, [1986] 1 CMLR 414   171
170/84 Bilka-Kaufhaus GmbH v Weber von Harz [1986] ECR 1607,
    [1986] 2 CMLR 701   196, 200, 204, 209, 211
178/84 Commission v Germany (Re Beer Purity Law) [1987] ECR 1262,
    [1988] 1 CMLR 780   124, 129, 130, 133, 139
205/84 Commission v Germany (Re: Insurance Services) [1986] ECR 3755,
    [1987] 2 CMLR 69   161, 162
222/84 Johnston v Chief Constable of the RUC [1986] ECR 1651,
    [1986] 3 CMLR 240   45, 196
53/85 AKZO Chemie BV v Commission [1986] ECR 1965 [1987] 1CMLR 231   186
59/85 Netherlands v Reed [1986] ECR 1283, [1987] 2 CMLR 448   145, 149, 157

66/85 Lawrie-Blum v Land Baden-Württemberg [1986] ECR 2121,
  [1987] 3 CMLR 389   144, 148
89, 104/85 & 125-29/85 Ahlström OY v Commission (Woodpulp case) [1988] ECR 5193,
  [1988] 4 CMLR 901   174, 176, 179, 181
133-136/85 Walter Rau v BALM [1985] ECR 2289   106
139/85 Kempf v Staatssecretaris van Justitie [1986] ECR 1741,
  [1987] 1 CMLR 764   144, 153
150/85 Drake v Chief Adjudication Officer [1986] ECR 1995, [1986] 3 CMLR 43   195
192/85 Newstead v Department of Transport [1987] ECR 4753, [1988] 1 CMLR 219   209
314/85 Foto-Frost v Hauptzollamt Lübeck-Ost [1987] ECR 4199, [1988] 3 CMLR 57   107
316/85 Centre Public d'Aide Sociale de Courcelles v Lebon [1987] ECR 2811,
  [1989] 1 CMLR 337   144, 158
407/85 Drei Glocken GmbH v USL Centro-Sud (Pasta Purity) [1988] ECR 4233   130
427/85 Commission v Germany (Re: Lawyers' Services) [1988] ECR 1123,
  [1989] 2 CMLR 677   150
39/86 Lair v Universität Hannover [1988] ECR 3161, [1989] 3 CMLR 545   29, 145
65/86 Bayer AG v Süllhöfer [1988] ECR 5249, [1990] 4 CMLR 182   171
68/86 UK v Council (Hormones) [1988] ECR 855, [1988] 2 CMLR 453   24, 25
80/86 Officier van Justitie v Kolpinghuis Nijmegen BV [1987] ECR 3969
  [1989] 2 CMLR 18   46, 51, 224
157/86 Murphy v An Bord Telecom Eireann [1988] ECR 673,
  [1988] 1 CMLR 879   200
302/86 Commission v Denmark (Re: Disposable Beer Cans) [1988] ECR 4607,
  [1989] 1 CMLR 619   134
18/87 Commission v Germany [1988] ECR 5427, [1990] 1 CMLR 561   131
29/87 Dansk Denkavit ApS v Danish Ministry of Agriculture [1988] ECR 2965,
  [1990] 1 CMLR 203   127
45/87 Commission v Ireland (Re: Dundalk Water Supply) [1988] ECR 4929,
  [1989] 1 CMLR 225   120
46/87 and 227/88 Hoechst AG v Commission [1989] ECR 2859,
  [1991] 4 CMLR 410   184, 185
85/87 Dow Benelux NV v Commission [1989] ECR 3137, [1991] 4 CMLR 410   185, 187
196/87 Steymann v Staatssecretaris van Justitie [1988] ECR 6159,
  [1989] 1 CMLR 449   144
242/87 Commission v Council (Erasmus) [1989] ECR 1425, [1991] 1 CMLR 478   23
274/87 Commission v Germany (Sausage Purity Law) [1989] ECR 250,
  [1989] 2 CMLR 733   124, 133, 134
267/87 R v Royal Pharmaceutical Society of Great Britain, ex parte Association
  of Pharmaceutical Importers [1989] ECR 1295, [1989] 2 CMLR 751   124
298/87 Proceedings for Compulsory Reconstruction against Smanor SA
  [1988] ECR 4489   130
302/87 European Parliament v Council (Comitology) [1988] ECR 5615   29
374/87 Orkem v Commission [1989] ECR 3283, [1991] 4 CMLR 502   185
33/88 Allué and Coonan v Università degli Studi di Venezia [1989] ECR 1591,
  [1991] 1 CMLR 283   144
C-47/88 Commission v Denmark [1990] ECR 3917   127
C-70/88 European Parliament v Council (Chernobyl) [1990] ECR I-2041,
  [1992] 1 CMLR 91   29
109/88 Handels- og Kontorfunktionaerernes Forbund i Danmark v Dansk
  Arbejdsgiverforening (Danfoss) [1989] ECR 3199, [1991] 1 CMLR 8   200, 204
C-143/88 & C-92/89 Zuckerfabrik Süderdithmarschen AG v Hauptzollamt Itzehoe
  [1991] ECR I-415, [1993] 3 CMLR 337   107
C-152/88 Sofrimport Sàr v Commission [1990] ECR I-2477,
  [1990] 3 CMLR 80   98, 101, 102, 103, 229

Table of Cases
XV

C-262/88 Barber v Guardian Royal Exchange Assurance Group [1990] ECR 1944,
[1990] 2 CMLR 513   31, 196, 203, 205, 206, 207, 208, 209, 210, 211
C-104/89 & 37/90 Mulder v Council [1992] ECR I-3061   98, 102, 228
C-106/89 Marleasing SA v La Comercial Internacional de Alimentación SA [1990]
ECR I-4135, [1992] 1 CMLR 305   46, 47, 51, 61, 202, 207, 224
C-188/89 Foster v British Gas plc [1990] ECR I-3313, [1991] 2 CMLR 217   45
C-213/89 R v Secretary of State for Transport, ex parte Factortame Ltd
[1990] ECR I-2433, [1990] 3 CMLR 1   56, 59, 61, 69, 220
C-221/89 R v Secretary of State for Transport, ex parte Factortame Ltd
[1991] ECR I-3905, [1991] 3 CMLR 589   69, 149
C-246/89R Commission v UK (Factortame) [1989] ECR 3125,
[1991] 3 CMLR 601   80, 234
C-246/89 Commission v UK (Factortame) [1991] ECR I-4585 [1991] 3 CMLR 706   160, 232
C-292/89 R v Immigration Appeal Tribunal, ex parte Antonissen [1991] ECR I-745,
[1991] 2 CMLR 373   144, 149, 157
C-294/89 Commission v France (Re: Lawyers Services) [1991] ECR I-3591,
[1993] 3 CMLR 569   150
C-300/89 Commission v Council (Re: Titanium Dioxide Directive) [1990] ECR I-2867,
[1993] 3 CMLR 359   25
C-309/89 Codorniu SA v Commission [1994] ECR I-1853,
[1995] 2 CMLR 561   88, 89, 93, 94
C-357/89 Raulin v Netherlands Ministry of Education and Science
[1992] ECR I-1027 [1994] 1 CMLR 227   148
C-3/90 Bernini v Netherlands Ministry of Education and Science
[1990] ECR I-1017   145
C-6 & 9/90 Francovich v Italy [1991] ECR I-5357, [1993] 2 CMLR 66, [1992] IRLR 84
46, 47, 51, 57, 74, 80, 85, 111, 202, 207, 220, 224, 233
C-60/90 European Parliament v Council [1992] ECR I-4593   18
C-76/90 Säger v Dennemeyer and Co. Ltd [1991] ECR I-4221,
[1993] 3 CMLR 639   151, 159, 162
C-159/90 Society for the Protection of Unborn Children Ltd (SPUC) v Grogan
[1991] ECR I-4685, [1991] 3 CMLR 849   104
C-195/90R Commission v Germany (Re: Lorry Tax) [1990] ECR I-3351   80
C-295/90 European Parliament v Council (Students Residence Directive)
[1992] ECR I-4193, [1992] 3 CMLR 281   25, 29
C-83/91 Meilicke v ADV/ORGA [1992] ECR I-4871   105
C-109/91 Ten Oever v Stichting Bedriftspensioenfonds voor het Glazenwassers
[1993] ECR I-4879, [1995] 2 CMLR 357   211
C-111/91 Commission v Luxembourg [1993] ECR I-817, [1994] 2 CMLR 781   158
C-152/91 Neath v Hugh Steeper [1993] ECR I-6935, [1995] 2 CMLR 357   211
C-155/91 Commission v Council (Waste Directive) [1993] ECR I-939   25
C-169/91 Stoke-on-Trent City Council v B & Q plc [1992] ECR I-6635,
[1993] 1 CMLR 426   138
C-200/91 Coloroll Pension Trustees ITD v Russell [1994] ECR I-4389,
[1995] 2 CMLR 357   211
C-220/91P Stahlwerke Peine-Salzgitter v Commission [1993] ECR I-2393   98, 101
C-267 & 268/91 Keck and Mithouard [1993] ECR I-6097,
[1995] 1 CMLR 101   122, 134, 136, 138, 139
C-325/91 France v Commission [1993] ECR I-3283   94
C-36/92 P Samenwerkende Elektriciteits-produktiebedrijven NV v Commission
[1994] ECR I-1911, [1992] 4 CMLR 434   185
C-91/92 Faccini Dori v Recreb Srl [1994] ECR I-3325, [1995] 1 CMLR 665   45, 46, 51
C-127/92 Enderby v Frenchay Health Authority, [1993] ECR I-5535,
[1994] 1 CMLR 8   200

C-188/92 TWD Textilwerke Deggendorf GmbH v Germany [1994] ECR I-833,
[1995] 2 CMLR 145   105
C-334/92 Wagner Miret v Fondo di Garantia Salarial [1993] ECR I-6911,
[1995] 2 CMLR 49   47
C-401 & 402/92 Tankstation't Heukste vof and JBE Boermans [1994] ECR I-2199,
[1995] 3 CMLR 501   139
C-32/93 Webb v EMO Air Cargo (UK) Ltd [1994] ECR I-3567   195
C-46 & 48/93 Brasserie du Pêcheur SA v Germany and Factortame v UK
[1996] ECR I-1029, [1996] 1 CMLR 889   46, 47, 57, 72, 85, 86, 111, 220, 224, 233, 234
C-57/93 Vroege v NCIV Instituut [1994] ECR I-4541, [1995] 1 CMLR 881   211
C-128/93 Fisscher v Voorhuis Hengelo BV [1994] ECR I-4583, [1995] 1 CMLR 881   211
C-384/93 Alpine Investments BV v Minister of Finance [1995] ECR I-1141,
[1995] 2 CMLR 209   160
C-392/93 R v HM Treasury, ex parte British Telecommunications plc [1996] ECR I-1631,
[1996] 2 CMLR 217   47, 51, 81, 225
C-5/94 R v Ministry of Agriculture, Fisheries and Food, ex parte Hedley Lomas
(Ireland) Ltd [1996] ECR I-2553, [1996] 2 CMLR 391   47, 80, 85, 225, 234
C-13/94 P v S and Cornwall County Council [1996] ECR I-2143,
[1996] 2 CMLR 247   202
C-55/94 Gebhard v Consiglio dell'Ordine degli Avvocati [1995] ECR I-4165,
[1996], 1 CMLR 603   151, 159, 162
C-63/94 Groupement National des Négociants en Pommes de Terre
de Belgique v SA ITM Belgium (Belgapom) [1995] ECR I-2467   139
C-68/94 France v Commission [1998] ECR I-1375,
[1998] 4 CMLR 829   177, 182, 189–90
C-84/94 UK v Council [1996] ECR I-5755, [1996] 3 CMLR 671   26
C-178, 179, 188 & 190/94 Dillenkofer v Germany [1996] ECR I-4845,
[1996] 3 CMLR 469   51, 81, 85
C-30/95 Societe Commerciale des Potasses et de l'Azote (SCPA) v Commission
[1998] ECR I-1375, [1998] 4 CMLR 829   177, 182, 190
C-68/95 T. Port GmbH & Co. KG v Bundesanstalt für Landeswirtschaft und
Ernährung [1996] ECR I-6065, [1997] 1 CMLR 1   112, 227
C-94 & 95/95 Bonifaci v Instituto Nazionale della Previdenza Sociale,
[1997] ECR I-3969 [1998] 1 CMLR 257   51
C-368/95 Vereinigte Familiapress Zeitungsverlags- und vertriebs GmbH v Heinrich
Bauer Verlag, [1997] ECR I-3689 [1997] 3 CMLR 1329   122, 139
C-392/95 Parliament v Council [1997] ECR I-3213, [1997] 3 CMLR 896   18
C-400/95 Handels-og Kontorfunktionaerernes Forbund I Danmark v Dansk Handel &
Service [1997] ECR I-2757, [1997] 2 CMLR 915   201
C-408/95 Eurotunnel SA et al v Sea France [1997] ECR I-6315,
[1998] 2 CMLR 293   106
C-409/95 Hellmut Marschall v Land Nordrhein-Westfalen [1997] ECR I-6363
[1998] 1 CMLR 547   196, 201, 205
C-22/96 European Parliament v Council (data exchange) [1998] ECR I-3231,
[1999] 1 CMLR 160   25
C-54/96 Dorsch Consult Ingenieurgesellschaft mnH v Bundesbaugesellschaft
Berlin mbH [1997] ECR I-4961, [1998] 2 CMLR 237   109
C-324 & 325/96 Deutsche Telekom v Vick Judgment of the ECJ 10 February 2000   194
C-394/96 Brown v Rentokil [1998] ECR I-4185, [1998] 2 CMLR 1049   201
C-395 & 396/96P Compagnie Maritime Belge Transports SA et al v Commission
[2000] All ER (EC) 385   175, 180, 190
C-158/97 G Badeck et al v Land Hessen [2000] All ER (EC) 289, The Times,
31 March 2000   202, 205
C-185/97 Coote v Granada [1998] ECR I-5199, [1998] 3 CMLR 958   201

C-333/97 Susanne Lewen v Lothar Denda [2000] 2 CMLR 38   201
C-387/97 Commission v Greece (Re Non-Compliance Penalties) Judgment of the
  ECJ 4 July 2000   80

Decisions of the Court of First Instance

T-7/89 SA Hercules Chemicals NV v Commission [1991] ECR II-1711,
  [1992] 4 CMLR 84   174
T-9/89 Hüls Ag v Commission [1992] ECR II-499   174
T-11/89 Shell International Chemical Co. Ltd v Commission [1992] ECR II-757   174
T-30/89 Hilti A G v Commission [1990] ECR II-163 [1990] 4 CMLR 16   185
T-51/89 Tetra Pak Rausing v Commission [1990] ECR II-309, [1991] 4 CMLR 334   175, 181
T-3/90 Prodifarma v Commission [1991] ECR II-1   28

Decisions of the European Commission

80/334 Fabbrica Pisana [1980] 2 CMLR 354   185
88/172 Konica v Commission [1988] 4 CMLR 848   171
IV/M37 Matsushita/MCA [1992] 4 CMLR M36   176

UK Courts

B & Q Ltd v Shrewsbury and Atcham Borough Council [1990] 3 CMLR 535   138
Bourgoin SA v Ministry of Agriculture, Fisheries and Food [1986] QB 716
  [1986] 1 CMLR 267 and [1987] 1 CMLR 169   85
British Railways Board v Pickin [1974] AC 765   63
Burmah Oil Co. Ltd v Lord Advocate [1965] AC 75   63
Doughty v Rolls Royce plc; see Rolls-Royce plc v Doughty
Duke v GEC Reliance Ltd [1988] AC 618, [1988] 1 CMLR 719, [1988] 1 All ER 626,
  [1988] 2 WLR 359   45, 68, 73
Ellen Street Estates Ltd v Minister of Health [1934] 1 KB 590   63
Garland v British Rail Engineering Ltd [1983] 2 AC 751, [1982] 2 CMLR 174   64, 68
Litster v Forth Dry Dock & Engineering Co. Ltd [1990] 1 AC 546, [1989] IRLR 161   68
Macarthys Ltd v Smith [1979] ICR 785, [1979] 3 All ER 325, [1979] 3 CMLR 44;
  subsequent proceedings [1981] QB 180 at 199, [1980] ICR 672 at 692,
  [1981] 1 All ER 111 at 120, [1980] 2 CMLR 217   64, 67, 70, 233
Marshall v Southampton and South West Hants Health Authority [1988] 3 CMLR 389   224
Mortensen v Peters (1906) 8 F(J) 93   63
Pickstone v Freemans plc [1989] AC 66, [1988] 3 CMLR 221   68, 195
R v Secretary of State for Employment, ex parte EOC [1995] 1 CMLR 395   65, 69
R v Secretary of State for Transport, ex parte Factortame Ltd (No. 1)
  [1989] 3 CMLR 1, [1990] 2 AC 85
R v Secretary of State for Transport, ex parte Factortame Ltd (No. 2) [1991] 1 AC 603
  at 645, [1991] 1 All ER 70 at 106 (sub nom. Factortame Ltd v Secretary of State
  for Transport (No. 2))   65, 233
Rolls-Royce plc v Doughty [1992] ICR 538, [1992] 1 CMLR 1045
  (sub nom. Doughty v Rolls Royce plc), [1992] IRLR 126   45
Torfaen Borough Council v B & Q plc [1990] 3 CMLR 455   138
Vauxhall Estates Ltd v Liverpool Corporation [1932] 1KB 733   63

Belgian Courts

Minister for Economic Affairs v SA Fromagerie 'Le Ski' [1972] CMLR 330   71

Table of Cases

German Courts

Internationale Handelsgesellschaft ('Solange I') [1974] 2 CMLR 540   36, 71
Brunner v European Union Treaty (TEU) [1994] 1 CMLR 57   72
Federal Tax Case of 9/1/1996, 7 EuZW 126 (1996)   72
Wünsche Handelsgesellschaft ('Solange II') [1987] 3 CMLR 225   71

Italian Courts

Fragd, SpA v Amministrazione delle Finanze, noted by Gaja in (1990)
    27 CML Rev pp 93–5   73
Granital, SpA v Amministrazione delle Finanze Judgment of 8 June 1984
    [1984] 1 Giur It 1521, noted by Gaja in (1984) 21 CML Rev pp 756–72   73

French Courts

Boisdet [1991] 1 CMLR 3   74
Café Vabre [1975] 2 CMLR 336 & noted in 16 CML Rev 367   73
Dangeville, Société J. (1 July 1992 decision of the Paris Administrative Court
    of Appeal)   74
Garage Dehus Sarl v Bouche Distribution [1984] 3 CMLR 452   74
Minister of the Interior v Cohn-Bendit [1980] 1 CMLR 543   74
Nicolo [1990] 1 CMLR 173   74
Rothmans International France SA [1993] 1 CMLR 253   74

Table of Primary Legislation

EC Legislation

EC Treaty   vii, 2, 3, 8, 11, 12, 13, 15, 27,
28, 30, 33, 36, 37, 38, 39, 40, 42, 43,
44, 46, 53, 54, 55, 57, 58, 59, 63, 65,
67, 69, 74, 75, 80, 94, 96, 105, 111,
114, 115, 118, 119, 120, 122, 128, 142,
143, 150, 152, 161, 165, 176, 183, 184,
193, 197, 198, 199, 204, 213, 214, 216,
217, 219, 225, 229, 232
Preamble   13, 119, 165, 169, 173, 186,
187, 194
Part 3
Title 1   118
art.2   13, 119, 159, 165, 166, 167, 168,
169, 173, 186, 187, 196
art.3   13, 14, 114, 119, 159, 165, 169,
173, 186, 196, 218
art.3(g) (ex 3(f))   166, 167, 173, 187
art.4 (ex 3a)   13
art.10 (ex 5)   46, 51, 54, 55, 57, 62, 119,
166, 214, 222, 224, 231
art.12 (ex 6)   54, 57, 62, 119, 157, 158,
160, 214
art.12 (ex 7)   55, 145
art.13   197
art.14(2) (ex 7a)   119
art.23-art.24 (ex 9–10)   118, 120, 123,
125, 126, 127, 128, 130
art.25 (ex 12)   38, 118, 120, 123, 125,
126, 127, 128, 130, 131, 216
art.26-art.27 (ex 28–29)   118, 119, 120
art.27 (ex 29)   118, 119, 120

EC Treaty – *continued*
art.28 (ex 30)   118, 119, 120, 121, 122,
123, 124, 125, 126, 127, 128, 129,
130, 131, 132, 133, 134, 135, 136,
137, 138, 139
art.29 (ex 34)   80, 118, 120, 121, 128,
134, 135, 136, 137
art.30 (ex 36)   118, 119, 120, 121, 122,
127, 128, 129, 130, 132, 133, 134,
135, 136, 137, 138
art.31 (ex 37)   118
art.34 (ex 40)   229
art.34(2) (ex 40(3))   101, 225, 228, 229
art.39 (ex 48)   13, 142, 143, 144, 148,
152, 156, 157, 230, 231, 233
art.39 (ex 48(2))   153
art.39 (ex 48(3))   149, 232
art.39 (ex 48(3)(b))   157
art.39 (ex 48(4))   144, 151, 153, 232
art.40 (ex 49)   23, 142, 143, 148, 152,
156
art.41-art.42 (ex 50–51)   142, 143, 148,
152, 156
art.43 (ex 52)   142, 143, 145, 148, 160,
161, 163
art.44 (ex 54)   17, 18, 148, 160
art.45 (ex 55)   148, 160
art.46 (ex 56)   18, 148, 160
art.47 (ex 57)   148, 160, 161
art.48 (ex 58)   148, 160
art.49 (ex 59)   145, 148, 150, 160, 161,
162
art.50 (ex 60)   145, 148, 160

EC Treaty – *continued*
art.50 (ex 60(1))   160
art.50 (ex 60(3))   161
art.51 (ex 61)   114, 148, 160
art.52 (ex 63)   148, 160
art.53-art.55 (ex 64–66)   148, 160
art.70-art.71 (ex 74–75)   114
art.80 (ex 84)   114
art.81 (ex 85)   13, 87, 164, 166, 167,
    169, 171, 172, 173, 174, 176,
    178, 179, 183, 186, 187, 188,
    189, 190
art.81 (ex 85(1))   170, 171, 172, 173,
    174, 175, 179, 181, 187, 190
art.81 (ex 85(1)(a))   180
art.81 (ex 85(1)(b)-(c))   174
art.81 (ex 85(2))   169, 172, 173, 179,
    187
art.81 (ex 85(3))   170, 171
art.82 (ex 86)   13, 87, 164, 167, 169,
    173, 174, 175, 176, 177, 178, 180,
    181, 182, 183, 186, 187, 188, 189,
    190
art.82 (ex 86)(a)   181
art.82 (ex 86)(b)   181
art.83 (ex 87)   183
art.85 (ex 89)   167, 183
art.90 (ex 95)   73, 120, 123, 125, 126,
    127, 128, 130
art.90 (ex 95(1)-(2))   126
art.94 (ex 100)   15, 25, 26
art.95 (ex 100a)   24, 25
art.140 (ex 118)   208, 210
art.141 (ex 119)   14, 44, 45, 47, 50,
    51, 193, 194, 196, 197, 199,
    200, 202, 204, 206, 207, 208,
    209, 210, 211
art.141(4)   201, 202, 205
art.189 (ex 137)   16, 20
art.192 (ex 138b)   21
art.202 (ex 145)   15, 16, 20
art.203-art.210 (ex 146–154)   15
art.211 (ex 155)   16, 231
art.212-art.219 (ex 156–163)   16
art.220 (ex 164)   28, 35
art.221-art.223 (ex 165–167)   27
art.226 (ex 169)   28, 75, 77, 78, 79,
    80, 81, 82, 84, 85, 106, 197,
    221, 222, 223, 230, 231, 232,
    234
art.227 (ex 170)   28, 75, 84, 106
art.228 (ex 171)   28, 54, 75, 79, 80, 214,
    222, 223, 232
art.229 (ex 172)   29, 79, 223, 232

EC Treaty – *continued*
art.230 (ex 173)   28, 29, 35, 75, 86,
    87, 88, 89, 91, 92, 94, 95, 96,
    97, 100, 105, 111, 112, 113,
    115, 116, 117, 185, 219, 225,
    226, 227, 229
art.231 (ex 174)   28
art.232 (ex 175)   28, 75, 96, 100,
    111, 112, 113, 114, 117, 219,
    226, 227
art.233 (ex 176(1))   114
art.234 (ex 177)   28, 72, 73, 75, 80, 82,
    84, 91, 95, 103, 104, 105, 106, 107,
    108, 109, 110, 117, 158, 200, 220,
    221, 229, 233, 235
art.234 (ex 177(3))   106
art.235 (ex 178)   28, 75, 85, 95, 96, 228
art.236-art.240 (ex 176–183)   28
art.241 (ex 184)   28, 75, 115, 116, 117,
    219, 226, 227, 229
art.242 (ex 185)   28
art.243 (ex 186)   28, 80, 234
art.244-art.245 (ex 187–188)   28
art.249 (ex 189)   33, 35, 37, 38, 40, 41,
    46, 48, 51, 54, 55, 58, 60, 62, 88, 92,
    93, 214, 216, 224
art.250 (ex 189)   13
art.251 (ex 189)   13
art.251 (ex 189b)   19, 21, 23
art.252 (ex 189)   13, 19
art.253 (ex 190)   94
art.272 (ex 203(8))   20
art.288 (ex 215)   75, 95, 99, 100, 186
art.288(2) (ex 215(2))   36, 47, 85, 96,
    100, 117, 219, 224, 226, 227, 228,
    234
art.292 (ex 219)   54, 58, 62, 214, 222
art.300 (ex 228)   35
art.308 (ex 235)   17, 25, 26
art.310 (ex 238)   35
EC Treaty (old numbering)
art.7   25
art.43   25
art.118a   26
art.130s   25
Euratom Treaty   8
European Coal and Steel Community
    Treaty   7

Single European Act 1986   11, 14, 15, 16,
    17, 18

Treaty of Amsterdam   vii, 2, 3, 11, 15, 17,
    21, 34, 118, 120, 196, 199, 204, 232

Treaty on European Union 1992   vii, 2, 11,
    12, 14, 15, 17, 18, 21, 74, 79, 112,
    223
art.6 (ex F2)   34
art.6(2) (ex F2)   220
art.49 (ex O)   34
German Accession Statute   72
Protocol II   206

Statute of the Court of Justice
    art.18   27

Member States'
Constitutions and Legislation

Belgium
Constitution
art.25a   71

France
Constitution
    art.55   73, 74
    art.88   74, 83

Germany
Constitution (Grundgesetz)   71, 72
    art.24   71, 72
    art.25   71
    art.101(1)   72

Italy
Constitution
    art.11   73

United Kingdom
European Communities Act 1972   61,
    63, 64, 65, 66, 67, 68, 69, 229, 231,
    233
    s.2(1)   64, 67, 68
    s.2(2)   67
    s.2(4)   64, 67, 68, 69, 70
    s.3(1)-(2)   64, 67
Merchant Shipping Act   86

International Treaties and
Conventions

European Convention on Human
    Rights   34, 36, 220
EEC-Portugal association agreement   35

GATT   35

Yaoundé Convention   35

Table of European Community Secondary Legislation

Directive 64/221   148, 153, 156
    art.1   153
    art.3(1)   149, 159
    art.3(2)   149, 154
    art.3(3)   154
    art.4   154
    art.6   159
    art.7   148, 153, 156
    art.9   148, 153, 156
    annex   150
Directive 68/360   153
Directive 70/50   120, 129, 136
    art.2   120, 124, 136
    art.3   124, 133, 137
Directive 75/117   45, 195, 200, 209
    art.5   201
Directive 76/207   195, 196, 201, 209
    art.2   200
    art.2(4)   201, 204
    art.3(1)   205
    art.6   46, 201, 202, 205
Directive 187/77   69
Directive 77/249   150
    art.4(1)   150
    art.5   150
Directive 79/7   195
Directive 86/378   47, 48, 195, 196, 211
Directive 86/613   195, 196
Directive 90/364   157
    art.1   157
Directive 90/366   25
Directive 91/156   25

Directive 92/85   195, 201
    art.11   201
Directive 96/34   195
Directive 96/97   211
Directive 97/7
    art.7   206
Directive 97/80   195
Directive 97/81   195
Directive 89/428   25

Regulation 17/62   87, 113, 167, 183, 184
    art.1-art.3   184
    art.4   170, 184
    art.5-art.10   184
    art.11   184
    art.11(5)   184
    art.12-art.13   184
    art.14   184, 185
    art.14(2)-(3)   184
    art.15   184, 185
    art.15(1)(c)   185
    art.16   184
    art.16(1)(c)-(d)   185
    art.17-art.18   184
    art.19   184, 186
    art.20   186
Regulation 1612/68   154, 157
    art.7(2)   145, 149, 150, 153, 157, 158
    art.10   157
    art.10(1)(b)   150
    art.10(2)   158
    art.12   150

Regulation 1483/83   169
Regulation 1484/83   169
Regulation 4087/88   169
Regulation 4064/89   176, 178, 179, 181,
   182, 188, 189, 190
   art.1   176, 181, 182
   art.1(3)   181
   art.2   177, 182
   art.4(1)   177, 182

Regulation 4064/89 – *continued*
   art.14   177, 182
Regulation 2/99   91
Regulation 4/99   91
Regulation 2790/1999   169
   art.2(1)   170
   art.3-art.5   170
   art.9   170

Abbreviations

AG	Advocate General
CAP	Common Agricultural Policy
CFI	Court of First Instance
CMLR	Common Market Law Reports
Court of First Instance	The Court of First Instance of the European Communities
Court of Justice	The European Court of Justice
EC	European Community/ies
ECA	European Communities Act 1972
ECB	European Central Bank
ECHR	European Convention on Human Rights
ECJ	European Court of Justice
ECR	European Court Reports
EEC	European Economic Community
EMU	Economic and Monetary Union
EP	European Parliament
ERTA	European Road Transport Agreement
EU	European Union
GATT	General Agreement on Tariffs and Trade
plc	Public Limited Company
QMV	Qualified Majority Voting
SDA	Sex Discrimination Act
SEA	Single European Act
TEU	Treaty on European Union
ToA	Treaty of Amsterdam

1 Introduction

This book is written to provide a number of example questions on EC law which should be fairly typical of those met on degree level courses on EC law. The questions are then followed by a few sentences or paragraphs of comment on the type of question, the main aspects to be considered in the question, advice on particular issues to be aware of and advice on structuring your answer. The commentaries are then followed by suggested answers. These are designed to demonstrate how the particular questions should be answered to get a good mark, i.e., an upper second or better. They are not model answers which can be learnt by heart and applied to answer any question on a particular topic, although I have often seen this attempted. It doesn't work because for the most part the candidate simply fails to answer the question set. There is no harm, however, in being able to adapt parts of these answers to particular questions provided that you are answering the question. The answers have been designed as exam type answers rather than answers for assessed course work, which would usually require far more detail.

Furthermore, this book is not a replacement for work, either for preparation for tutorials or seminars or for revision for the examination. If used carefully, it will help you prepare answers but will not help you learn the material in the first place. It does not present the answers in a systematic way but instead selects particular issues within questions on which to concentrate. It also worth pointing out that the choice of example cases provided within some if not most of the answers is rather limited, especially in comparison with textbooks and some of the cases and materials books. This is deliberate because for the most part, one case will be sufficient authority for the points of law you wish to convey in answer to the question set. This is also a realistic approach bearing in mind that in an examination you will not have time to reproduce a large number of cases, but by necessity must concentrate your attention upon a smaller number of clearly relevant cases. For the most part I have sought to use the leading and more popular cases in EC law as example cases. Don't worry however if these do not coincide with the cases you have read, learnt or have been referred to. As long as they cover the same issue or point, they are perfectly acceptable alternatives in an examination. It is the legal point at issue and not necessarily the particular case authority.

A brief mention will be made here in respect of the terms European Union and European Community as their use can be confusing. The term European Union was brought in by the Treaty on European Union (also known and referred to as the Maastricht Treaty) and describes the extension by the Member States into additional policies and areas of cooperation. The EU consists of three pillars comprising the existing Communities (the three original treaties), a common foreign and security policy and, following the reorganisation by the Treaty of Amsterdam, a third pillar now called Provisions on Judicial and Police cooperation in Criminal Matters. Although most text books describe themselves now as textbooks on EU law, the Court of Justice has very little jurisdiction over the two new pillars, and most Community law courses, whether called EU law or EC law are not likely to consider the law of the second and third pillars in any depth, if at all. Most courses will study EC law only, as contained in the EC Treaty and will not consider the parts of the EU outside of the EC Treaty. Hence then the term EC law has been retained for this book.

It must be assumed in a book of this nature that you have already completed your course, or in the case of particular topics, that you have completed those topics before consulting the suggested answers here. It is also assumed that you are already familiar with the statutory provisions of Community law and the case law of the European Court of Justice so that references to a case by one name or by a short title will be enough for you to identify the case. Therefore, in order to avoid cluttering up the text, the references to cases will be to the name of the case and the case docket number as given to it by the European Court of Justice (C) or the Court of First Instance (T). This number identifies a case uniquely, although it is not often used to identify cases for the purposes of examinations. However, by adopting this method it does allow you to look the case up in either the alphabetical or numerical case lists in textbooks for further details.

Furthermore, because you will be working directly from the text of this book, i.e., you will be reading each question and answer as a complete whole, you will be unlikely to enter the book via the case references, and so it was considered appropriate only to include one set of case tables. Given that some cases are often known by more than one name, or the case names can commence with different words and letters, it seems safer to offer the numerical list, especially as these numbers identify the case uniquely and are also contained in the text.

As far as the choice of topics included in the book is concerned, this is becoming slightly more difficult as EC law extends its scope and degree courses change to reflect this or to reflect the particular topics of interest to those examining the course. There is, however, an irreducible minimum largely because EC law is a core subject for the Law Society and the Bar. So, whilst the subject matters contained in this volume will cover virtually all of the requirements of the Law Society course, it may not cover all the topics on your particular course.

All references to the Treaty mean the EC Treaty and where appropriate to the predecessor EEC treaty, unless where otherwise stated. The entry into force of the Treaty of Amsterdam on 1 May 1999 brought with its substantive changes to the EC and EU Treaties, the renumbering of the EC and TEU treaties. Although new numbering now applies, the old numbering must still be learnt as all previous case law will refer to old numbering only and as some cases take up to 13 years to final judgment on appeal before the ECJ, the problem will remain a current one for at least the next decade. The policy adopted in this book is to refer predominantly but not exclusively to the new numbers in the text followed by the old numbers in brackets, e.g., Art 234 (ex 177). For the most part, even when referring to pre-Amsterdam case law or legislative provisions, the new number will be given first although this may not be technically correct. Occasionally, when close attention to the old numbers and content of provision is essential, the old numbers will be retained but that this will be made clear, e.g., old Art 5 (now 10). It is hoped confusion may be avoided.

It may be useful here to make one or two comments in respect of the use of statutory materials in the examination room if these are permitted on your course.

Most institutions allow reference to statutory materials during the examination. One real advantage is that there is no need to concentrate too heavily on memorising statutory provisions whilst revising. It leaves you more time to consider the application and interpretation, rather than having to waste time on the regurgitation of particular provisions. It also makes it pointless to reproduce the whole of a legislative provision in an answer if the examiner knows that you have it in front of you during the examination. Indeed, there is no need for such reproduction even if statutory materials are not allowed to be used in the examination. However, to ignore completely the legislative provisions prior to the examination means you will be unfamiliar with them and will probably waste time finding the relevant provisions, e.g., some candidates, when provided with such materials, seem to spend an inordinate amount of time browsing or flicking through them during the examination. If you can, try to treat these materials as a last resort or a mental crutch to which you can refer should your memory fail you. There is no compulsion to look at them at all, but you may still need to cite specific parts of provisions to support your answer.

Open-book examinations, where you are able to take in other materials as well, are less common and vary considerably as to the materials that the candidate is allowed to use during the examination and the time allowed to complete the examination. You still have to revise and prepare thoroughly for the examination and not rely on finding the information whilst in the exam hall. They are a hybrid between the closed-book examination and assessed work in the form of extended essays or dissertations, but still require a structured answer at the end of the day.

Finally, and I hope this advice is not too late, the best preparation for an examination is to have worked consistently over the period of your course on EC law. If you have, some of the questions and answers suggested here might actually make sense to you and not be the first time you have come across the issues, cases or law involved. If you are still in need of further advice for the examination or for revision, you will find the first two chapters of the SWOT: EC Law book devoted to general study and examination techniques and to the study of Community law. I suggest you get hold of a copy and read through those chapters. The SWOT also contains additional example questions and answer advice you might wish to consult. Apart from that, I wish you 'all the best' in the examination.

2 The Origins, Institutions and Development of the Communities, the Legislative Process and Budgetary Process

INTRODUCTION

Questions on the topics in this chapter cover a number of related subjects and can consequently give rise to a very wide range of questions, the exact form or content of which will be determined by the emphasis given to the topics in your courses. Given that these topics might be covered by introductory lectures rather than tutorials or seminars, it is likely that most of the questions posed will be of the essay type rather than problem questions. Therefore a range of questions and framework answers to cover these areas has been included. However, because the coverage of these topics can vary significantly between courses, it is consequently more difficult to predict with accuracy the range and type of questions which may be encountered. Direct questions on the history and development of the Communities would be rare because the answers could only be very descriptive and not therefore particularly suitable for the level of examination you are taking. Questions therefore tend to be concentrated on the institutions and in particular on the interrelationship of these institutions in the legislative and other processes of the Community.

Other exam questions may concern the role and legality of the Management Committees and procedures, the budget or legislative procedures in further detail or questions may focus on the powers and rights of the European Parliament (EP), the Council or the Commission separately.

The first questions will, however, concern the more general aspects of Community law courses.

QUESTION 1

The United Kingdom has been described as a reluctant partner as far as its attitude to the European Union is concerned.

Discuss this statement in the light of the development of the European Union.

Commentary

This question is looking for an historical analysis, not just of Britain's attitude but also of the general development of the Communities. This is because Britain's attitude was originally a direct response to the setting up of the European Economic Community and as further developments took place to the EEC and the other two Communities, so further reactions from Britain were prompted.

The answer could be divided into time periods to help in the presentation; such divisions are often artificial, however, and the facts may not always fit comfortably. The answer should thus include a brief outline of the setting up of the Communities and in particular, the reasons for this. Periods could, however, include the 1950s and the setting up of the Community; the attempts of the UK to enter in the 1960s and the reasons for this; the 1970s when Britain entered, but had second thoughts; and the 1980s to date. The latter period includes the at-times hostile relations of the UK with the rest of Europe and also a change in attitude as a result of the landslide Labour Party victory in the May 1997 General Election.

Much of the explanation for Britain's attitude lies in the realm of politics rather than law, in a strict sense. The degree to which this is then covered in your course will determine whether such questions will be set in an examination and the amount of discussion expected in your answer.

Finally, you could provide a paragraph summarising Britain's attitude to the EC.

Suggested Answer

Although there had been ideas to unify Europe before the Second World War, it was only afterwards that they found fruition. This was prompted by the horrific events and the devastation of Europe in the Second World War which left much of Europe in economic and political ruins. Political and economic co-operation and development between nations was regarded as crucial to replace the economic competition which was viewed as a major factor in the outbreak of wars between European nation states. Thus plans were put forward to eliminate harmful national jealousies and to promote economic and political stability, especially in the face of the rising Soviet threat. The first forms of co-operation concentrated on these aspects and led to the set-up of the United Nations in 1945, the Organisation for European Economic Co-operation (OEEC) in 1948 and the North Atlantic Treaty Organisation (NATO) and the Council of Europe in 1949.

The direct impetus for the Communities came in the form of the plan proposed in 1950 by the French Foreign Minister, Robert Schuman, in conjunction with the research and plans of Jean Monnet, head of the French Economic Planning Commission, to link the French and German coal and steel industries. The Schuman Plan would not only help economic recovery but also remove the disastrous competition between the two states. It was aimed to make future war not only unthinkable but also materially imposs-ible. It was left open for other European countries to join in the discussions and Italy and the Benelux nations (Belgium, the Netherlands and Luxem-bourg) took full part. The establishment of the Communities was not intended to exclude Britain which was invited to participate in negotiations but took no further role than that of observer, despite the seeming enthusiasm of Winston Churchill and many in the UK about the unification of Europe and the apparent leading role that Britain might play. Britain, however, did not envisage a role as a key participant and was reluctant to involve itself further in the negotiations.

To try to explain some of the reasons for this attitude it must be pointed out that Britain had at the time an historical legacy which involved quite different economic and social ties, including the Empire and Commonwealth and the Atlantic alliance, which were the result of both historical colonisation and the alliances which had found victory in the war. These ties of security and common language are often overlooked but played no small part in the attitude of Britain to Europe in the immediate post war years. Britain also regarded its status as remaining a world power whose sovereignty and independence could not be compromised by membership of such an organisation.

Hence six nations went on without the UK to sign the European Coal and Steel Community Treaty (ECSC) in 1951. As a result of the success of this first Community, the six Member States decided to extend the scope of their co-operation. The Spaak Report was prepared to consider the establishment of a Economic Community and an Atomic Energy Community for energy and the peaceful use of nuclear power. Britain was again invited to participate fully but again declined. On 25 March 1957 the two Treaties of Rome were signed establishing the European Economic Community and the European Atomic Community. Britain instead embarked on what might have seemed the potentially wrecking path of establishing, with other non EC European States, a European free trade area (EFTA) under the lead of Reginald Maudling in 1958; a common market but with no further political aims and no desire to create a supranational organisation capable of superseding the Member States in any way.

Following this initial reluctance, a change of mind by the UK occurred in 1961 when the Conservative government, under Prime Minister Harold Macmillan, applied for membership. The previous reasons for not joining included the view that because Britain retained its world power status and direct links with most of the world membership was neither desirable nor necessary. However, these had been weakened by the economic demise of the UK, the Suez débâcle and continuing conversion of the Empire into the Commonwealth of independent states. Trade patterns were shifting towards Europe and the Atlantic alliance was less prominent. The Commonwealth started to appear as not such a promising long term trading relationship. Britain had observed the much faster economic improvements taking place in the EEC of six and was jealous of this. It was clear that this certainly provoked the main interest in membership. Whether the UK had now become fully supportive of the entire package and aims of the Community is less clear. However Britain had now to bargain from the outside and the application was in any case vetoed by President de Gaulle of France. The second attempt, the 1967 application by the Labour government, under Prime Minster Harold Wilson, was also vetoed by de Gaulle. Neither of the vetoes came as any surprise.

The third attempt in 1970, under the Conservative government of Edward Heath, was successful and in 1973 the UK joined the Communities with Ireland and Denmark, mainly because of their trade dependence on the UK. This was regarded by some as a panic measure spurred on by the view that if the UK was unable to get in at this stage Europe would leave the UK behind. Thus, the UK joined in 1973, but in 1975 the UK re-negotiated entry terms and held a referendum on membership.

The timing of this entry was in fact unfortunate. Instead of the UK being able to participate equally in the post war boom and recovery, the economy of

Europe had received a set-back and Britain along with the rest of the western world became the victim of oil price increases. Instead of a period of economic prosperity, the 1970s witnessed high inflation and economic stagnation. To aggravate matters still further, the high and arguably inequitable level of the British budget contribution became the focus of attention. It did not take long before disquiet with the terms of entry arose. It seems that we paid too high a price to join the club and that the budget wrangles that polarised opinion both in Europe and the UK were inevitable, given the pattern of trade in the UK which initially favoured imports from Commonwealth, non-EEC countries, and having to pay the higher CAP regulated food prices, all of which added to the economic problems.

In 1974 a new government was elected in the UK and a re-negotiation of the terms of entry was started. This was climaxed by the approval of the British public in the unprecedented 1975 referendum which not only approved membership but also the re-negotiated terms regarding budget contributions. However, it was only a partial cure for the level of contributions, and this dispute was later re-opened by Margaret Thatcher. Its effect was, however, to cast the UK firmly in the role of the reluctant partner and as a trouble maker in Europe.

Viewed politically, the UK had decided to cast in its lot with the EEC, aware that some loss of sovereignty was involved and that a potentially high monetary contribution was required. One side of the bargain was not, as with other Member States, the security of nationhood or the stamp of approval and stability of the democratic political system that membership gave. The fact that the UK had been on the winning side in the war and had centuries of stability meant that these were so well secured in the UK that the EEC could never seriously be considered for these advantages, nor to keep the peace, which Britain had secured for itself by victory in the last war. The other side of the bargain was to share in the spoils of European economic progress. Given the changing circumstances, this proved to be a dubious economic gain. No wonder that there was a feeling by some, that still remains, that membership had sold Britain short.

In the 1980s, the first part of the decade was occupied with further wrangles over the British budget contribution which hindered progress on other matters in the Community and did not engender relaxed relations with Britain's partners in the Community. The budget contributions were settled in 1984, only to be questioned again in the 1990s.

Latterly, the discussions and agreements made in Maastricht demonstrate how Britain continued to be out of line with its other partners by demonstrating its reluctance to participate fully. Part of the agreement reached in Maastricht was that the UK opted out of the Social Policy but all other Member States went ahead with this. Maastricht also agreed to a process and timetable for moving towards economic and monetary union. The UK negotiated another opt-out here over the decision whether to join the final stage in which a single currency would be established.

The change of government in the United Kingdom on 1 May 1997 saw a change in the relationship with Europe, with the new Labour government announcing soon afterwards the intention to sign up to the social chapter, which was carried through soon afterwards, and generally to take a more participatory role in Europe. The UK opposition to monetary union seems to have been removed, although uncertainty about when the UK might join continues.

Finally, a much more positive attitude by the UK was displayed during the Nice IGC in 2000, although as with other member states certain items were still subject to a national overriding veto.

Trying to summarise Britain's attitude over the four decades, it has to be said, is no easy matter, as it is a complex of many concerns and influences. Whether Britain is a reluctant or just hesitant partner is itself still unclear. The fact that the UK is not committing itself to adopting the Euro must still leave room for doubt. There is, however, certainly no serious talk of withdrawal these days by any of the political parties likely to the members of a UK Government.

QUESTION 2

European integration is initially a wholly political concept whose implementation proceeds by the formulation of economic policies and decisions.

Comment on this statement by the European Commission from the 1960s.

Commentary

This question basically addresses the questions of why the Communities were set up and how they were designed to achieve their aims. The term 'European integration' in the question clearly focuses on the Communities and must be defined in the answer as meaning this. This question also focuses initially on the original reason or reasons for setting up the European Communities, i.e., the initial impetus which prompted moves to pursue European integration. Hence, the answer must commence with a review of these reasons. The fact that these reasons find their base in politics is stressed and must be addressed in the answer in contrast to suggesting that the reasons were based purely or merely on economic grounds, although it is very difficult to distinguish the two terms completely.

This in turns leads you on to considering the form of integration envisaged, i.e., the process by which the implementation of the political concept was to be achieved. This brings in considerations of initial theories of European integration including federalism and functional integration.

Next, you should look at how the implementation was to be achieved. This will involve you in considering the overall objectives of the EC Treaty and the way in which further laws and decisions could be reached to assist integration.

Since you are informed that the quotation arises from the 1960s you will be aware that it pre-dates the discussions which surrounded the Treaty on European Union negotiations about where the Communities were considered to be heading. However, don't limit your answer to an intention as viewed in the 1950s and 1960s. You should also include in your answer, a discussion on developments since that time including the Single European Act (SEA), the Treaty on European Union, the Amsterdam Treaty and the Nice IGC in 2000. You could consider the further question of whether the eventual goal of the Communities, that of political union to be achieved by progressive economic integration, will ever be reached.

Suggested Answer

The term 'European integration' is taken to refer to the European Communities which were set up in the 1950s. What were the reasons for setting up these Communities by treaties between nation states? The Communities were a political response to the Second World War and the massive destruction that had taken place in Europe as a consequence. They represented both an attempt to ensure that such a war could not occur in Europe again and to provide a better and hopefully more stable means by which the reconstruction of Europe could take place. They aimed to remove the rivalries between nation states by legally binding them together in economic communities. So, the reason for setting up the Communities was the result of entirely political motives to eliminate war and provide a new basis for economic reconstruction of Europe. Thus the primary motivation was political but economic reasons were also inevitably involved.

What was then the political concept of European integration? At the time the Communities were being contemplated and even after the establishment of the Treaties, different views were adopted on the form of integration. These ranged from the view that a European Federal State was envisaged to the view that the member states were participating in the erection of a common market concerned only with economic co-operation.

It was, however, originally widely considered that because there was success in certain policies this would automatically cause a spillover from one area to another to lead to increasing integration and that the whole process of integration was a dynamic and not a static process. This process is termed functional integration. In fact, it was considered that in order for the original policies to work properly there must be continuing integration. Thus sector by sector integration and the process of European integration was regarded as an inexorable process. For example, common tariffs and the establishment of the Common Market would lead to exchange rates being stabilised to ensure that production factors and costs in the Member States were broadly equal. This in turn requires monetary union to be established to ensure exchange rates do not drift apart and this requires full economic union to be achieved so that the value of different components of the common currency is not changed by different policies in different countries. This economic integration would also mean that the political integration would eventually follow. Whilst the above is a rather simplistic account of the theories of integration, it also helps explain the suggestion that any decision on the part of the Community to go no further in terms of integration would in fact not maintain a stable position but would ultimately be regressive as it would start to undermine or undo the previous successes and integration achieved.

Federalism may therefore be the argued goal of the Communities if the aims are not limited to the distinct policies thus far agreed. In order to make the goal of the Communities more acceptable, the term 'a closer union' has been used in both the EEC and Maastricht Treaties. Its exact meaning is unclear as to whether it refers to federalism or something short of that. The UK's view on this during the negotiations for the Treaty of European Union was that it falls somewhat short and whilst the Community does operate on the supranational level, it does not signify an inevitable move to federalism. That view may now have changed under the Labour government and because the two leading European nations, France and Germany, remain keen to see greater integration.

Secondly, the way in which these fundamental political objectives were to be converted into economic and social integration must be considered. This was initially by the agreement to establish a Treaty providing the legal basis for economic and further integration. The aims and objectives of the Community are clearly set out in the EC Treaty. The preamble and Arts 2 and 3 set out in general terms the type and range of policies the Community will pursue to achieve the general objective of European integration.

Article 2, for example, sets the general goals as the establishment of a common market and an economic and monetary union. This is to be achieved by the implementation of the common policies or activities referred to in Articles 3 and 4 (ex 3a). Article 3 notably includes policies on customs duties, a common commercial policy, free movement of goods, persons, services and capital, agriculture and fisheries, transport, and competition. Newer developments include activities and policies in the social sphere, economic and social cohesion, the environment, research and technological development, trans-European networks, health protection, education and training, culture, development co-operation, overseas policies, consumer protection and energy, and civil protection and tourism.

Those objectives and policies outlined in Arts 2 and 3 are expanded upon in specific parts of the Treaty, for example, free movement of workers in Art 39 (ex 48) and competition law in Arts 81 and 82 (ex 85 and 86). The Treaty articles were not to be the only source of legal provisions formulating the economic policies and decisions. The Community institutions, notably the Council, Commission and to a (at first) very limited extent, the European Parliament, were also empowered by the Member States with their own law making powers to establish further laws to achieve European integration and the objectives of the Treaties. These powers are summarised in Arts 250–252 (ex 189) EC. Furthermore, a European Court of Justice was established for the Community to adjudicate on Community law and provide rulings binding on the Member States. These further help to implement the concept of European integration.

Thus, whilst it would be true to agree that the original concept was a political one, which has been and is being implemented by economic policies, the debate continues and it is clear from the intense discussions surrounding the

Single European Act, the Treaty on European Union and the further enlargement in the 1990s that the eventual goal of the Community is far from clearly or definitively determined. European integration is still dependent on further political impulses. Implementation of European integration can only proceed by further political policy and not just by economic decisions. Indeed it can be observed from the very modest scope of social policy in the original EEC Treaty, Art 119 (now 141), that considerable advances or inroads have been made into the social areas of the Member States' economies. See the policies noted above from Art 3 of the Treaty. The underlying political nature of the EU was clearly seen during the negotiations at the Nice 2000 IGC where only after very hard political bargaining was sufficient agreement reached to open up the way for further European expansion and integration.

QUESTION 3

The Council of Ministers is by its very nature the federal institution of the Community. (Walter Hallstein.)

Discuss.

Commentary

This question appears to be quite simple but in order to get a respectable mark, it would involve you in more work than meets the eye. In order to answer this fully, a little lateral thought is required rather than just simply describing or analysing the position and the work of the Council. However, it clearly involves the Council as the central element in any answer. The term 'federal' is also a decisive element of the question. In order to provide a meaningful answer there should be a definition of what is meant by federal, both generally and with particular respect to the European Community. If your answer only included those aspects it would be adequate but only just, and would probably not attract more than a 2(ii) mark. To get more you would have to place these central elements of your answer in context. The context relevant here would be in relation to other institutions of the Community as the question implicitly requires an answer to this point, i.e., that the council is 'the' federal institution as opposed, or in contrast, to the others. You would need therefore to consider the position and role of the Commission and the European Parliament and compare these with the Council.

First of all you should describe the pertinent features of the Council and its main tasks.

Suggested Answer

The Council is governed by Treaty Arts 202–210 (ex 145–54) and is the principal legislative organ of the Communities. Its composition is outlined in Art 203 (ex 146) and consists of representative government Ministers of the Member States, depending on the subject matter under discussion. Foreign Ministers attend the general Council and the agriculture or finance Ministers, for example, attend the specialist Councils.

Article 202 (ex 145) EC imposes on the Council the duty of ensuring the co-ordination of the general economic policies of the Member States and confers upon it the power to take decisions and to delegate decision making powers to the Commission.

The Council has the final power of decision for the adoption of legislative proposals made by the Commission. Depending on the Treaty requirements it may have to consult the EP, the Economic and Social Committee or the Committee of the Regions and, by later amendments to the Treaty made by the SEA, the Treaty on European Union and the Treaty of Amsterdam, share the law making process with the EP. It reaches its decisions by voting, but the majority required differs depending on which Treaty Article the legislative proposal is based. Article 205 (ex 148) provides three different proceedings consisting of a simple majority, qualified majority or unanimity voting. The qualified majority is 62 votes from a possible total of 87. After Nice is implemented this will be 258 out of 342. For example, Art 94 (ex 100), which details the procedure for the approximation of laws not catered for by any of the specific parts of the Treaty, requires unanimity.

Next, the term 'federal' needs to be analysed. Whether the Council can be considered to be 'the' federal institution first requires a consideration of what is meant by federal. Federalism is defined as a form of government in which two or more states constitute a political unity while remaining independent in respect of their internal affairs. It involves the construction of political institutions which oversee integration on many fronts as agreed by the constituent states. A federal state is usually achieved by democratic means and can be otherwise referred to as a confederate state. Examples of federal nations are the USA, Nigeria, Switzerland, Germany, Australia and Canada. These consist of federal and state governments with appropriate spheres of power.

Is this applicable to the Council of Ministers? The Council is federal in that it consists of representatives of the Member States who meet together to act in a legislative capacity, creating rules binding on the constituent Member States. However, it is more often the case that national interests are pursued by the individual members rather than the Council acting collectively first and foremost in the interest of the Community. Furthermore, it is not the equivalent of a federal government as other institutions in the Community play a part in the legislative and executive processes, namely the European Parliament and the Commission. Thus to describe it as federal was perhaps too optimistic. By its method of action it is more intergovernmental and was described so by the Italian member of the European Parliament, Spinelli, who was largely responsible for the Parliament's Draft Treaty on European Union published first in 1984.

However, before you can conclude that it is not the only federal institution, you need to look at the other institutions.

The Commission, the executive of the Community, was given the sole right as the proposer of legislation under Art 155 (now 211) of the original EEC Treaty, although this has been in effect partially circumvented by the Council and European Council. It has its own powers of decision and is able to exercise powers delegated to it by the Council. This is now subject to the measures under Art 202 (ex 145), regulating the Management Committee structure.

The tasks and composition of the Commission are now determined by Arts 211–219 (ex 155–163) EC. It presently consists of 20 members, made up of two from France, Germany, Italy, Spain and the United Kingdom and one each from the other Member States. These are appointed by common accord of the Member States and are required to act independently (Arts 213–214 (ex 157–158)). The Commissioners are required under oath to act in the interest of the Community rather than in the interest of their host Member States. The Commission is, however, described as multinational or supranational, and not federal, because the Commissioners are not representing or acting for the constituent states but for the Community.

The European Parliament, originally called the Assembly and consisting of members nominated from the Member State governments, is now directly elected and presently consists of 626 members. It is arguably more aptly named an Assembly, consisting of only one chamber whereas a Parliament usually consists of two chambers and a head of state.

Before the SEA, the Parliament had largely advisory and consultative powers, which under Art 137 EEC (now 189 EC) provided that the Assembly shall 'exercise the advisory and supervisory powers which are conferred on it by this Treaty'. The treaty specified only 17 instances where the EP had to be consulted. Under its advisory role, certain provisions of the Treaty required that the EP be consulted before a decision could be adopted by the Council, see old Arts 54 and 235. The participation in the legislative process was increased by the conciliation procedure of 1977, and the introduction of the co-operation procedure by the SEA. The Treaty on European Union has now introduced a co-decision procedure by which the EP enjoys an ultimate power of veto over proposed legislation, which was extended into more areas by the Treaty of Amsterdam and will be further by the Treaty of Nice.

However, despite these improvements, the legislative role of the EP is still limited, to such an extent that the term 'democratic deficit' is used to describe this state of affairs. Parliament at the moment thus lacks the power really to be described as federal. It is federal in as much as, in limited circumstances, it participates in the legislative process to create binding legislation on the constituent Member States, but this is very limited. It does consist of representative members from each of the constituent states but they are elected to represent regional constituencies and political parties and not state governments.

Thus, of the three political institutions, leaving the Court of Justice to one side, it may be true to say that the Council by its nature is 'the federal institution'. However, because the Council does not act in that manner, and the other two have at present little capacity to do so, it cannot therefore be truly described as such.

QUESTION 4

As far as its legislative and budgetary procedures are concerned, the EC is neither efficient nor democratic.

(a)   Discuss this statement in the light of the powers and the decision making procedures of the Council, Commission and European Parliament.

(b)   What reforms would you advocate which would overcome these criticisms?

Commentary

This question is quite complex because it is in three parts. The first part can be broken down to determine what issues must be considered. You must

consider the legislative and budgetary procedures, i.e., they must be described as concisely as possible because there is a lot more of the question
to answer and because specific features of these procedures will be considered in the answer to (a), thus they need only briefly be outlined at the outset.
Having basically described the two procedures, you must then address the
issues that, in respect of the two procedures, the EC is neither efficient nor
democratic in respect of the powers and activities of the three political
institutions in the second sentence of the question.

This final section is probably the hardest to prepare for in that it really
requires you to have read particular advocated reforms during your course
such as the EP's own Draft Treaty on European Union, rather than try to
consider reforms in the exam. Although good suggestions will pick up a few
extra marks, it is not the major part of the answer and it is not worth spending
an excessive amount of time trying to think up reforms, if you have not
previously prepared such suggestions. In other words, in order to do well in
this question, you must have at least prepared for the possibility of a question
on institutional reforms in your revision. If you have not, it would probably
be better to find another question to answer.

Suggested Answer

All the legislative procedures commence with a proposal from the Commission. At present there are four forms, the original consultation, the conciliation, the co-operation procedure introduced by the SEA and the conciliation
and veto procedure, also known as the co-decision procedure, introduced by
the Treaty on European Union. The EP also has a limited power of assent on
international agreements and new Member States.

Under its advisory role a limited number (17) of Treaty Articles provided that
the Council was required to consult the EP as to its opinion before coming
to a decision on Community secondary law, see, for example, old Arts 54 or
56. The *Isoglucose* cases (Roquette Frères) (138–9/79) confirmed the EP had
to be consulted. However, on receipt of that opinion the Council could
proceed to ignore it and override any view given by the EP. In two cases *EP
v Council* (C-60/90) and *Parliament v Council* (C-392/95), the Court
annulled two Regulations which had been amended by the Council without
a further consultation of Parliament taking place when the Council had
amended its draft legislation.

The conciliation procedure was introduced by the Joint Declaration of the
Council, Commission and Parliament in 1975 as a result of the view that,

because the EP had no say over compulsory expenditure in the budget, it should nevertheless be given an opportunity to participate in the decisions concerning substantial compulsory expenditure. The EP is able to give its opinion but this may be disregarded by the Council.

The two reading co-operation procedure (now Art 252 EC) was introduced to establish a form of first and second reading in areas largely affecting the internal market. After the Council has received a proposal from the Commission and the opinion of the EP, it adopts a common position on the basis of a qualified majority vote. Then, rather than proceed immediately to decide on the matter as it would have done under the old consultation procedure, this common position is sent to the EP which has three months in which to act. It can approve the proposal, do nothing, or reject the common position, in which case the Council can nevertheless adopt it but only if it does so within three months and by a unanimous vote. Finally, if the EP makes amendments, the Commission must re-examine the proposal and resubmit it to the Council within one month. The Council then has three months to act. It can adopt by a qualified majority, amend by unanimity or do nothing, in which case the proposed measure will lapse.

Finally, Art 251 (ex 189b) introduced a co-decision procedure whereby ultimately the EP can reject a legislative proposal. After the EP has given its opinion on a legislative proposal, the Council must adopt a common position by a qualified majority. The EP can, within three months, either approve or take no decision in which case the Council can adopt the measure. Alternatively the EP can reject or amend the proposal by an absolute majority. In which case the Council can within three months approve those amendments by a qualified majority, but if the Commission has issued a negative opinion on the amendments, the Council can only approve by unanimity. If the Council does not accept the amended proposal the matter is referred to a new Conciliation Committee to attempt to achieve a compromise within six weeks. If a joint text is approved, the Council and the EP may adopt the provision together within six weeks. If there is no agreement the Council must confirm its position within six weeks and the EP may finally reject it within six weeks by an absolute majority.

The budgetary procedure is that the Commission proposes the first draft and the maximum increase for non-compulsory expenditure which the Council and Parliament are unable to exceed. The Council then prepares the draft budget by a qualified majority and sends it to the EP which can approve it within 45 days in which case it will be adopted. Modifications can be made by the EP in respect of compulsory expenditure which can be rejected by the Council by a qualified majority. Ultimately, however, the EP cannot interfere with compulsory expenditure which includes the Common Agricultural Policy and thus consumes between 65-80% of the total budget. Amendments can be made by a majority to non-compulsory expenditure such as the regional and social funds. These can be modified by the Council by a qualified majority within 15 days. The draft is returned to the EP which can modify these within 15 days by a majority and at least three-fifths voting. The EP can then either adopt or reject the budget under Art 272 (ex 203(8)) as it did in 1979 following the direct elections and again in 1984.

The questions of efficiency and democracy must now be considered in the light of the features and powers of the institutions which support or contradict the view expressed in the question.

The powers of the Council are basically set out in Art 202 (ex 145) EC. The Council disposes of Community legislation which must be initiated by the Commission. The power of the EP is set out in Art 189 (ex 137) EC which provides that the Assembly is to 'exercise the powers conferred on it by this Treaty'. EP budgetary powers stem from the Treaty of July 1975 and the Joint Declarations on budgetary procedure.

The Commission's powers are to initiate the legislative procedure by making proposals and to act under powers delegated to it by the Council. The Commission's right to act under delegated powers is extremely restricted by the Management Committee structure by which the Council retains much of its original powers.

Features that support the first statement are the limited role played by the EP in the legislative procedure, the fact that at present four procedures exist and the slowness of these procedures. In particular, the co-operation procedure only applies to a limited number of Treaty articles. Finally the most fundamental feature is that with the exception of the co-decision procedure, the EP can be overruled at the end of the day. Even in the latter procedure the EP's ultimate power is only that of a negative veto.

With regard to the budget, the EP can only effect non-compulsory expenditure to a set maximum and, although it can reject the whole budget, the Community then goes on the one-twelfth rule, so that the Community is not brought to a grinding halt.

Addressing the criticism concerning the lack of efficiency, the delays that were often and still are experienced in the legislative procedure can be cited, and also the fact that there are a number of procedures depending on the Treaty Article. The procedures are also becoming more complex and, as evidence, the stagnation of the legislative process in the 1970s and 1980s could be highlighted. Further evidence is that the Council could not cope with the amount of work necessary and had to devise ways in which decision making power could be delegated, but control could nevertheless be retained, by setting up a number of complex management committees. The Council by its nature acts in the interests of the Member States and not the Community, hence compromises must be reached which have delayed some legislation by very many years.

The question of democracy is easier to address and clearly points both to the role of the EP as the only directly elected body through only having a minor role in the legislative process and to the question of delegation to Committees controlled by the Council and not the EP. This whole argument is described as the democratic deficit in the Community, i.e., because the EP is the only directly democratically elected element, in order to maintain the democratic right or justification of Community laws, the legislative process must be more in the hands of elected bodies. If this democratic deficit is real then something needs to be done.

Finally to move onto reforms. To help you in this part, the reforms put into affect under the Maastricht Treaty and the Treaty of Amsterdam should be considered to determine whether these have answered the criticisms before suggestions for further reform are made.

The criticisms of the Maastricht reforms are that the power of co-decision still does not go very far and only gives the EP a negative power of veto and Art 251 (old 189b) still only applies to limited specific areas. The ability under Art 192 (old 138b) to request the Commission to make legislative proposals in areas of Community policy is also uncertain as to whether it can insist a proposal is made. The changes introduced by the Treaty of Amsterdam, whilst welcome and beneficial to the EP, are also limited. They increase the use and streamline the co-decision procedure. The Treaty also extends the areas in which the assent of the Parliament is to be required to incorporate the structural and cohesion funds. However, these do not actually increase the level of participation of the EP and its ability to insist on particular measure and thus do little to reduce the democratic deficit and make the Union more democratic. Finally, the discussions and conclusions of the intergovernmental conference in Nice 2000 must be mentioned into your answer, although as with Amsterdam, these were more limited in scope than hoped and planned for. However, QMV was extended into 39 new areas and the codecision procedure was also extended to more Treaty articles but further discussions about the revision of institutional relations was postponed until 2004.

What ever other reforms you suggest will depend on your views as to whether the Community is inefficient or undemocratic or, whether Maastricht or Amsterdam and now Nice has improved the situation, i.e., does it answer the democratic deficit? Your suggested reforms might be to increase the EP's powers to give equal power of decision making and equal say in the approving of the budget, and generally to speed up the procedures, but it would not do to simply to state this. You must say how this is to be done and the consequences for the other institutions. Any increase of the powers of the EP has to be at the expense of some other organisation, not the national parliaments but the Councils of Ministers and/or the Commission.

QUESTION 5

The choice of legal base of a Community legislative provision can become a matter of dispute.

Discuss.

Commentary

First of all you need to consider exactly what the legal base is. Thus a definition of the legal base must be provided and the relevance of its choice must be explained, as must the consequences for the various parties involved in the legislative processes. The use of different legal bases in the Treaty determines which particular legislative procedure is employed in enacting the provision. This in turn determines the extent of the role played by the various institutions. You should determine which institutions are concerned and why. The choice of a certain legal base is important to the Member States, the Council, the Commission and the EP. Each of these could be considered briefly in turn. Then the reasons why it can and does give rise to legal disputes must be provided. Better candidates will be able to refer to decided cases to help them and to demonstrate how the Court of Justice has resolved these disputes.

Suggested Answer

The legal base or authority for the enactment of Community secondary legislation is initially determined by the subject matter of the legislative proposal. This can be seen in the area of free movement of persons which provides a legal base for the Council and European Parliament to enact further secondary legislation for the free movement of workers. Article 40 (ex 49) is the provision and requires that the co-decision procedure under Art 251 be used. Hence, the legal base of each particular proposal for a Regulation, Directive or Decision determines the procedure to be used. This in turn then determines which participants (e.g., Council plus European Parliament or Economic and Social Committee or the Committee of the Regions) participate in the legislative process and also the level of their participation. The choice of legal base therefore is fundamental to the relative powers and ability of the institutions to affect the content of Community law.

The Member States and each of the major institutions is affected in the following ways.

The Commission

The Commission is concerned because the use of qualified majority voting in the Council of Ministers is extremely important to the Commission who stand a greater chance of having proposals accepted by a majority rather than by all Members States. The extreme views can thus be ignored rather than taken into account at the draft stages and in the legislative proposal put forward by the Commission.

The Commission may wish to see a proposal go through on a majority vote if it was of the opinion that one or two Member States may object. Thus the Treaty base may affect the precise content or formulation of the proposals, in that, if they know a qualified majority vote applies then they can ignore the objections of the extreme views in Council as these will be outvoted, hence they need not water down proposals to take into account all views. See *Commission* v *Council* in the *Erasmus* decision (case 242/87).

The European Parliament

The EP is clearly concerned as the legal base is also vital to the level of participation of the EP in the legislative process. For example, whether it can participate in the consultation process, the conciliation process or the cooperation process, all of which give the final say to the Council or whether it can participate in the co-decision process in which case the EP has marginally more say in the process. Its opinion in the consultation procedure can be ignored by the Council whereas for example, under Art 95 (ex 100a), measures for the single market, the co-decision procedure is more likely to reflect the views of the EP.

The Member States and the Council of Ministers

The Members States are represented in Council by the relevant ministers of the national Governments. As such they are subject to whatever political pressures are present in the Member States and the degree to which this is important depends on the strength of the Government concerned and the strength of the pressure groups and lobbies who might object to certain legislative proposals. In some Member States the farming lobbies are very influential and the governments in these Member States may therefore wish to take into account their protests. If these States are a minority in Council, the consequence for the Member States is that if a legal base is used which does not require unanimity to enact legislation, they would not be able to veto the measure or at least water down the requirements significantly. An example of where a Member State has taken an action to try to protect such an interest is the *UK* v *Council* (the Hormones case (68/86)).

The Council might therefore continue to prefer to use a base requiring unanimity because as a body it retains full unshared power in the legislative process, other bases weaken its position as a Community institution.

Hence, differences of opinion can arise as to the correct legal bases and the institutions and Member States have often fought over legal base, because it is possible to base measures on more than one Treaty provision due to the fact that the subject matter can straddle more than one Treaty section. Measures in support of the single market require majority voting rather than unanimity in the Council. Because this makes life easier for the Commission, it tries to exploit this by introducing as much legislation as possible under Art 95 (old 100a), whereas one or more Member States and/or the Council have argued the proposals should have as their legal base other Articles requiring unanimity. Looked at it from the other side, a single Member State which objects to a particular measure would wish to veto it and would want unanimity in Council to have that chance. It would object to the Council deciding to adopt the measure under a legal base requiring qualified majority voting (QMV). The subject matter may simply lend itself to both and thus give rise to a genuine dispute. The EP has not refrained from challenging the Council for the use of the incorrect legal base and regularly brings cases before the ECJ (See e.g., case C-22/96 *EP* v *Council* (data exchange)) claiming that by using a legal base which gives it less participation, its prerogatives are being eroded. An early example of the many cases which have reached the ECJ on legal base is the case of *UK* v *Council* (the Hormones case (68/86)) concerned with a ban on growth producing hormones. It was argued that old Art 100, an internal market measure, which required unanimity was more suitable than old Art 43 (the CAP measure) under which the measure was actually adopted and required only a qualified majority. The adoption by qualified majority was objected to by the UK. The Court of Justice was required to consider whether the subject matter more concerned the free movement of goods and thus a single market measure or really agricultural policy and thus the CAP. The use of the qualified majority procedure under the CAP was held to be appropriate by the Court of Justice.

In the 1992 case of *European Parliament* v *Council* (Students residence C-295/90), Parliament successfully challenged the adoption of Directive 90/366 on the residence of students which the Council adopted under old Art 235 requiring only consultation rather than under old Art 7 which would require the cooperation procedure to be used. The Directive was annulled and has been re-enacted.

A further case to focus on the issues raised above is *Commission* v *Council* (Re: Titanium Dioxide Directive C-300/89). The Council adopted a Directive on the basis of old Art 130S as an environmental measure which then required unanimity and only consultation of the EP, despite the protests of the EP at the time. The Commission argued it should have been adopted using Art 100A as a single market measure, which then required QMV and the cooperation procedure instead. Whilst the Court acknowledged that both could be a valid base, the use of Art 130S instead of Art 100A deprived the EP of its greater role in the legislative process. Even if both were used, as suggested by the Council it would still have to decide unanimously and thus overrule any opinion objections of the EP.

In a similar challenge, in case C-155/91 *Commission* v *Council* (Waste Directive), to a Directive (91/156) on waste disposal, adopted under old Art 130s by the Council, the Commission challenged it on the basis that old Art 100a in respect of the internal market should have been used as the legal base. On this occasion, the Court disagreed and held that the protection of the environment stated in the Directive was the real reason and not the free movement of waste. Therefore the challenge by the Commission was rejected. The view of the ECJ was that it was not so much the right to move waste around but the promotion of the most efficient way of dealing with waste to protect the environment, i.e., by not preventing its movement to the most efficient waste disposal operators.

A further case concerned the adoption by the Council in June 1993 of a Directive specifying a minimum working week, albeit with the ability of workers to work longer voluntarily. The UK which was opposed to this was unable to veto the proposal as it was introduced under the Health and Safety of workers provision under the old Art 118a of EEC Treaty (social policy) which requires only a qualified majority in the Council. The UK requested the annulment of the Directive in case C-84/94 *UK* v *Council*, arguing that it would have been more appropriate to base the measure on Art 308 (old 235) or 94 (old 100) either of which would have required unanimity on the part of the Council thus allowing the UK the chance to veto the measure. The Court of Justice was, however, satisfied with the choice of Art 118a.

The view of the Court of Justice is essentially that the democratic process which now involves the EP demands that where two legal bases are available requiring differing procedures, the one allowing the EP the greater role must be used so as not to deprive the EP and the Community of its democratic right, unless it can be shown the matter is primarily more concerned with a particular Treaty base.

Given the simplification of the legislative procedures by the Treaties of Amsterdam and Nice and the change of legal procedure for many provisions in favour of the EP, it might not be such an important issue in the future.

QUESTION 6

In the light of the roles of the Advocate General and the European Court of Justice and with reference to the jurisprudence of the Court, consider whether the ECJ possesses law making powers in the Community legal order.

Commentary

This is a relatively straightforward question dealing generally with the Court of Justice and the Advocates General and their impact in the Community legal order. The question can be broken into easier sections. First, you clearly need to outline the position and function of the Advocate General and the role and powers of the European Court of Justice. The place to start for both of these is the Treaty.

You have then to decide whether the role played by the ECJ in the decisions it reaches constitutes a law making power and thus whether it adds to the body of Community law, or whether it merely interprets and applies existing Community law. The reference to the jurisprudence of the ECJ is simply asking you to refer to the case law of the ECJ where necessary to support your arguments and answer.

The amount of detail you include for the first part of the answer will depend on the coverage in your course and whether, for example, you have considered in detail the Protocol on the Statute of the Court of Justice or the Rules of the Court of Justice. If not, then supply as much detail as you can.

Suggested Answer

As an introduction, it would be useful to state that the Court of Justice presently consists of 15 judges and eight Advocates General, nominated and appointed by unanimous agreement by the governments of the Member States. This may be increased after further enlargement of the European Union. They must be chosen from persons whose independence is beyond doubt and who possess the qualifications required for appointment to the highest judicial office in their own countries (Arts 221–223 (ex 165–7)).

The position of the Advocates General is established under Art 222 (ex 166) of the EC Treaty. The role of an Advocate General is to assist the Court by giving an opinion, in complete independence and impartiality, on the issues of a case.

In doing so the Advocate General will examine the legal issues in depth and critically review the jurisprudence of the Court on the subject. The reasoned submissions of the Advocates General are to be made in open court. It is a mandatory requirement that the opinion of the Advocate General be heard before judgment is given (Art 18 of the Statute of the Court of Justice (Art 20 after Nice)). The Advocate General can therefore take a public view of things and consider the submissions of all the parties but cannot be bound to present or represent any particular view. Additionally, the opinion of the Advocate General is not binding on the Court but it acts like a sort of persuasive precedent. Alternatively it can be considered that the opinion of the Advocate General acts like a first instance decision subject to an automatic and instant appeal. The Advocate General plays no part in the actual decision of the Court and once the Advocate General has delivered an opinion it brings to an end his or her role in the case.

Whilst not having the formal impact on Community law that the Court has, the Advocates General have nevertheless also helped in the development of Community law. This arises indirectly from their detailed research for cases often involving comparative research of the laws of Member States. At times this has led to a direct influence by the introduction of national legal principles into the Community legal order, e.g., in the case of *Transocean Marine Paint Association* v *Commission* (17/74), the principle of *audi alterem partem* (the right of the other party to be heard) was introduced by the Advocate General and adopted later by the Court. An opinion of an Advocate General may be referred to in later cases as a sort of persuasive precedent, as in the case of *Prodifarma* v *Commission* (T-3/90) when the Advocate General's opinion in a previous case was taken up by the Court of First Instance (CFI).

Article 220 (ex 164) EC outlines the general function of the Court of Justice. It states 'The Court of Justice shall ensure that in the interpretation and application of this Treaty the law is observed' . Originally it had exclusive jurisdiction over Community law but it has now been joined by the Court of First Instance. The European Court of Justice has been divided into chambers to help expedite the business of the Court. The jurisdiction and tasks of the Court are laid down in Arts 226–245 (ex 169–88).

As a result of the fact that the European Treaties and some of the secondary legislation are framework measures, they often require considerable amplification and interpretation. This, coupled with the style of interpretation which has been adopted by the Court to give effect to the aims of the Treaty, has given a wide scope to the Court of Justice to engage in judicial activism.

A primary form of interpretation is described as teleological, in that the Court tries to determine in the light of the aims and objective of the Treaties and legislation, what was intended and what result would assist those goals. These methods are applied in addition to the usual array of methods of interpretation found in the Member States' legal systems. The Court often refers to the spirit of the Treaty and Community to come to a particular conclusion. See in particular in this context the case of *CILFIT Srl* v *Ministro della Sanita* (283/81), concerned with the necessity of national courts to refer a question under Art 234 (ex 177). This form of interpretation allows the

Court to be more adventurous in its decision making than could be assumed from a literal reading of the legal provisions. For example, in certain circumstances it has been held that persons who are unemployed or studying can be classified as workers under Community law, see the cases of *Hoekstra v BBDA* (75/63) and *Lair v Universität Hannover* (39/86).

Past decisions are often cited in Court, but they only carry a form of persuasive rather than any formal authority. For example, the *CILFIT* case can also be observed to give rise to a form of precedent in that the ECJ stated that it was possible for national courts to refer to previous judgments of the ECJ in identical cases to achieve a solution without the need for reference to the ECJ. However, it must be stated there is no formal system of precedent but the Court, as do courts in civil law jurisdictions, tries to maintain consistency in its judgments. An example of a reversal of the Court's decisions is in the case of *EP v Council* in the *Comitology* case (302/87) in which the EC was denied the right to take action under Art 230 (ex 173) but it was later allowed in the case of *EP v Council* (C-70/88) concerned with a Euratom decision Treaty base by Council to protect Parliament's prerogatives.

One aspect which may hinder a law-making role is the requirement to give a single judgment of the Court. This is because a single judgment is at times difficult to interpret because it does not reveal whether the decision was reached on an unanimous or majority verdict. It can be confusing and terse and thus difficult to apply in future cases as 'established' law.

It can be observed that the Court has played a crucial role in the establishment and development of the Community legal order by the establishment and development of leading principles of Community law. Notable judgments are those concerned with what are now fundamental decisions of the Court including direct effects and supremacy and case rulings in actions concerning the rights of the Community institutions, notably the EP. In the case of *Les Verts v EP* (294/83), an action against the EP under Art 230 (ex 173) was admitted despite the lack of any mention in the Article that the EP could be a defendant and in *EP v Council* (C-295/90) concerned with the Treaty base, the extension of the rights of the EP to take action under Art 230 (ex 173) was confirmed despite not having been given the right under the provision of the Article itself.

A number of cases could then be cited to provide evidence that the ECJ enjoys some form of law-making role. It would be best, however, to rely on leading cases in which the ECJ has established the fundamental principles of Community law of direct effects and supremacy of Community law, e.g., *Van Gend en Loos* (26/62) and *Costa* v *ENEL* (6/64). Quotations from these cases could be employed to great effect.

In *Van Gend en Loos* the ECJ held:

> . . . the Community constitutes a new legal order of international law for the benefit of which the States have limited their sovereign rights, albeit in limited fields, and the subjects of which comprise not only member States but also their nationals.

From *Costa* it was held:

> By contrast with ordinary international treaties the EEC Treaty has created its own legal system which became an integral part of the legal systems of the Member States and which their courts are bound to apply. By creating a Community of unlimited duration, having its own institutions, its own personality, its own legal capacity and more particularly real powers stemming from a limitation of sovereignty or a transfer of powers from the states to the Community the Member States have limited their sovereign rights and have created a body of law to bind their nationals and themselves.

Also:

> It follows . . . that the law stemming from the treaty, an independent source of law, could not because of its special and original nature, be overridden by domestic legal provisions, however framed, without being deprived of its character as Community law and without the legal basis of the Community itself being called into question.

These cases must demonstrate more than the simple interpretation and application of law, as there is nothing in the Treaty expressly to establish these two fundamental principles of Community law. Furthermore the introduction of new principles to the Community legal order also establishes new principles and rules of Community law.

Inevitably in reaching a conclusion an answer to such a question depends on how you define 'law making'. It is at least arguable that given the width of the scope that the ECJ enjoys it would not be incorrect to describe it as having law making powers. Indeed during the Intergovernmental Conference in 1996/7, some of the Member States had expressed their dissatisfaction with the ECJ in cases such as *Barber* (C-262/88). No changes resulted from this, but it may be regarded as evidence that the Member States consider the ECJ to be doing more than just interpreting law.

3 The Sources and Forms of Community Law

INTRODUCTION

This chapter includes questions on a wide variety of often overlapping topics concerned with the sources of Community law. The sources of law are the Treaties which are regarded as primary sources, and legislation enacted by the institutions of the Community by virtue of the powers given by the Member States and contained in the Treaties and this is termed secondary Community law. Additional sources of law in the Community legal order are agreements with third countries, general principles, and the case law of the ECJ establishing, amongst other case law developments, the doctrine of direct effects, supremacy of Community law and state liability.

The prime candidate for questions in this area, because of its far-reaching ramifications, must be the doctrine of direct effects. Questions about this topic will be posed in all manner of forms and mixed with more general questions on the sources of law so that you may also be required to consider, for example, the direct effects, if any, of international agreements entered into by the Community. A sample of such questions is included in this chapter.

QUESTION 1

Identify the sources of law (other than treaty provisions and secondary Community legislation) invoked by the European Court of Justice. What is the justification for the recognition and application of such sources in the Community legal order?

Commentary

This question by-passes a consideration of the prime sources of Community law, namely the Treaties and Regulations, Directives and Decisions, to consider other sources of law and legal rules which have had an impact in the Community legal order. First of all you need to identify those other sources according to different types, if it is possible to categorise them conveniently. You will most likely concentrate on the provisions of international agreements, general principles of law and fundamental rights provision. Having identified other sources of law, you must then account for their recognition and application in the Community legal order which requires you to address your answer both from the point of view of whether there are any direct or indirect legal justifications arising from the EC Treaty for the ECJ to employ these other sources in its judgments, and whether there are any non-legal arguments which would either justify or demand their application.

Suggested Answer

The Community Treaties and the secondary forms of Community law sanctioned by the those Treaties, in particular Regulations, Directives and Decisions under Art 249 (ex 189) EC, are not the only sources of law or legal rules which have an impact in the Community legal order. Whilst the Treaties and secondary Community legislation are clearly the most important and abundant sources, other sources have been recognised and employed by the ECJ. These other sources can be broadly classified into two categories.

A first additional source of law arises from the international agreements entered into by the Community on behalf of the Member States, or those, such as the European Road Transport Agreement or the North-East Atlantic Fisheries Convention, the Community has taken over the competence of the Member States as agreed. Most notable are the GATT agreements on import duties and trade, association agreements with other European states and the Lomé Conventions between the Member States and many third world nations.

The second major additional source of law includes the categories of general principles and fundamental rights. These will be considered as essentially one category as there is a considerable degree of overlap. General principles of law have been used to assist the Court of Justice in the interpretation and application of Community law and by the parties to assist them in challenging the Community institutions or law and the actions of the Member States in the application of Community law. These principles are also referred to in actions for damages against the Community institutions.

General principles from external sources can arise from particular provisions of other legal systems, in particular the constitutions of Member States, principles of natural law or justice found in common law or in written form in some Member States, or international law and agreements, for example, the European Convention on Human Rights (ECHR). Sometimes the actual articles of the ECHR are referred to directly, as in the *Hauer* (44/79) and *Kirk* (63/83) cases. The public law and legal systems of Germany, France and now the UK have all had a considerable impact on the supply of general principles for the Community legal order. The principles which form a source of Community law need not be present in all of the Member State legal systems nor indeed in a majority. The Court of Justice will often conduct a comparative review of whether, or in what form, the principle exists in some or all of the Member States. In particular now, Art 6 (old F2) TEU provides that the Union shall respect fundamental rights, as guaranteed by the ECHR and as they result from the Member States' constitutional traditions as general principles of Community law. The Amsterdam Treaty has amended Art 6 (old F) (2) of the TEU which now obliges the European Union to respect the articles of the ECHR and those human rights common to the Member States as general principles of Community law. Furthermore, any applicant states joining the European Union are now obligated by Art 49 (old O) TEU to have respect for human rights. At the Nice ICG in 2000, the Member States further agreed to produce a European charter of fundamental rights, although it would not be a part of the Treaties and its legal force was not agreed at the time.

Often too, it is the nationality of the Advocate General and judges in the case which may be particularly influential in the introduction of a certain principle into the Community legal order. Thus the Advocates General from particular countries are more easily able to identify the principles, which may be common in one form or another in a number of the Member States and thus more likely to introduce these principles to the Court of Justice. For example, the Latin maxim *audi alterem partem* was introduced by the Advocate

General in *Transocean Marine Paint Association* v *Commission* (17/74). He argued that in the absence of Transocean being allowed to present their views on the matter, the Commission's Decision would be in breach of a general principle of law, clearly applicable in the UK and other legal systems.

When it comes now to considering the rationale for these additional sources of Community law, it is to be noted that the justification for the recognition and application differs according to the type of other source.

The conclusion of agreements with countries associated with the Member States and agreements with other third countries is specifically catered for under Arts 300 and 310 (ex 228 and 238) EC. In the *Haegemann* v *Belgium* (181/73) case, an agreement between the Community and Greece was held to be binding on the Member States even though such agreements are not envisaged by Art 249 (ex 189). Furthermore, although there is no statement in the Treaty that such agreements entered into by the Community or by the Member States can give rise to direct effects, the Court of Justice has held that they may give rise to direct effects providing they satisfy the criteria established in the leading case of *Van Gend en Loos* (26/62). These criteria tend, however, to be more strictly applied. To this extent an investigation of one of the GATT provisions in the case of *International Fruit* (No. 3) (21-22/72) was held not to be directly effective. However, provisions of the Yaoundé Convention and the EEC-Portugal association agreement were held to be directly effective in the cases of *Bresciani* (87/75) and *Kupferberg* (104/81).

With regard to general principles, whilst some are clearly imported into the legal system from external sources, others have been developed by the Court of Justice from the Treaty. There are three Treaty Articles which provide some justification for the Court of Justice to introduce general principles into the Community legal order.

Article 220 (ex 164) is a general guideline set by the Treaty for the functioning of the Court of Justice. It states 'The Court of Justice shall ensure that in the interpretation and application of this Treaty the law is observed'. This is taken to mean the law outside the Treaty. Article 220 (ex 164) has been invoked to introduce very many different general principles of law, most notably human rights. More specifically, two further articles of the Treaty mandate the court to take account of general principles of law. Article 230 (ex 173) refers to the infringement of any rule of law relating to the application of the Treaty as one of the grounds for an action for the challenge to the validity of Community law, and Art 288 (ex 215)(2), concerned with damages claims, specifically allows the settlement of claims by the Community on the basis of the general principles of the laws of the Member States. The latter two are specific to the claims raised under those Treaty articles but they serve to reinforce the Court of Justice's claim that it can rely on general principles as a source of law in the Community legal order.

The Treaty has also supplied the basis for one or two principles coinciding with the general principle of non-discrimination which applies both in relation to nationality and sex and has been developed into a general principle of equality and non-discrimination.

More widespread and logical arguments for the inclusion of general principles are that the Community and Court was morally and socially, if not legally, obliged to observe fundamental human rights, especially those upheld in the constitutions of the Member States. No self respecting legal system in Europe could ignore, or be seen to be ignoring, such ideologically important rights such as these. Failure to observe them might lead to serious clashes with Member States' constitutional law, which might have led to severe strains on the Community legal system. The *Internationale Handelsgesellschaft* ([1974] 2 CMLR 540) case showed the potential for conflict and ultimate harm to the Community legal order if the Community failed to uphold human rights provisions.

Another argument stems from the fact that the Treaty is only a framework Treaty and requires completion by reference to other laws. For the most part this is done by the specific secondary legislation of the Community, but this only provides the substantive law rules which also often require interpretation by the Court of Justice. The Community legal order was established anew and does not have the traditions of the Member States' legal systems to rely on which are rich in developed principles of law. Therefore something is needed to assist the Court of Justice in its task and, general principles, many of which are borrowed from the Member States' legal systems, do just that.

While it has been the subject of discussion for many years, there are at present no plans for the European Union to join as a signatory to the European Convention for the Protection of Human Rights and fundamental Freedoms (ECHR). The European Council Presidency Conclusions of 3 and 4 June 1999 proposal to establish the Community's own catalogue of Fundamental Human rights has been agreed during the Nice IGC in 2000.

QUESTION 2

Article 249 (ex 189) provides that Regulations shall be directly applicable in all Member States. Does this mean that they are also necessarily directly effective?

Commentary

This is a seemingly straightforward question but it might be deceptive to answer. Clearly, the starting point for the answer to this question lies with Art 249 (ex 189) and a definition of 'directly applicable' and, furthermore, an explanation of the consequences of this concept. Once that has been set out you need to define the concept of 'directly effective' and decide whether Regulations, by virtue of the fact they are directly applicable, are by necessity directly effective.

Suggested Answer

Direct applicability refers to a means or mode of incorporation, or the way in which international law finds validity in national legal systems. This is recognised in international law and means that international law is automatically binding (otherwise described as self-executing) in national states.

Article 249 (ex 189) declares that Regulations shall have general application and that they shall be binding in their entirety and directly applicable in the Member States. They are designed as general provisions of legislation applicable to all rather than specific individuals or groups and are often termed normative acts (see case 17/62). Regulations are detailed forms of law so that the law in all Member States is exactly the same. They are also described as self executing because of the way they obtain legal validity in the Member States without the need for any implementation or transformation into national law by the Member States. Article 249 (ex 189) carries an obligation that the Member States are not to transform Community Regulations into national legislation. It was held in the case of *Commission v Italy* (slaughtered cows) (39/72) that Member States cannot subject a Regulation to any implementing measures other than those required by the act itself. There may, however, be circumstances where the Member States are required to provide implementing measures to ensure the effectiveness of the Regulation, as in the case of *Commission v UK* (tachographs) (128/78). This obligation also applies to Treaty Articles as these satisfy the requirement

of directly applicable law by automatic validity in transformation, and they
are also generally binding because they can obligate individuals.

The special elements or criteria, therefore, are that Regulations are automatically binding and general, because they apply to citizens directly and not just
to nation states.

In contrast to the above definition it is now necessary to define and explain
the concept of directly effective. Directly effective is the term given to
judicial enforcement of rights arising from provisions of Community law
which can be upheld in favour of individuals in the courts of the Member
States. It may also be referred to as 'direct effects' and it describes the right
to rely directly on Community law in the absence of national law, or in the
face of conflicting national law.

Direct effects can apply to Articles of the Treaty, Regulations, Directives and
Decisions, in fact any binding law in terms of Art 249 (ex 189) and, in some
circumstances, outside Art 249 (ex 189) as with international agreements.
However, in contrast to provisions of law which are directly applicable such
as Regulations, certain criteria have to be fulfilled before the ECJ can declare
a particular Community law provision to give rise to direct effects. The
criteria for specific provisions to be declared directly effective were determined by the ECJ in a series of cases commencing with the leading
Community law case of *Van Gend en Loos* (26/62). In *Van Gend en Loos* a
private legal individual company challenged a new import duty imposed by
the Dutch authorities and claimed it was contrary to Arts 12 and 13 of the
EEC Treaty (now 25). The Dutch authorities in their defence claimed that the
obligation was one imposed by the Treaty on the Dutch state alone and could
not be invoked by an individual of that state. The Court of Justice held that
the institutions of the Community are endowed with sovereign rights, the
exercise of which affects not only Member States but also their citizens, and
that Community law was capable of conferring rights on individuals which
become part of their legal heritage. For a particular provision of Community
law to be upheld before a national court in the face of non-implementation,
or incorrect implementation of national law, the provisions have to be clear
and precise; they should leave no discretion to the authorities of the Member
State; they are unconditional and require no further implementation by either
the Community or the Member State. Hence in the *Van Gend en Loos* case
the company could rely directly on the Treaty Article to avoid paying the
unlawful duty imposed by the Dutch authorities.

Thus to contrast these two concepts: direct applicability is a mode of incorporation, whereas direct effects is a judicial development for the enforcement of rights. Another difference is that direct effects can apply to all forms of Community law whereas directly applicable applies just to certain types. Directives are not, for example, directly applicable but only apply to persons to whom they are addressed. They are not self executing and in most cases must be transformed by national legislation into national law.

Direct effects was sometimes considered to be a sub concept of direct applicability, or direct applicability a pre-requisite for direct effects. The Court of Justice has spoken in the *Verbond van Nederlandse Ondernemingen* (51/76) and *Grad* (9/70) cases of Regulations which are directly applicable but which by their very nature can have direct effects, which suggests that direct effects must be automatically attributable to directly applicable legislation. In *Grad* the Court also stated that the ability of an individual to invoke a Decision before a national court leads to the same result as would be achieved by a directly applicable provision of a Regulation, again as if to suggest the concepts are the same.

The question whether Regulations which are directly applicable are necessarily directly effective is really asking if it follows that a directly applicable provision must, without exception, be capable of direct effects. The answer must be no, because direct effects are not automatic. For example, individual provisions, including those of Regulations and Treaty Articles, still have to satisfy the criteria laid down by the Court and do not do so in all instances, whereas direct effects can arise from all forms of legislative provision.

Therefore, whilst Regulations are capable of direct effects, it is not necessarily the case that they will give rise to direct effects capable of enforcement by an individual, see e.g., *Eridania* v *Ministry of Agriculture and Forestry* (230/78).

QUESTION 3

While the EC Treaty suggests that Regulations and Directives are very different types of legislative instruments, in practice, as a result partly, but not exclusively, of the doctrine of direct effects, the distinction between Regulations and Directives has become blurred.

Discuss.

Commentary

This is a question which concentrates on the debate which ensued and continued for a long time following the ECJ's gradual development of the doctrine of direct effects. It was considered that direct effects was undermining the distinction between the two forms of secondary Community legislation established by the Treaty by the suggestion that if both Regulations and Directives could give rise to direct effects then no real difference existed between the two. To some extent these concerns were answered by the first *Marshall* (152/84) case to reach the ECJ, which decided that a Directive could not give rise to rights capable of enforcement by individuals against other individuals, the so-called 'horizontal direct effects'. Thus a distinction remains as Regulations are capable of horizontal direct effects. Nevertheless the issue is still relevant and topical.

In answering the question you clearly need first to outline both forms of law from their Treaty base and then to explain that they were intended to have different functions. You then need to consider why in practice the distinction has been undermined. The question itself indicates that you should concentrate your answer on the influence of the doctrine of direct effect on this practice. This requires therefore a definition and explanation of direct effects.

Suggested Answer

The question concerns Regulations and Directives which are the two most important forms of secondary law to be enacted by the institutions of the EC under the power granted by Art 249 (ex 189) EC. This provides:

> A regulation shall have general application. It shall be binding in its entirety and directly applicable in all Member States. A directive shall be binding, as to the result to be achieved, upon each Member State to which it is addressed, but shall leave to the national authorities the choice of form and methods.

Regulations are general or normative provisions of legislation applicable to all legal persons in the Community rather than to specific individuals or groups. They are usually very detailed forms of legislation to ensure that the law in all Member States is exactly the same.

Regulations become legally valid in the Member States without any need for implementation and this process is sometimes described as self executing. In fact it was held in the case of *Commission* v *Italy* (slaughtered cows) (39/72) that Member States cannot subject the Regulation to any implementing measures other than those required by the act itself. There may, however, be circumstances where the Member States are required to provide implementing measures to ensure the effectiveness of the Regulation as in the case of *Commission* v *UK* (tachographs) (128/78).

Directives, in contrast, set out aims which must be achieved but leave the choice of the form and method of implementation to the Member States. This was done to ease the way in which national law could be harmonised in line with Community law and give the Member States a wider area of discretion to do this. If, for example, a Member State considers that the existing national law is already in conformity with the requirements of a new Directive then it need not do anything, apart from the requirement now in Directives that the Member State inform the Commission of how the Directive has been implemented. Member States are given a period in which to implement Directives which can range from one year or even less to five years or more depending on the complexity of the subject matter and the urgency for the legislation.

It may be useful at this stage to try to summarise the notable differences in the forms of legislation. Directives are aimed at the Member States or named individuals, whereas Regulations apply to everyone. Regulations were designed to be directly applicable but it would seem from Art 249 (ex 189) that Directives require some form of implementation in order to take effect or have validity in the Community legal order. Directives were designed with the harmonisation of different national rules in mind whereas Regulations were aimed to be prescriptive by providing one rule for the whole of the Community. Hence Regulations would be detailed and precise and Directives more likely to be framework provisions laying down general guidelines and so less precise by nature. Furthermore Regulations are required to be published in the Official Journal, whereas only Directives addressed to all Member States must be published, although all invariably are.

Thus by design these are very different forms of legislation. The answer can now consider why the distinction seems to have been blurred in practice. This can be covered in two parts, first generally and then with specific attention to direct effects. In practice a less rigid or distinct division has been observed.

It is not always the case that Regulations are precise and complete, as noted above in the case of the tachographs and further action may be required on the part of the Member States. Regulations should be normative but they are often used in respect of specific individuals: see, e.g., anti-dumping regulations and regulations in the area of competition law. On the other hand, directives can very often be very detailed.

The biggest assault on the distinction arose when the ECJ held that it was not only Treaty Articles and Regulations which could give rise to rights directly enforceable by individuals before the national courts but also other forms of Community law could give rise to such rights. This has come to be known as 'direct effects' in the Community legal order. This is the term given to judicial enforcement of rights arising from provisions of Community law which can be upheld in favour of individuals in the courts of the Member States. The term 'directly effective' may also be used and it describes the right to rely directly on Community law in the absence of national law or in the face of conflicting national law. The cases of *Grad* (9/70) and *Van Duyn* v *Home Office* (41/74) confirmed that Directives could also give rise to direct effects, providing they satisfy the criteria required for direct effects as initially laid down in the case of *Van Gend en Loos* (26/62) and that the time limit given to the Member States has expired. Therefore although Directives are not directly applicable in that they are not automatic and general in application and give rights without further implementation, Directives have been held to give rise to directly enforceable rights in specific circumstances, i.e., where they have not been implemented or have been incorrectly implemented.

The argument then arises as to whether the distinction has been eroded as both Regulations and Directives can be enforced by individuals in the national courts and in practice there is really not a great deal of difference between them. This might have been, or become, more likely if the Court of Justice had not decided in the case of *Marshall* (152/84) that Directives could not give rise to rights which could be enforced against other individuals, the so-called 'horizontal direct effects'. To date, the Court has upheld this position.

Thus whilst it may be argued that in practise the gap between Regulations and Directives has narrowed, clear distinctions remain and they are still used for different purposes as the occasion demands, i.e., either as a harmonising rule to accommodate different previous positions, or as a new rule entirely. Furthermore even when it comes to considering direct effects, Directives are only enforceable by individuals in a limited of number of cases where approved by the ECJ and not universally and they do not provide rights enforceable between individuals.

QUESTION 4

Does the distinction between vertical and horizontal direct effects cause difficulties for individuals in actions involving Community law? If so, what has been done to mitigate these difficulties?

Commentary

This question picks up the detail where the last one left off, in that it asks you to consider the arguments in respect of horizontal direct effects and whether this causes problems for individuals in certain circumstances. The circumstances are those in respect of the consequence that the ECJ ruling in *Marshall* (152/84) and subsequent case law denied individuals the ability to enforce Directives against other individuals.

The answer requires a definition of what is meant by both types of direct effects and requires you to know and explain that it is impliedly referring to the direct effects of Directives which cause the difficulties. The distinction was highlighted by the *Marshall* case which should be discussed along with the consequences of the decision which have given rise to difficulties, if you agree that this is the case. One point you should note is that you should not refer to national definitions of direct effects in your answer as it is a Community and not national law concept.

The final part then asks you how the difficulties have been avoided or circumvented. This requires you to refer to the developing case law of the ECJ which has already provided some alternative solutions where individuals are deprived of the protection of horizontal direct effects from Directives.

Suggested Answer

Direct effects is a Community concept developed by the Court of Justice to apply to Treaty Articles, Regulations, Directives and Decisions. It is the term given to judicial enforcement of rights arising from provisions of Community law which can be upheld in favour of individuals in the courts of the Member States. To be capable of direct effects a provision must satisfy the criteria established by the Court of Justice, initially in the case of *Van Gend en Loos* (26/62), that the provision should be clear and precise; unconditional; should not require implementing measures by the state or Community institutions or leave room for the exercise of discretion by the Member State or Community institutions. In *Van Gend en Loos* it was held that the institutions of the Community are endowed with sovereign rights, the exercise of which affects not only Member States but also their citizens and that Community law was capable of conferring rights on individuals which become part of their legal heritage.

Direct effects have been found to arise from many Treaty Articles, which often confer an obligation not just on organs of the state as in a vertical relationship, but on other individuals, in particular in the Community context, employers. It was confirmed by the Court of Justice that employers must comply with the requirements of a Treaty Article and other individuals may enforce corresponding rights directly against the obligated party who has failed to comply with Community law. In this case the resultant rights are termed horizontal direct effects. The first case to confirm this was that of *Defrenne* v *Sabena (No. 2)* (43/75) in which the rights of an air hostess for equal pay guaranteed under Art 119 (now 141) were upheld against the employing airline, Sabena, which was in breach of the obligation.

For a considerable time the question of whether Directives could be held to give rise to horizontal direct effects and thus be enforceable against other individuals was open to speculation. However, the Court of Justice decided in the case of *Marshall* (152/84), which concerned a claim for equal treatment in retirement against a health authority, that Directives could only be enforced against the state or arms of the state and not against individuals. The health authority was held to be an arm of the state. A claim against private employers would fail in the same circumstances.

Marshall decided that there could be no horizontal direct effects of Directives mainly as a result of the fact that Directives are not addressed to individuals, therefore individuals should not be obligated by them. The result of this decision is that the scope of the concept of public service as opposed to a private body is crucial. Rights contained within Directives cannot be enforced by individuals against other individuals. This has the result that there is not a uniform application of Community law either in a Member State or between Member States. There is no uniformity in the application of Community law between public employers and private employers within Member States and between Member States, because there are different concepts of what is the state and what are private and public employers. Furthermore this position can be further complicated by the movement of utilities and companies in and out of public ownership. Certain individuals are thus denied rights that employees in the public sector can enforce in the face of non-compliance by Member States. The uniformity of Community law is undermined in important areas of law dealing with employment rights, where many Directives are relevant to private employers and the protection of individuals and their rights; e.g., Art 141 (ex 119) can create horizontal direct effects but the Directive providing the same rights cannot (Directive 75/117). An example of the dire consequences for individuals is the *Duke* case ([1988] AC 618) in the UK, which considered the same question as *Marshall* (152/84). However, in *Duke* a private employer was involved and the House of Lords held that, Mrs Duke could not uphold her claim for equal treatment in retirement because Directives could not give rise to direct effects which could be relied on horizontally. The decision has thus led to an arbitrary and uneven protection of individual rights (see more recently the case of *Dori* (C-91/92)).

There are various arguments for and against having horizontal direct effects of Directives but as these go beyond the required answer for this question they should not be rehearsed here.

Once you have identified that in certain circumstances the decision concerning Directives is unfortunate, case law which mitigates the harsh consequences can be considered.

One way pursued by the ECJ is by expanding the concept of public sector in the case law and thus including more individuals capable of protection by Community law; see, e.g., the cases of *Johnson* v *RUC* (222/84) and *Foster* v *British Gas* (C-188/89) which showed that, although the concept was wide enough to include a nationalised industry and includes any form of state control or authority, a distinction nevertheless remains between public and private employers. Although it may be considered that tinkering with the scope of what is meant by an 'emanation of the state' will broaden the concept and protect more people, it does not get to the heart of the matter. It still allows a variation between public and private employees and between the Member States. The difficulties and limits to this approach are demonstrated in the UK case of *Rolls-Royce plc* v *Doughty* ([1992] ICR 538), in which the Court of Appeal considered that the nationalised Rolls Royce company was not a public body for the purposes of the claim to direct effects. Privatisation of once nationalised companies also affects the rights of individuals.

Another line of case law has developed, however, which may provide an alternative for individuals defeated by the absence of horizontal direct effects. The first cases in this line are *von Colson* (14/83) and *Harz* (79/83) both concerning Art 6 of the Equal Treatment Directive (76/207) but concerning a public and a private employer respectively, thus the contrast of remedies was starkly visible. Rather than highlight the unfortunate results of the lack of horizontal direct effects of Directives, which would have helped *von Colson* (14/83) but not *Harz* (79/83), the Court of Justice concentrated on Art 5 (now 10) EC which requires Member States to construe with Community obligations. The Court held that this requirement applies to all authorities of Member States including the courts, and so the courts are obliged to interpret the implementing national law in such a way as to ensure that the obligations of a Directive are obeyed. The difficulty with the *von Colson* line of argument is that it requires there to be national law to interpret, or rules with which the national court can, and is willing to construe to achieve the correct result. Further cases which develop the boundaries of this principle are *Marleasing* (C-106/89), which required the national courts to apply Community law regardless of whether the national law was based on any particular Directive and regardless of the intent or even existence of national law, and *Kolpinghuis* (80/86) which held that a Member State which has not implemented a Directive cannot invoke it against an individual, i.e., direct effects must not be used to worsen the position of an individual. Neither go as far to protect the rights of individuals as would be achieved by the extension of horizontal direct effects to Directives. However, the denial of horizontal effects of Directives by the ECJ has been confirmed in the case of *Dori* (C-91/92).

A significant alternative development by the ECJ is the use of general provisions of the Treaty, such as Arts 5 and 189 (now 10 and 249) as in the *Francovich* case (C-6 & 9/90), to impose liability on the state for the non implementation of Directives and more recently for other breaches of Community law obligations by Member States. In *Francovich* the relevant Directive was not capable of giving rise to direct effects, but the requirements of the effective and uniform application of Community law gave rise to a liability on the part of the state to compensate for its failure to implement the Directive where the Directive had conferred rights on individuals and that there was a link between the breach and the damage caused. It does, however, take the emphasis away from the difficulty caused by the lack of horizontal direct effects of Directives. *Francovich* has now been followed by the *Brasserie du Pêcheur* case and *Factortame III* (46 & 48/93) in which the ECJ held that all manner of breaches of Community law by all three arms of state could lead to liability to individuals. Thus it expands the circumstances which might give rise to liability in cases where there would be no rights because either there are no horizontal direct effects or even no direct effects at all. But the focus has been moved to the seriousness of the breach. *Factortame III* introduced the revised criteria that the breach must be analogous to that applied to liability of the EC institutions under Art 288 (old 215) (2). This is known as the Shöppenstedt Formula and in order for liability to arise on the part of the Member State, there must have been a sufficiently serious breach of a superior rule of law designed for the protection of individuals. This has provoked further case law to help decide how serious a breach is required for Member States to incur liability. *British Telecom* (C-392/93) takes a generous view of what constitutes a breach but this can be contrasted with the *Hedley Lomas* case (C-5/94) where a mere infringement will invoke potential liability. Thus, if there is a breach, Member States must compensate according to the principles established in *Francovich*. Further, the *Wagner Miret* case (C-334/92) creates a bridge or link between *Marleasing* and *Francovich* because the ECJ held that if Member States can't construe national law to read in conformity, which is a distinct possibility as a result either of the court being incapable or unwilling, it must be assumed that Member States nevertheless intended to comply with its Community Law obligations. Thus, if there is a breach, Member States must compensate according to the principles established in *Francovich*. In other words, a *von Colson* failure under EC law should not be the end of the litigation line. It may be concluded that the difficulties caused by the *Marshall* (152/84) decision, whilst not overcome, have been mitigated in most other circumstances.

QUESTION 5

As part of its social programme under Article 141 of the EC Treaty, the Council adopted two Directives on 1 January 1999. The first Directive provides *inter alia* that 'Member States shall take such steps as they consider appropriate to encourage employers to adopt the same pension arrangements for men and women doing the same kind of work'. The second Directive provides that 'Member States shall ensure that employers do not discriminate between men and women doing the same kind of work in respect of holiday entitlement'.

Member States were given one year in which to implement both Directives. At the present time (January 2001) the United Kingdom has taken no steps to implement either Directive.

In December 1999 the Inland Revenue engaged Mrs Evans and Mr Rees as clerks. Their work is the same and they are paid the same. However, Mr Rees's contract of employment provides that he is entitled to four weeks holiday a year and is included in the company's own pension scheme, whereas Mrs Evans's contract of employment provides that she is entitled to three weeks holiday a year and is excluded from the company's pension scheme.

In January 2000, the Inland Revenue engaged a further clerk, Mrs Jones, who is employed on the same terms as Mrs Evans.

Mrs Evans and Mrs Jones are unhappy with their contracts of employment. Advise Mrs Evans, who made a claim in December 1999, and Mrs Jones who now claims, whether there are any provisions of EC law on which they could rely in an action brought before an English court or tribunal.

Would your advice be different if the place of employment at which they were working had been privatised?

Commentary

This question concerns the rights provided by two Directives and the ability of individuals to rely on those rights directly before the courts of their own country as a result of the fact that the Member State has not implemented the Directives within the time period for implementation.

It is necessary to discuss direct effects and the problems associated with the direct effects of Directives and where necessary, the alternative remedies where direct effects are not found to exist. In order to provide a solution you should identify the issues or particular problems arising as a result of the facts of the case. Then apply the legal rules to the issues and come to conclusions on each issue. Where helpful or necessary you should introduce any relevant case law to come to a conclusion on the problems or aspects of it.

Suggested Answer

The facts here are that there are two Directives which have not been implemented by the UK, which provide rights in respect of pensions and holiday entitlement for workers. Both Directives should have been implemented by 1 January 2000. One complaint relates to discrimination from December 1999 and the other from January 2000. In both claims, the discrimination relates to pension arrangements and holiday entitlement.

The applicable law for these claims is Art 249 (ex 189) which requires Member States to achieve a required result when implementing Directives, and the doctrine of direct effects which will allow individuals to enforce Community rights before their national courts. It would be useful briefly to define direct effects and the particular considerations applicable in respect of Directives. Directives can be subject to direct effects providing they satisfy the criteria as laid down in *Van Gend en Loos* (26/62) and subsequent cases. The special concerns of Directives and the time limits given for their implementation were considered in *Pubblico Ministero v Ratti* (148/78) which concerned the prosecution by the Italian authorities for breaches of national law concerning product labelling. Ratti had complied with two Community Directives; the expiry period for implementation of one of them had not expired. The Court held he could rely on the one for which the time period had expired provided it satisfied the other requirements, but not on the Directive whose implementation period had not expired. So, when the time period has expired, an individual can rely on the Directive if it fulfils the criteria. The case of *Verbond van Nederlandse Ondernemingen* (51/76) extended the situation to where a Directive had been implemented but that implementation was not faithful to the requirement of the Directive. The Court of Justice held that to deny the rights of individuals would be to weaken the effectiveness of Community obligations and that individuals helped to ensure that Member States kept within the realms of the discretion granted. In the case of *Marshall* (152/84), the ECJ held, however, that Directives could not be enforced against other individuals but could only be enforced vertically against the state to which they were addressed.

So, with the facts and law established the claims of the two workers must be considered.

Mrs Evans and Mrs Jones seek to rely on both Directives, Mrs Evans from December 1999 and Mrs Jones from January 2000. It is necessary to know whether in the absence of the UK implementing legislation at the material time they can rely directly on the Directive to give them rights enforceable in the national courts. To determine this the criteria adopted by the ECJ must be applied. Two questions arise, both of which must be answered. They are: have the time limits for the implementation of the Directives expired, and are the relevant provisions directly effective?

Only if the time limit has expired can the Directives be relied on. So in respect of any claim to rely on either of the Directives before January 2000, as the time limits will not have expired the claim will fail. The UK should have implemented the Directives by 1 January 2000. Applying the *Ratti* (148/78) case, when Mrs Evans's first claim was made the time limit had not expired and so the Directive could not have given rise to direct effects at that time.

The time limit had expired for the second claim made in January 2001, i.e., Mrs Jones's claim so we can move on and consider whether both of the Directives can now give rise to direct effects.

The claim in respect of equal pensions is covered by the first Directive, but does it satisfy the criteria for direct effects? Is it clear, precise and unconditional, etc.? The answer to this is probably that it is not clear enough given the words 'Member States shall take such steps as they consider appropriate to encourage'. Therefore there will not be direct effects and the Directive cannot be relied upon before the national courts, see generally the cases of *Van Gend en Loos* (26/62) and *Van Duyn* (41/74).

The second Directive relates to the holiday entitlement. Does it satisfy the criteria for direct effects? Yes, the Directive is clear, precise, legally perfect, complete and requires no further legislative intervention or implementation. It imposes a clear and unconditional obligation on Member States to ensure that employers do not discriminate between men and women doing the same kind of work in respect of holiday entitlement. The word 'shall' is a clear obligation. The provision therefore meets the requirements for direct effect, and can be relied on before a national court.

Any claim made before January 2000 by Mrs Evans, therefore, will fail due to the fact that the time limit for implementing the two Directives has not expired and the Member State cannot be held under any obligation before this date. Any claim in respect of pensions under the first Directive will also fail because it does not give rise to direct effects. However, alternatively it may be argued that as pensions have been held to constitute pay, which is covered by Art 141 a claim is therefore not dependent on the Directive and can be lodged relying on Art 141 itself. This is clear and precise and has been held to give rise to direct effects in the case of *Defrenne* v *Sabena (No. 2)* (43/ 75) and applied to pensions in the case of *Worringham* v *Lloyds Bank Ltd* (69/80). Whether holiday entitlements could also be interpreted as 'pay' is uncertain as there is no previous case which has considered this. The case of *Garland* (12/81) held that low-fare travel facilities for the family of ex-workers could be considered to be pay under Art 119 (now 141), but whether this would extend to holiday entitlement is not guaranteed.

In answer to the final part of the question relating to the status of the Inland Revenue as a private concern, it can be generally stated that the Court of Justice has repeatedly emphasised that direct effects so far as Directives are concerned only arises as against the Member States, and not against private individuals (see *Marshall* (152/84) and *Dori* (C-91/92), thus none of the claims will succeed here. However, whilst Directives cannot give rise to horizontal direct effects, Treaty Articles can, so a claim for equal pension provisions will succeed if lodged under Art 141, as discussed above.

In respect of the holiday entitlements, other remedies may be available using the *von Colson* (14/83) line of case law. The ECJ held in *von Colson* that, although a Directive may not be horizontally directly effective, the Member States' courts should take the provisions of the Directive into account when applying national law. With the second Directive, however, there are no rights in national law, so a national court cannot make an interpretation according to EC law. In these circumstances the *Marleasing* (C-106/89) and *Kopinghuis* (80/86) cases should be applied to state that there are general obligations under Arts 10 and 249 (ex 5 and 189) of the Treaty for the Member States to ensure compliance with Community law. Finally, the case of *Francovich* (C-6 & 9/90) might apply to obtain damages for the failure to implement the Directive. If an individual suffers damage as a result of the failure of a Member State to implement a Directive, the Member State may be liable to pay damages, if the Directive itself defined and conferred a right on individuals, the content of which was clear and not open to differing interpretations (*British Telecommunications* (C-392/93)). The fact that the UK has not taken any steps to implement the Directives by the prescribed time has been held by the Court of Justice to be sufficient to found a sufficiently serious breach of Community law (*Dillenkofer* (C-178, 179, 188 & 90/94)). It may well be, therefore, that both Mrs Jones and Mrs Evans have a claim for compensation against the UK. Any damages they do obtain must compensate them in full for losses directly incurred because of the breach (*Bonifaci* (C-94 & 95/95)).

4 The Supremacy of Community Law and its Reception in the Member States

INTRODUCTION

The subject matter of this chapter should be clear immediately. It is likely that many of you reading this will already have considered this topic from the national point of view in constitutional law courses. Inevitably questions on this topic in EC courses in the UK will most likely concentrate on the relationship between the EC and the UK and many will involve a consideration of the reasons for the supremacy of EC law before looking at the reception of EC law in the UK. Some questions, however, may look at these two aspects independently. Additionally, and depending on whether a consideration of the reception of Community law in other Member States has been covered in your course, a look at the reception in one or two or more other Member States may be undertaken and examined.

Both the legal arguments for supremacy and the political logic will often be considered in establishing the reasoning for Community law supremacy.

The first question in this chapter concentrates on the reasons for EC law supremacy from the point of view of the Community and in the view of the ECJ.

QUESTION 1

Is it the case that 'the doctrine of the supremacy of Community law is a logical if not a necessary inference from Community Treaties'?

Commentary

This clearly concerns the now well established doctrine or principle of constitutional law of supremacy. As with most questions, a definition of the subject matter of the question would be required. So, with the above question you need to state clearly and concisely what you understand by the phrase 'the doctrine of the supremacy of Community law', i.e., that established by the Court of Justice in the leading cases, of *Van Gend en Loos* (26/62) and *Costa* v *ENEL* (6/64).

You are then asked whether 'it is the case that it is logical if not a necessary inference' and you have to determine exactly what this cryptic part of the question is demanding for an answer. It suggests the supremacy of Community law is *logical,* but that it is not a *necessary inference* from the Treaties. You must address both these contentions.

Although the word logical appears first you should consider addressing the part about the necessary inference first, because this refers you to the Treaty provisions. It also makes sense to consider whether the Treaties provide for the supremacy before having to consider the logic of whether Community law is supreme. Then finally you must decide, if it is the case, how the Treaties logically provide for supremacy. This should be done with reference to any assistance from the Treaty and from the jurisprudence of the ECJ in which statements on supremacy are made.

Suggested Answer

The question has already hinted that the Treaties do not expressly provide for supremacy, i.e., there is no Article which clearly states that Community law is supreme. By a direct reading of the Treaty you might not necessarily infer that Community law is supreme. However, whilst there is no express statement of supremacy in the Treaty, it can be argued that some of the articles of the EC Treaty impliedly or logically require supremacy. Thus a conclusion as to whether Community law supremacy is to be inferred from the Treaty depends upon a consideration of some of its provisions. For example, Art 10 (ex 5), the good faith or fidelity clause; Art 12 (ex 6), the general prohibition of discrimination on the grounds of nationality; Art 249 (ex 189) in respect of the direct applicability of Regulations; Art 292 (ex 219), the obligation of Member States to submit only to Treaty dispute resolution and Art 228 (ex 171), the requirement to comply with rulings of the Court of Justice. So you could conclude that Community law requires supremacy but cannot state that the Treaty expressly or categorically imposes it.

It is through the decisions and interpretation of the Court of Justice that the reasons and logic for the supremacy of Community law have been developed. The Court of Justice's view on this is quite straightforward. From its case law, notably *Van Gend* (26/62), *Costa* v *ENEL* (6/64) and *Simmenthal* (106/77), it is clear that Community law is assumed to be an autonomous legal order which is related to international law and national law but nevertheless distinct from them.

The *Van Gend en Loos* case affirmed the Court's jurisdiction in interpreting Community legal provisions, the object of which is to ensure uniform interpretation in the Member States. The Court of Justice held that the Community constitutes a new legal order of international law for the benefit of which the states have limited their sovereign rights.

Further elaboration of the new legal order in *Van Gend* was given in *Costa* v *ENEL*. The case raised the issue of whether a national court should refer to the Court of Justice if it considers Community law may be applicable or, in the view of the Italian government, simply apply the subsequent national Law. The Court of Justice stressed the autonomous legal order of Community law in contrast with ordinary international treaties. It held that the EEC Treaty has created its own legal system which became an integral part of the legal systems of the Member States and which their courts are bound to apply. By creating a Community of unlimited duration, having its own institutions, its own personality, its own legal capacity and more particularly real powers stemming from a limitation of sovereignty or a transfer of powers from the states to the Community, the Member States have limited their sovereign rights and have created a body of law to bind their nationals and themselves.

The Court also established that Community law takes priority over all conflicting provisions of national law whether passed before or after the Community measure in question:

The integration into the laws of each Member State of provisions which derive from the Community, and more generally, the terms and spirit of the Treaty, make it impossible for the states, as a corollary, to accord precedence to a unilateral and subsequent measure over a legal system accepted by them on the basis of reciprocity. Such a measure cannot therefore be inconsistent with that legal system.

That is, a later national law does not overrule an earlier Community law. As additional justifications, the Court of Justice also invoked some of the general provisions of the Treaty: Art 5 (now 10), the requirement to ensure the attainment of the objectives of the Treaty and Art 7 EEC (now 12), regarding discrimination, both of which would be breached if subsequent national legislation was to have precedence. Furthermore the ECJ considered that Art 189 (now 249), regarding the binding and direct application of Regulations, would be meaningless if subsequent national legislation could prevail. The Court summed up its position:

> It follows . . . that the law stemming from the treaty, an independent source of law, could not because of its special and original nature, be overridden by domestic legal provisions, however framed, without being deprived of its character as Community law and without the legal basis of the Community itself being called into question.

Therefore Community law is to be supreme over subsequent national law.

There are two cases which additionally consider the conflict between Community law and national constitutional law.

The *Internationale Handelsgesellschaft* case (11/70) concerned the claim that Community levies were contrary to German constitutional law. The German Constitutional Court purported to reserve this question to itself but the ECJ held that the national courts did not possess the power to review Community law. The Court of Justice held that if there were no violation of Community fundamental rights, the Community measures were acceptable, i.e., there should be no reference to national constitutions to test the validity of Community law.

The second case of *Simmenthal* (106/77) arose from a conflict between the Italian constitution and Community law. In Italy the constitutional practice existed that the power to disregard or declare invalid a provision of national law was the sole right of the Constitutional Court. A lower court was faced with inconsistency between a Community law provision and a national provision but was aware that a reference to the Italian Constitutional Court would have the effect of subrogating Community law to national law, inconsistent with existent Community case law on the matter in the *Costa* v *ENEL* (6/64) case. However, disregarding the national law was contrary to constitutional requirements. The Italian magistrate made a reference to the ECJ and asked whether subsequent national measures which conflict with Community law must be disregarded without waiting until those measures are formally repealed or declared unconstitutional.

The ECJ firstly declared that the doctrine of direct effects of Community legislation was not dependent on any national constitutional provisions but a source of rights in itself. Therefore national courts which are called upon to apply provisions of Community law are under a duty to give full effect to those provisions including a refusal to apply conflicting national legislation, even if adopted subsequently. The ECJ also ruled that directly effective provisions of Community law also preclude the valid adoption of new legislative measures to the extent that they would be incompatible with Community provisions and that any inconsistent national legislation recognised by national legislatures as having legal effect would deny the effectiveness of the obligations undertaken by the Member State and imperil the existence of the Community.

In the *Factortame (No. 2)* case (C-213/89), the Court of Justice, building on the principle laid down in *Simmenthal* (106/77), i.e., that a provision of EC law must be implemented as effectively as possible, held that a national court must suspend national legislation that may be incompatible with EC law until a final determination on its compatibility has been made. In the case of doubt national law should be suspended. The *Factortame (No. 2)* case represents another confirmation that national constitutional practises or rules, in this case the doctrine of parliamentary sovereignty in the UK, must not be allowed to stand in the way of a Community law right. In the case this was the clear understanding of the courts that they had no power to set aside or not apply an Act of Parliament. The ECJ held that even though the Community law rule was still in dispute, the national procedure should be changed so as not to possibly interfere with the full effectiveness of the Community law right.

Hence, the Court of Justice in the cases of *Van Gend en Loos* (26/62), *Costa* v *ENEL* and *Simmenthal,* amongst others, has held that Community law supremacy is a logical conclusion. It can also be inferred from the doctrine of direct effects that Community law should be supreme both because of the transfer of powers from the Member States and because by having its own law making machinery, it must have precedence if the Community is going to work. The voluntary limitation of sovereignty and the need for an effective and uniform Community law requires supremacy. To give effect to subsequent national law over and above the Community legal system which Member States have accepted would be inconsistent and illogical.

Finally, in this context it is worth mentioning the consequences of a Member State not giving primacy to Community law when it should have done. Liability on the part of the state will be incurred as first established by the Court of Justice in the *Francovich* case (C-6/90) and later confirmed in *Factortame III* (C-46 and 48/93).

QUESTION 2

Consider how the Court of Justice's argument for the supremacy of Community law tempers traditional views of international law implementation and the principle that later laws overrule previous laws.

Commentary

This question requires you to consider the reasons for the supremacy of EC law according to the ECJ and to explain the consequences of this supremacy on previously held or valid international law principles. In your answer you need to outline the view of the ECJ or its grounds for stating that Community law should be supreme over the law of the Member States. The question then requires you to compare and contrast this view with the usually older relationship between international law and national law and the generally accepted principle that a later rule overrules a previous law. The answer should thus focus on the new legal order created by the founding of the Community which has upset or altered traditional views.

Suggested Answer

The first thing to consider is the reason why the Court of Justice has explained that Community law should take priority over conflicting national law. Whilst it is the case that there is no express declaration or specific legal base for the supremacy of Community law in the Treaties, it can be argued that some of the articles of the EC Treaty impliedly require primacy, for example, Art 10 (ex 5), the fidelity clause; Art 12 (ex 6), the general prohibition of discrimination on the grounds of nationality; Art 249 (ex 189), the direct applicability of Regulations and Art 292 (ex 219), the reservation of dispute resolution. It is through the decisions and interpretation of the Court of Justice that the reasons and logic for the supremacy of Community law have been developed. The Court of Justice's view on this is quite straightforward. From its case law, notably *Van Gend en Loos* (26/62), *Costa v ENEL* (6/64) and *Simmenthal* (106/77), it is clear that Community law is assumed to be an autonomous legal order which is related to international law and national law but nevertheless distinct from them.

The *Van Gend en Loos* (26/62) case affirmed the Court's jurisdiction in interpreting Community legal provisions, the object of which is to ensure uniform interpretation in the Member States. The Court of Justice held that the Community constitutes a new legal order of international law for the benefit of which the states have limited their sovereign rights.

Further elaboration of the new legal order in *Van Gend* was given in *Costa v ENEL* (6/64) in which the Court of Justice held:

By contrast with ordinary international treaties the EEC Treaty has created its own legal system which became an integral part of the legal systems of the Member States and which their courts are bound to apply. By creating a Community of unlimited duration, the Member States have limited their sovereign rights and have created a body of law to bind their nationals and themselves.

The Court also established that Community law takes priority over all conflicting provisions of national law whether passed before or after the Community measure in question by holding that:

The integration into the laws of each Member State of provisions which derive from the Community, and more generally, the terms and spirit of the Treaty, make it impossible for the states, as a corollary, to accord precedence to a unilateral and subsequent measure over a legal system accepted by them on the basis of reciprocity. Such a measure cannot therefore be inconsistent with that legal system.

That is, a later national law does not overrule an earlier Community law.

The Court summed up its position:

It follows . . . that the law stemming from the Treaty, could not because of its special and original nature, be overridden by domestic legal provisions, without the legal basis of the Community itself being called into question.

Therefore Community law is to be supreme over subsequent national law.

In *Simmenthal* (106/77), the Court of Justice ruled that national courts which are called upon to apply provisions of Community law, are under a duty to give full effect to those provisions and if necessary to set aside any conflicting provisions of national legislation, even if adopted subsequently. It held that directly effective provisions of Community law preclude the valid adoption of new legislative measures to the extent that they would be incompatible with Community provisions. Any inconsistent national legislation recognised by national legislatures as having legal effect would deny the effectiveness of the obligations undertaken by the Member State. Therefore, to give effect to subsequent national law over and above the Community legal system which Member States have accepted would be inconsistent and imperil the existence of the Community.

In the *Factortame* case (C-213/89), the Court of Justice, building on the principle laid down in *Simmenthal,* i.e., that a provision of EC law must be implemented as effectively as possible, held that a national court must suspend national legislation that may be incompatible with EC law until a final determination on its compatibility has been made. In case of doubt the national law should be suspended.

Next, it is necessary to consider whether the legal position established in the Community upsets traditional international law theories and practices.

Traditional international law implementation conforms to one of two theories of incorporation, either that of monism or dualism. The views of the ECJ contrast with both of these. Monism basically assumes that international law and national law form part of a single world system or hierarchy of laws. This means in relation to the acceptance of international law there would have to be no formal incorporation of international law into the national legal system by legislative transformation. The international law would be self-executing within the nations who adopt the monist position, i.e., it would be directly applicable within the state. All that is required by such a state to achieve this is a simple assent to, or ratification of an international Treaty.

Dualism, on the other hand, regards international law and national law as belonging to fundamentally different systems of law which exist alongside each other but are distinctly separated, as in watertight compartments. In order to overcome the barrier existing between the two systems, legislation is required to transform rules of international law into the national legal system before it can have any binding effect within the state.

If a Member State conformed to monism, international law joins the national hierarchy of law but enjoys no special status and it can be overruled by later national law, However, there is a presumption that, in the case of inconsistency, there was no intention by the national Parliament to be inconsistent unless this was express.

If a Member State continued to adhere to dualism in respect of Community law and there was no transformation, the Community law would remain outside the legal order. However, when transformed it would merely take on the status of national law and would be subject to the usual rules including the view that later laws overrule earlier laws.

The EC legal order, as a new legal order, does not conform to this strict division. For example, Treaty articles and certain forms of Community legislation, e.g., Regulations, are not transformed in the national legal orders to have validity but are directly applicable, see Art 249 (ex 189) EC. Member states which previously had conformed to the dualist approach did not in fact transform these types of legislation into the national legal orders but instead simply acceded to the Community and adopted Treaty Articles and Regulations automatically, see for example, the UK and Germany. In addition to this, other forms of Community law, whilst not directly applicable, can also have effect in the Member States without transformation in certain circumstances. See the Court of Justice development of the doctrine of direct effects in the cases of *Van Gend en Loos* (26/62), *Van Duyn* (41/74) and *Grad* (9/70).

The traditional view that the later law will prevail was not just limited to an express overruling or inconsistency but also to implied overruling in cases of inconsistency, whether intentional or not. Thus that any later inconsistent law impliedly repealed the earlier was recognised in both common law and civil law jurisdictions. The case law of *Van Gend en Loos* (26/62), *Costa* v *ENEL* (6/64) and *Simmenthal* (106/77), noted above, contradict this form of repeal in the Community legal order which must now be adopted in the Member States, although it has taken some time for this to be accepted in some of the Member States, e.g., the UK, Germany and France. Community law supremacy when in conflict is regardless of whether it is later or even earlier than the national law. Therefore, the principle that later laws overrule earlier may still be valid domestically but it is now possible for an earlier EC law to overrule a later national law, see the case of *Marleasing* (C-106/89) in this respect.

QUESTION 3

Comment on the view that the biggest obstacle to accepting the supremacy of EC law in the UK was and is the doctrine of Parliamentary sovereignty.

Commentary

This question concerns the supremacy of EC law and how this was catered for when faced with the difficult constitutional issue of Parliamentary sovereignty in the UK.

The subject matter of this question is clear and can be divided into three parts.

First, it is necessary to outline the reasoning for the supremacy of Community law from the Community point of view, largely achieved by considering the leading cases from the Court of Justice. Secondly, a definition and the consequences of the doctrine of Parliamentary sovereignty must be given. Both these parts are reasonably straightforward and would thus be fairly descriptive passages. You should try to be more concise in your description of the meaning and scope of Parliamentary sovereignty than for courses in constitutional law but could certainly employ much of the work done for this topic in that subject. Certainly you should consider the limitations which have been acknowledged and point out that the doctrine of Parliamentary sovereignty itself is subject to criticism and qualification.

The third part requires more thought, especially in structuring your answer. Set out the issues to be tackled and explain that at first sight these two doctrines appear to be incompatible. You should then consider the European Communities Act 1972 and whether this has reconciled the two doctrines. Finally, consider how the UK courts have considered this relationship. Given the system of precedence in the UK the latest cases should now be overriding the dicta of older cases, e.g., the judgments of Lord Bridge in *Factortame* (C-213/89) are of more use than the judgments of Lord Denning in *Macarthys* (129/79) and Lord Diplock in *Garland* (12/81).

Suggested Answer

The Treaties do not contain a specific legal base or express declaration for the supremacy of Community law but some articles logically imply supremacy.

See Art 10 (ex 5), the fidelity clause; Art 12 (ex 6), prohibiting discrimination on the grounds of nationality; Art 249 (ex 189), providing for the direct applicability of Regulations and Art 292 (ex 219), ensuring Community dispute resolution autonomy. The Court of Justice has basically developed the reasons and logic for the supremacy of Community law.

The *Van Gend en Loos* (26/62) case affirmed the Court's exclusive jurisdiction in interpreting Community legal provisions to ensure uniform interpretation in the Member States. In the *Costa* v *ENEL* (6/64) case, its autonomous nature was emphasised. The case questioned whether a national court ʿshould refer to the ECJ if it considers Community law may be applicable or, in the view of the Italian government, simply apply the subsequent national law. According to the ECJ the voluntary limitation of sovereignty and the need for an effective and uniform Community law requires its supremacy. To give effect to subsequent national law over and above the Community legal system would be inconsistent.

To summarise the Community view on supremacy according to the Court of Justice is that, Community law, because of it's unique nature, denies the Member States the right to resolve conflicts of law by reference to their own rules or constitutional provisions. Community law obtains its supremacy because of the transfer of state power and sovereignty to the Community by the Member States in those areas agreed. Furthermore, the Member States have provided the Community with legislative powers to enable it to perform its tasks. There would be no point in such a transfer of power if the Member States could annul or suspend the effect of Community law by later national law or provisions of their constitutions. If that were allowed to be the case, the existence of the Community legal order and the Community itself would be called into question.

A precondition of the existence and functioning of the Community is the uniform and consistent application of Community law and the Community legal order in all the Member States. It can only achieve such an effect if it takes precedence over national law. Therefore the legal and logical consequences of this are that any provision of national law which conflicts with Community law must be invalid.

The meaning of Parliamentary sovereignty must now be considered.

Basically, in the terms of Dicey, the doctrine of Parliamentary sovereignty means that there are no legal limitations of Parliament and it has the right to make or unmake any law whatsoever. Further, no person or body is recognised as having a right to override or set aside the legislation of Parliament. The doctrine also implies that it is impossible to bind future Parliaments. Any subsequent Act expressly or impliedly overrides a prior Act and even international treaties can be expressly overridden by municipal law. See generally the cases of *Vauxhall Estates* ([1932] 1 KB 733), *Ellen Street Estates* ([1934] 1 KB 590) and *Mortesen* v *Peters* ((1906) 8 F(J) 93) to support these contentions. There is no constitutional role for UK courts: they cannot review the validity of Acts passed by Parliament. They must enforce and apply Acts of Parliament equally. See the cases of *Burmah Oil Co.* v *Lord Advocate* ([1965] AC 85) and *British Railways Board* v *Pickin* ([1974] AC 765) to support these views.

There are, however, limitations to Parliamentary sovereignty, most notably those devolving power externally and concerned with a change of state. Dicey admitted that there were political limits to the sovereign power of Parliament. Parliament could abdicate or divest itself of power to another body. This may be irreversible and although it would be possible to pass an amending Act, it would be politically impossible to regain power once surrendered, unless by the acceptance of the entity to whom power had been surrendered. Dicey was referring not only to complete abdication but also to partial abdication or transfer of powers.

The arguments of abdication of political sovereignty must also apply in favour of the European Communities. The issue thus focuses on how the UK tried to resolve the clash of Parliamentary sovereignty and Community law supremacy. The European Communities Act 1972 was passed in an attempt to overcome this.

In contrast to the earlier practice of incorporation, the European Communities Act 1972 did not reproduce the whole of the Treaties or subsequent secondary legislation as Acts of Parliament. If this was so, the words of any future Act could override the prior Treaty. The Community Treaties were adopted by a simple assent. The Act therefore impliedly recognises the unique new legal system and is regarded as a very special form of UK legislation by its attempt to bind future Parliaments. It had still, however, to ensure that Community law was supreme, not only as against prior UK legislation but also future UK legislation.

Section 2(1) recognises the legal validity and direct applicability of Community Treaties and Regulations already existing and provides that all such future Community legal provisions shall also be recognised. The subsection recognises the doctrine of direct effects and allows for future developments by the Court of Justice. This is termed in the Act as an 'enforceable Community right . . . and similar expressions'.

Section 2(4) is the subsection which recognises the supremacy of Community law and therefore concerns sovereignty. Any such provision and any enactment passed or to be passed (that refers to any Act of Parliament past or future) shall be construed and have effect subject to the foregoing provisions of this section. That is a reference to the entire section and in particular s. 2(1) and means any future Act of Parliament must be construed in such a way as to give effect to the enforceable Community rights. This is achieved by denying effectiveness to any national legislation passed later which is in conflict with Community law.

Section 3(1) instructs the courts to refer questions on the interpretation and hence the supremacy of Community law to the Court of Justice if the UK courts cannot solve the problem themselves by reference to previous Court of Justice rulings. This follows the *Costa* v *ENEL* (6/64) ruling and is backed up by s. 3(2) which requires the courts to follow decisions of the Court of Justice on any question of Community law. This would include direct effects and supremacy although it does not expressly say so.

Therefore it can be argued the combination of s. 2(1) and s. 2(4) with the control of s. 3(1) and (2) achieve the essential requirements of the recognition of direct effects and the supremacy of Community law for past and future UK legislation.

It is contended that the 1972 Act purports to bind future Parliaments and negates the doctrine of Parliamentary sovereignty. However, the effect of a cleverly drafted piece of legislation may be negated by the judicial reception it receives in the courts. The acid test of any piece of legislation is the interpretation given to it in the Courts and in order to assess its worth we must consider the case law of the UK courts.

As yet the courts have made no express statement on how these two seemingly conflicting doctrines can be resolved. Whilst a number of cases have provided views, expressed as *obiter dicta,* on what they might do in the case of an intention on the part of Parliament to legislate in conflict with the Community, it has not yet arisen in reality (see the judgments of Lord Denning in *Macarthys* [1979] ICR 785 and Lord Diplock in *Garland* ([1983]

2 AC 751)). The best statement to date on this topic comes from the case of *Factortame* ([1991] 1 AC 603 at 645). In this case Lord Bridge commented on the view that the earlier decisions in favour of Community law were an attack on Parliamentary sovereignty. He considered that if the supremacy of Community law over the national law of Member States was not always inherent in the EEC Treaty, it was certainly well established in the jurisprudence of the Court of Justice long before the United Kingdom joined the Community. He thus considered that the limitation of its sovereignty which Parliament accepted when it enacted the European Communities Act 1972 was entirely voluntary. He concluded that, under the terms of the 1972 Act, it has always been clear that it was the duty of a United Kingdom court to override any rule of national law found to be in conflict with any directly enforceable rule of Community law. According supremacy to Community law in those areas to which they apply was therefore nothing new. National courts must not be inhibited by rules of national law from granting interim relief in appropriate cases because it is no more than a logical recognition of supremacy. In *R v Secretary of State for Employment ex parte EOC* ([1995] 1 CMLR 395), the House of Lords confirmed the conclusion reached in *Factortame* and held that in judicial review proceedings the UK courts could declare an Act of Parliament to be incompatible with EC law, although this does not extend to being able to annul the UK Act of Parliament nor indeed command a Government to repeal the act or compel or command a minister to change the law.

The conclusions are that it is true that the European Communities Act 1972 has transferred sovereignty in certain areas as agreed for an indefinite period, but whether it has completely overruled the doctrine cannot be stated. The real problem in trying to reconcile these doctrines is that legal reasoning is not fully reconcilable with the practical realities of Community membership. Whilst it may be *legally* possible to repeal the 1972 Act and leave the Communities, it is *practically* and *politically* untenable. Thus, as far as membership of the Communities is concerned, the doctrine of Parliamentary sovereignty is, at least, in abeyance, if not completely undermined. As such the UK seems to have gone further than some of the other Member States. Areas of law which are still the exclusive jurisdiction of the UK are still subject to the full weight of the doctrine.

QUESTION 4

How does the European Communities Act 1972 seek to ensure that Community law which is directly effective or directly applicable has that status in the United Kingdom and prevails over conflicting UK law?

What problems, if any, have been experienced in practice in attaining the aims of the Act?

Commentary

This is a question which concentrates on the practical clash of Community and national legislation and puts the theories of the last question to the test. It requires you to consider the legal argument of how membership was accommodated in the UK legal system and the reception of Community law in the UK courts.

First, you should look in detail at the Act and how it sets out to achieve its aims. Then you need to see how it works in practice, i.e., to look at how the UK courts have interpreted and applied it.

Whilst there are a number of earlier cases which discuss the perceived relationship and the effect of the European Communites Act (ECA) 1972, it would be better to concentrate on the latest cases which provide a truer reflection of the present situation. However, a brief review of earlier case law would still be acceptable.

Suggested Answer

Community law implementation in the UK is primarily concerned with how the 1972 Act observes and takes account of such well established Community law concepts or doctrines as direct effects and supremacy of Community law, and the difficulties in respect of sovereignty.

In contrast to the earlier practice of incorporation which followed the dualist approach to international law, the ECA 1972 did not reproduce the whole of the Treaties or subsequent secondary legislation as Acts of Parliament. If it had done so, the words of any future UK Act could impliedly override and thus repeal the prior Treaty as it would simply have the status of any other UK Act of Parliament.

All prior Community legislation was adopted by a simple Act of Accession, except for those Directives which required national law implementation. The ECA therefore impliedly recognises the unique new legal system and is regarded as a very special form of UK legislation by its attempt to bind future Parliaments.

The most important provisions of the Act, which concern the acceptance of Community law, are as follows. Section 2(1), recognises the direct applicability and thus validity of Community Treaty provisions and Regulations and arguably the doctrine of direct effects. This is termed in the Act 'enforceable community right and similar expressions'. Thus those rights or duties which are, as a matter of Community law, directly applicable or effective are to be given legal effect in the UK. It also provides that all such future Community legal provisions shall also be given legal effect and enforced and followed in UK.

Section 2(2) allows for the implementation of Community obligations such as Directives or Decisions, which are not automatically applicable in the UK, via Orders in Council or Statutory Instruments. The Executive has power to make secondary legislation to give effect to Community obligations and any ensuring developments.

Section 2(4) recognises the supremacy of Community law and therefore concerns sovereignty. It states that any such provision and any enactment passed or to be passed (that refers to any Act of Parliament past or future) shall be construed and have effect subject to the foregoing provisions of this section. That is a reference to the entire section, in particular s. 2(1), and means any future Act of Parliament must be construed in such a way as to give effect to the enforceable Community rights in existence. This is achieved by denying effectiveness to any national legislation passed later which is in conflict. This is further controlled by the directions to the courts. Section 3(1) instructs the courts to refer questions on the interpretation and hence the supremacy of Community law to the Court of Justice if the UK courts cannot solve the problem themselves by reference to previous Court of Justice rulings. This follows the *Costa* v *ENEL* (6/64) ruling and is backed up by s. 3(2) which requires the courts to follow decisions of the Court of Justice on any question of Community law. Therefore it can be argued the combination of s. 2(1) and s. 2(4) with the control of s. 3(1) and (2) achieves the essential requirements of the recognition of the doctrine of direct effects and the supremacy of Community law for past and future UK legislation.

The views of the courts in decided case law are thus now paramount in answering this question because the application of Community law is dependent on the national judiciary.

The most important of the earlier cases is *Macarthys Ltd* v *Smith* ([1979] ICR 785) in which Lord Denning MR expressed the view that it was the court's bounden duty to give priority to Community law under s. 2(1) and (4) of the ECA 1972 in as of deficient or inconsistent national law, i.e., unintentional inconsistency. Lord Denning *(obiter)* thought that with regard to an express or intentional repudiation of the Treaty or expressly acting inconsistently, the courts would be bound to follow the express and clear intent of Parliament to repudiate the Treaty or a section of it by the subsequent Act. Following a reference made to the ECJ (case 129/79), the Court of Appeal ([1981] QB 180 at 199) later confirmed that Community law is now part of UK law and whenever there is any inconsistency Community law has priority.

In *Garland* v *BREL* ([1983] 2 AC 751), UK and Community law were regarded by the House of Lords as clearly inconsistent. A reference was made to the Court of Justice (12/81), which ruled that Community law covered the situation in the case. The House of Lords considered themselves bound in view of the Court of Justice ruling and ECA 1972 to interpret the national law in such a way as not to be inconsistent with the UK obligations under Community law. They concluded *(obiter)* that UK courts should interpret UK law consistently with Community law, no matter how wide a departure from the words of the UK Act the interpretation needed to be.

In a case brought at roughly the same time as the *Marshall* (152/84) case, *Duke* v *GEC Reliance* ([1988] AC 618), also dealing with equal retirement ages but involving a private employer, the House of Lords rightly concluded that the Directive itself could not be enforced by Mrs Duke against individuals, i.e., it had no horizontal direct effects. However, when seeking an alternative solution via the ECA, the House of Lords held that s. 2(4) and (1) only refer to directly effective or directly applicable Community law so that Mrs Duke's claim was defeated. At the time this judgment was considered to be a very backward step by a UK court and seemed to uphold the supremacy of the UK Parliament over Community law.

In the case of *Pickstone* v *Freemans plc* ([1989] AC 66) the House of Lords followed the advice of the Court of Justice in the *von Colson* (14/83) case to interpret and apply national legislation adopted for implementation of a Community Directive in conformity with the requirements of Community law, but suggested this could only be done under s. 2(4) ECA where the actual words used are reasonably capable of being interpreted to read in conformity with EC law.

In the case of *Litster* v *Forth Dry Dock & Engineering Co. Ltd* ([1990] 1 AC 546) the UK secondary legislation which purported to implement the obligations contained in the EEC Council Directive 187/77 was considered to be ambiguous. The Directive did not give rise to direct effects because a private employer was involved. The House of Lords could not achieve a satisfactory result in keeping with the European Directive and the case law of the Court of Justice, by a literal attempt, and concluded that under s. 2(4) it must use the Community legislation to interpret the later UK legislation and imply additional provisions to achieve consistency.

Two cases known as *R* v *Secretary of State for Transport, ex parte Factortame Ltd* (C-213/89 and C-221/89) are particularly important cases in respect of the supremacy of Community law. A party seeking to rely on Community law sought an interim injunction against the Crown not to apply a disputed national regulation issued under a UK Act whilst the merits of the case were being referred to the Court of Justice. This was something not previously acceptable as courts could not set aside UK law. The House of Lords considered that if Community law rights were to be found to be directly enforceable in favour of the appellants those rights would prevail over the inconsistent national legislation, even if it has been passed later. It was said (*obiter*) that:

This [s. 2(4)] has precisely the same effect as if a section were incorporated into [the national statute] which in terms enacted that the provisions [of an Act] were to be without prejudice to the directly enforceable Community rights of nationals of any Member State of the EEC.

Upon the return of the procedural aspect from the Court of Justice, the House of Lords held that, if a national rule precludes a court from granting an interim relief, in order to determine whether there is a conflict between national law and Community law, the court must set aside that rule: in effect ignore national law. Lord Bridge considered that if the supremacy of Community law over the national law of Member States was not always inherent in the EEC Treaty, it was certainly well established in the jurisprudence of the Court of Justice long before the United Kingdom joined the Community. He concluded that under the terms of the 1972 Act it had always been clear that it was the duty of a United Kingdom court to override any rule of national law found to be in conflict with any directly enforceable rule of Community law. Therefore, national courts must not be inhibited by rules of national law from granting interim relief in appropriate cases because it is no more than a logical recognition of supremacy. In *R* v *Secretary of State for Employment ex parte EOC*, the House of Lords confirmed the conclusion reached in *Factortame* and held that in judicial review proceedings the UK courts could declare an Act of Parliament to be incompatible with EC law, although this does not extend to being able to annul the UK Act of Parliament nor indeed command a Government to repeal the act or compel or command a minister to change the law.

The view now of s. 2(4) ECA is that it is a direct rule to give priority, rather than a rule of construction which requires there to be national law to construe or even to limit the function of the court to a reasonable construction. As far as the House of Lords is now concerned entry to the Communities and s. 2(4) of the ECA 1972 has led to the modification of the doctrine of parliamentary sovereignty because implied repeal of previous Acts of Parliament, as far as Community law obligations are concerned, would not be heeded by the courts. Whether this overrides the dictum in *Macarthys* v *Smith* ([1979] ICR 785) is open to question. It remains open for Parliament expressly to repeal the Act and the courts would of course have to observe this faithfully.

QUESTION 5

How have the courts of Member States other than the UK reacted to the Court of Justice's view on the supremacy of Community law?

Commentary

To be capable of answering this question, you must have at least taken account of the position of other Member States in your course on Community law. This is not always the case and the depth of treatment may vary considerably. The states which may have been concentrated on are those whose courts may have been reluctant to accept Community law supremacy in all cases, or whose legal orders presented seemingly intractable barriers. As a contrast with these states it may be worthwhile making a brief contrast with a state which found no difficulty in accepting the supremacy of Community law. Your choice of states to consider will very much depend on those considered in your particular course.

Suggested Answer

A number of states have not experienced any problems so far, see for example, Luxembourg, Netherlands and Belgium. The last state provides a good example of an unproblematic acceptance of the supremacy of Community law.

In Belgium, the constitution was amended to allow for the transfer of powers to institutions governed by international law (Art 25a). However, Belgium was a dualist country whereby later laws would prevail over earlier including international treaties if these were simply converted into national law. The courts in Belgium have no role in respect of judging the validity of international agreements but accepted Community law supremacy as if it were a monist country and not in reliance on a Belgian statute (see *Minister for Economic Affairs* v *SA Fromagerie 'Le Ski'* ([1972] CMLR 330)). It was held that in the case of conflict between national law and the directly effective law of an international Treaty, the latter would prevail even if earlier in time.

In Germany, in contrast, some difficulties were experienced, especially in respect of the provision of fundamental rights in the German constitution (*Grundgesetz*) and in the Community legal order.

Article 24 of the German constitution allows for a transfer of powers and membership of international organisations and was used to establish membership of the European Communities. Article 25 declares general rules of public international law to be an integral part of federal law and to take precedence over national law but it is silent as to the effect of international law on the German constitution.

Previously German courts had been divided as to the effect of Community primary law and secondary law and at times courts had refused to make a reference in cases of doubt or not accept Community law supremacy, thus denying the parties to the case the chance to see whether Community law would have affected the outcome of the case. However, the views of the Federal Constitutional Court are paramount because of its constitutional position in the German state.

In the *Internationale Handelsgesellschaft case* ([1974] 2 CMLR 540), the Constitutional Court held that as long as the recognition of human rights in the Community had not progressed as far as those provided for by the *Grundgesetz,* German courts had the right to refer questions on the constitutionality of secondary Community law to the Federal Constitutional Court with the possible result that Community law might be ignored if it did not have sufficient regard for basic rights. This position changed in the *Wunsche Handelsgesellschaft* decision ([1987] 3 CMLR 225). The Federal Constitutional Court accepted that Community recognition and safeguards of fundamental rights through the case law of the Court of Justice were now sufficient and of a comparable nature to those provided for by the *Grundgesetz*. Thus as long as Community law ensures the effective provision of fundamental rights the Federal Constitutional Court will not review Community law in the light of the rights provisions of the constitution. It also stated that it would not be prepared to accept constitutional complaints from lower courts on this basis. The basis for the decision is not, however, the inherent supremacy of Community law but the fact that Art 24 of the *Grundgesetz* allowed a transfer of powers to the Community and the subsequent accession Act obliged the German courts to accept the supremacy of Community law.

Following these cases there would seem to be no procedural difficulty in getting Community rights at least considered in the proper forum in Germany. Any court which refuses either to follow a previous ruling of the Court of Justice or make an Art 234 (ex 177) ruling may be subject to the review of the Federal Constitutional Court for an arbitrary breach of Art 101(1) of the *Grundgesetz*.

The Federal Constitutional Court held in the *Brunner* case ([1994] 1 CMLR 57) that, the German Accession Statute to the Treaty on European Union was compatible with the German constitution and thus rejected claims that it was unconstitutional, although again there was a dubious statement to the effect that a review function of the Constitutional Court would still be maintained to ensure Community law complied with the provision of fundamental rights.

The German courts are still able to provide conflicting evidence in respect of their recognition of the supremacy of Community law. In 1996, in one of a series of cases arising from the German courts challenging the Community Banana regime preference of ACP states and not the traditional south American countries supplying Germany (*Federal Tax* case of 9/1/1996, 7 EuZW 126 (1996)), the Federal Tax Court upheld German law on the basis of basic rights over the Community rules. In contrast is German Supreme Court ruling (Bundesgerichtshof) in the *Brasserie du Pécheur* v *Federal Republic of Germany* (C-46/93) case, which accepted the principle of state liability on the part of the German state for a legislative breach. In the case, however, the Court held that the breach had not been sufficiently serious enough to impose liability.

In Italy the position both constitutionally and judicially was and is very similar to Germany whereby both had new constitutions set up after the Second World War with strong provisions for fundamental rights. Both allowed a transfer of power to international organisations but were silent as to the effect on constitutional law (see Art 11 of the Italian constitution).

As in Germany, the focus in Italy is on the Constitutional Court. Given that two of the leading cases on supremacy, *Costa v ENEL* (6/64) and *Simmenthal* (92/78) arose from Italy, it should certainly have been clear to the Italian Constitutional Court what was expected of it. Again there has been a mixed reaction, also along the lines of the German Constitutional Court.

In *Granital SpA v Amministrazione delle Finanze* (see 1984) 21 CML Rev pp. 756–72) the supremacy of Community law was accepted on the basis of an interpretation of Art 11 of the Italian constitution allowing for the limitation of sovereignty in favour of international organisations, and by reason of the case law of the Court of Justice. The case did, however, make the reservation that Italian law should only be cast aside where directly applicable Community law exists, similar in effect to the judgment of the House of Lords in the *Duke* case ([1988] AC 618).

A later decision in *Fragd SpA v Amministrazione delle Finanze* (see 1990) 27 CML Rev pp. 93–5) suggests the Italian Constitutional Court is still prepared to review Community law in the light of the fundamental rights provision in the Italian constitution.

The French courts are divided into two hierarchies with their own appeal courts and final appeal. They have had, however, significantly different attitudes to Community law, despite the fact that both are subject to Art 55 of the French constitution which is monist and gives international law a rank above municipal law but is silent as to the effect on the constitution. This is the point that has led to discrepancies between hierarchies.

The courts of ordinary jurisdiction have felt no hesitation in making Art 234 (ex 177) references to the Court of Justice and giving supremacy to Community law on the basis of Art 55 of the constitution. The French Supreme Court of Ordinary Jurisdiction, the *Cour de Cassation*, has in fact gone further and found for the supremacy of Community law without direct reference to Art 55 of the Constitution and more on the basis of the inherent supremacy and direct effects of Community law itself. See the *Café Vabre* case ([1975] 2 CMLR 336) in which Art 95 EEC (now 90 EC) was held to prevail over a subsequent national statute. These rulings have been consistently followed by the lower courts and reference to either Art 55 of the

Constitution or even the above decisions is rarely made (see, for example, *Garage Dehus Sarl* v *Bouche Distribution* ([1984] 3 CMLR 452)).

French administrative courts deal with complaints by citizens against any acts of the state administration. The Supreme Administrative Court, the *Conseil d'Etat,* has from time to time completely denied the supremacy of Community law or the need to make reference to the Court of Justice, relying heavily on the French principle of law, known as the *acte clair* (see, for example, *Minister of the Interior* v *Cohn-Bendit* ([1980] 1 CMLR 543)). The French court held individuals could not directly rely on Directives to challenge an administrative act. The court declined to follow previous Court of Justice rulings or make a reference itself.

More recently, however, cases have demonstrated a much more cooperative attitude on the part of the French administrative courts. In *Nicolo* ([1990] 1 CMLR 173), the Conseil d'Etat reviewed the supremacy of international law including EEC Treaty Articles and held the latter to take precedence over subsequent national law, largely on the basis of Art 55 of the Constitution. In *Boisdet* ([1991] 1 CMLR 3), incompatible national law was declared invalid in the face of a Community Regulation. In doing so the Conseil d'Etat followed the case law of the Court of Justice. The *Rothmans* case ([1993] CMLR 253) confirms the supremacy of Community Directives over subsequent national law and that public authorities cannot enforce the incompatible national law.

Finally, in *Dangeville* (see (1993) PL 535), the Paris Administrative Court of Appeal upheld the ruling of the ECJ in *Francovich* (C-6 & 9/90) and imposed a liability on the French state to pay damages for the failure to implement a Community Directive.

The Treaty on European Union has been declared compatible with the constitution after amendments to the constitution and has been ratified and thus takes priority over French national law (Art 88).

Whilst it can be seen that there have been some problems in other Member States and there may continue to be problems, by and large the supremacy of Community law is increasingly recognised and applied in other Member States and the Community legal order continues to make its mark on the national legal orders.

5 The Jurisdiction of the Court of Justice

INTRODUCTION

This chapter deals with questions on the range of actions or types of procedure provided for under the EC Treaty. These are the actions under Arts 226–228, 230, 232, 234, 241 and 235 & 288 (ex 169–171, 173, 175, 177, 184 and 178 & 215). Whereas a division is often made in text books between the actions which are considered directly by the Court of Justice and those which are only heard indirectly by the Court of Justice in the course of litigation before a national court, such a division seemed rather artificial in a book on questions and answers on Community law. The reason for taking this view is that many questions ask for alternative actions or procedures to be considered in the event that the most obvious or first action proves to be too difficult or unsuccessful for the applicant. Another reason is that not all textbooks make the same division and whilst there is some consistency maintained between direct and indirect actions, some make further distinctions between actions seeking to enforce Community law in the Member State and other actions which are classified as administrative actions concerning challenges of the legality of Community law or actions of the institutions.

Grouping them all together in one chapter avoids having to split the subject matter, which concerns essentially one topic, i.e., the jurisdiction of the Court of Justice, into two, three or even four separate and smaller chapters. All questions concerned with the procedural jurisdiction of the Court of Justice are dealt with in this chapter with the exception of some mixed topic questions in the final chapter.

The range of questions is quite considerable under this broad heading. Questions can range from a straightforward consideration of the procedure of each action to the difficulties for applicants in these actions; the setting of difficult problem questions on the procedural aspects to questions requiring a consideration of more than one action. Mixed questions which concern both procedural law and the substantive law of the Community have, however, been reserved to the last chapter of the book.

This chapter includes a mixture of essay and problem type questions.

QUESTION 1

Discuss the effectiveness of the Art 226 procedure in ensuring compliance with Community law on the part of Member States.

Commentary

The question is concerned with the authority which has been provided by the Treaty under Art 226 (ex 169) to the Commission to prosecute Member States for a failure to comply with their obligations under Community law. It allows the Commission to police the application and implementation of Community law by the Member States. It requires, first of all, a description of the procedure for the actions under Art 226 (ex 169). In so describing the procedure you could, if these were featured in your course, give an idea of how many cases reach the Court of Justice under these actions.

Having provided a description, you are required to consider whether this procedure is effective in ensuring Member States' compliance with Community law. Whilst not an express requirement of this part of the answer it may nevertheless be useful to suggest other ways in which compliance may be required or encouraged.

Suggested Answer

The Art 226 (ex 169) procedure is provided to allow the Commission to pursue its task of policing the application and compliance with the Treaties and secondary Community law obligations. In order for a procedure to commence, a breach of an obligation by a Member State must be suspected by or brought to the attention of the Commission. A breach or failure to act is most often observed in the form that a Member State has failed to implement Community legislation, mainly Directives, or that the implementation was incomplete or dilatory, or the Member State has failed to remove national legislation which is in conflict or inconsistent with Community legislation or obligations. This includes decisions of the Court of Justice. A breach may also be the action of a Member State in enacting or maintaining legislation or national regulations incompatible with the Treaty or secondary Community law. The failure can be attributed to all organs of the state not just the government.

If the Commission thinks a breach is probable, Art 226 (ex 169) requires certain administrative procedural steps to be taken before a court action can result. The first part of Art 226 (ex 169) states: 'If the Commission considers that a Member State has failed to fulfil an obligation under this treaty, it shall deliver a reasoned opinion on the matter'. This means that the Commission must have reached a conclusion that the Member State is in breach of an obligation before it can commence an action before the Court. The matter can be brought to its attention by its own investigations and supervision of implementation by Member States, by the Member States, by the European Parliament or by individual citizens or companies.

Having decided that a state has breached its obligations the Commission will inform the state and give the state the opportunity to answer the allegation or correct its action or inaction before the formal procedure of Art 226 (ex 169) begins.

Not every suspicion by the Commission of infringement will result in the initial letter being sent to the Member State. The initial letter has been held to be essential for the commencement of proceedings before the Court (*Commission* v *Italy* (274/83)). In 1991 the Commission sent out 853 formal letters stating its point of view. Following the reply from the Member State, or after a reasonable time where no reply is received, the Commission will then deliver a reasoned opinion which records the reasons for the failure of the Member State. This is delivered to the Member State and is registered by the Court of Justice. Many of the 853 original complaints had been settled informally before this stage and the resulting number of reasoned opinions in 1991 was 411.

If the state should then fail to comply with the reasoned opinion of the Commission within a reasonable time, the Commission has the discretionary right to bring the matter before the Court of Justice. Sixty-five cases were brought in 1991. These figures are produced each year in a Report on monitoring the application of Community law. In 1998 there were 1,101 notices, 675 reasoned opinions and 123 referrals to the ECJ and in 1999, there were 1,075 formal notices, 460 reasoned opinions and 178 referrals to the ECJ.

The final stage of the procedure is action before the Court of Justice and its judgment which is merely declaratory. It is possible however for the Court to order interim measures. After the judgment the state is required to take the necessary measures to comply with the judgment. Judgments rendered by the Court of Justice in 1991 were 57. In 1998, 55 of the 123 cases were withdrawn before reaching the ECJ.

Having considered the actual procedure, its effectiveness in securing compliance must now be considered. Other international tribunals are unable to enforce their judgments against miscreant Member States, for example, the International Court of Justice at the Hague or the European Court of Human Rights in Strasbourg and the best that can really be achieved is the issue and discussion of a report on the failure or breach and the hope that the ensuing political storm will encourage compliance.

Whilst the initial judgment of the Court of Justice is only declaratory and carries no specific sanctions, Member States are placed under a further obligation by Art 228 (ex 171) to comply with the judgment by taking the necessary measures. If they do not do this a further action may lie against them by the Commission under Art 226 (ex 169) for a breach of Art 228 (ex 171). This has taken place a number of times and increasingly so; in 1989 e.g., it was used on 26 occasions and in 1998 the Commission commenced 39 actions for a breach of Art 228 (ex 171). The leading instance of this is *Commission* v *Italy* (second Art Treasures case) (48/71). The Commission decided that because Italy had not complied with the Court's judgment in the first *Art Treasures* case (7/68), judgment should be given that Italy had also failed in its obligation under Art 228 (ex 171). Despite the fact that Italy complied with the original decision prior to judgment the Court held that Italy had also failed to comply with Art 228 (ex 171).

Prior to the Treaty on European Union, the judgment was, however, only declaratory but other methods to secure the eventual compliance of the Member States were possible in the Community legal order. However, even prior to Maastricht it was rarely necessary to rely on other methods of enforcement. Despite the lack of direct sanctions the Art 226 (ex 169) procedure can be regarded as effective, in that in most actions the Member States complied with the judgment in good time.

Following the entry into force of the Treaty on European Union, Arts 228 and 229 (ex 171 and 172) provide that sanctions can be requested by the Commission in an action to establish that the Member States have failed to comply with a previous judgment of the Court of Justice. This has already occurred in a number of requests by the Commission for penalty payments to be imposed on 14 occasions to 1999 against France, Germany, Greece, Italy and Luxembourg. Eight of these referrals by the Commission were withdrawn after the infringement was corrected and 6 were awaiting judgment with the prospect of daily fines of hundreds of thousands of ECUs. After three more cases were settled in 2000, only one so far has resulted in judgment. This is *Commission* v *Greece* (C-387/97) in which a penalty of 20,000 Euros per day was imposed by the ECJ from the date of judgment (4/7/2000). The conclusion is that the revised Art 228 is having an effect in securing compliance.

There are also interim measures under Art 243 (ex 186) which have been used to prevent the continued breach by Member States (see, e.g., the *Factortame* litigation in the UK (C-246/89R) and *Special Road Tax for Lorries in Germany* (C-195/90R). The Commission successfully applied for interim measures in both cases to suspend the application of the national measures alleged to breach Community law whilst the substantive question in each case was being considered by the Court of Justice.

Alternatively, actions by individuals in the national courts to defend or establish their individual rights based on Community law, which are referred to the Court of Justice under Art 234 (ex 177), also serve to bring to the attention of the Commission and the Court of Justice a failure by the Member State. In most circumstances the Member States amend their laws to comply with their Community obligations without the need for an Art 226 (ex 169) action by the Commission. Many examples could be cited here but leading cases are *Van Gend en Loos* (26/62), *Marshall* (152/84) and there are similar cases where the doctrine of direct effects have upheld individuals' rights under Community law, in the face of conflicting national law.

Whilst straying from the direct question, it would nevertheless be acceptable to say that a recent development which may spur on Member States to comply far more than any of the above actions is the prospect of having to compensate in each case where an individual has suffered damage as a result of the failure of the Member State to comply with a Community obligation. In the case which decided this, i.e., *Francovich* (C-6 & 9/90), the provision of law was a Directive. There are three conditions to such an action. The Directive must provide an individual right, which could be determined by the provisions of the Directive alone, and there must be a link between the breach and the damage caused. There is an ever-growing number of cases in this area which have clarified the circumstances under which the Member State will be held liable. The Court of Justice held in *Hedley Lomas* (C-5/94) that a breach of Community law will be sufficiently serious to found liability where a State violated an established principle of Community law (Art 34 (now 29) on exports), especially where the Member State had legislated in direct contravention of a Treaty obligation. It was not necessary for a State to have been held in breach of Community law in a previous Art 226 (ex 169) action by the Commission. In fact, failure to take any measures to transpose the Directive within the time limit set will suffice to establish a sufficiently serious breach of Community law (*Dillenkofer* (C-178, 179, 188 & 90/94)). A Member State will not have seriously breached Community law where it can be shown that the Directive in question is open to several interpretations (see *British Telecommunications* (C-392/93).

Hence then if Art 226 (ex 169) itself is not sufficient to secure compliance then an action to impose liability on the state for failure to comply with Community law almost certainly will be.

QUESTION 2

In 1996 the Council of Ministers issued a Directive on washing machine specifications which was to be implemented by all Member States by 1 January 1999. The controversial nature of the Directive, which would have opened the ailing British washing machine industry up to competition from other Community Member States, and the pressure on Parliamentary time meant that the UK government did not alter its own regulations on the specifications which must be met by washing machines marketed in the UK. However, the UK government did issue a circular in June 1999 to all customs officers, advising them of the existence of the Directive and informing them that all washing machines which met the specifications in the EC Directive were to be granted access to the UK market, even if they did not meet the stricter requirements of the UK regulations.

In February 1999, Danny, an importer of washing machines, had a consignment of French washing machines held up at customs at Dover because, although they met the requirements of the EC Directive, they did not meet the specifications contained in the UK regulations. The washing machines were not released until mid June when the customs received the government circular.

In March 1999 the Commission instituted proceedings under Art 226 and, following the issue of a reasoned opinion, the UK government introduced a regulation to implement the directive.

The UK government, in response to the reasoned opinion, observes that:

(a) it was unable to comply with the Directive because of the lack of Parliamentary time;

(b) the circular issued in June was sufficient to comply with the requirements of the Directive;

(c) in any event, the Directive had now been implemented by the new regulation, and the proceedings under Article 226 no longer served any useful purpose.

(d) France had also failed to implement the Directive within the time limit.

1 Advise the EC Commission as to the validity of these arguments by the UK government.

2 Briefly outline if there are any other parties who could take action against the UK.

Commentary

This question concentrates on the ability of Member States to resist a conclusion under Art 226 (ex 169) that they have breached Community law obligations and the alternative actions which may be taken against Member States either to encourage compliance or obtain a remedy in the case of a breach of Community law.

It requires you initially to consider defences which have been raised by a Member State in an attempt to avoid being found in breach of Community law obligations. Various specific grounds are mentioned and you should therefore only address these in turn. To complete this part it would be helpful to provide a conclusion as to whether you would regard the UK to be in breach according to the case law of the ECJ.

You are further asked to discuss whether any other parties could take action against the UK. This part of the question is more open than the first part in that there are a number of possible alternatives to consider. These include action by the importers to challenge the right of the UK to prevent imports taking place and requesting a reference under Art 234 (ex 177), or action by the importers to claim damages as a result of the UK action.

Suggested Answer

1 Member states have raised various defences to justify their noncompliance with obligations, which may be acceptable in international law, but without success in the Community legal order.

(a)   The first reason given by the UK is similar to the argument *of force majeure* or overriding necessity raised in the case of *Commission* v *Belgium* (duty on timber) (77/69). Belgium failed to implement a Community Directive and was taken before the ECJ by the Commission. The Belgian government pleaded that it should not be held responsible for the negligence of the Belgian Parliament in not completing the implementation. This was rejected by the ECJ. Similarly, the argument raised by Italy in the *Art Treasures* case (7/68) that the delay in implementing Community measures was the consequence of political difficulties, was rejected by the ECJ.

(b)   The suggestion that the circular, which only advised the appropriate authorities but did not actually bring UK law into compliance, would be an adequate defence, is also likely to be held to be insufficient. See the case of *Commission* v *France* (French Maritime Code) (167/73) in which the formal rules were not amended but a change in practice was advised to the French authorities. The ECJ held that this was not sufficient to comply with Community law obligations.

(c)   The defence that no legal interest remained was raised in *Commission* v *Italy* (Italian Pigmeat case) (7/61). However, it was held that, as long as the Commission has an interest, it can bring a case before the Court of Justice and therefore the interest can continue even when the infringement no longer exists. Furthermore, in the case of *Commission* v *Italy* (slaughtered cows) (39/72) the ECJ held that where a legal issue remains unsettled an interest remains.

(d)   That an argument based on reciprocity, i.e., that another Member State's or Community institution's own failure to act justifies a defendant Member State's failure to comply with an obligation, is an acceptable defence was put forward in *Commission* v *Belgium and Luxembourg* (90 & 91/63). The states involved claimed that they were merely taking reciprocal action in disregarding Community Directives because the Council had delayed in passing legislation. The ECJ held that the Community was a new legal order whose structure involved the prohibition of Member States taking justice into their own hands. Similarly where other Member States have not complied with their obligations the ECJ has held (*Commission* v *France* (232/78)) that this does not justify non-compliance on behalf of the defendant Member State even where the Member State's constitution specifically allows for this (French Constitution Act 88).

It is likely therefore that all of the defences raised will be rejected by the ECJ and the UK will be found in breach of its Community law obligation.

2 In addition to the action under Art 226 (ex 169) by the Commission, individuals affected either by a refusal to allow imports or suffering damages resulting from delays may consider attempting the following actions.

Additionally French government might be interested in assisting the French manufacturers of washing machines whose products have been denied access for so long. It may consider taking an action under Art 227 (ex 170) to establish a breach by the UK. Such actions are, however, extremely rare in Community law (only two so far to 2000) and it is likely that they would leave it up to the Commission to take an Art 226 (ex 169) action.

An individual who is affected by the action of the UK may point to the breach of a Community obligation or duty by a Member State as a defence to prosecution by that Member State or where they seek to challenge national rules which operate against their interest. It was early in the life of the Communities that the Art 234 (ex 177) preliminary ruling procedure was seen to short-circuit the use of Arts 226 and 227 (ex 169 and 170). This was objected to by the Dutch Government in the *Van Gend en Loos* case (26/62), which thought that it was up to the Commission only and not individuals to take action or claim rights against Member States. This claim was firmly rejected by the Court and, by the establishment of the doctrine of direct effects was able to place the policing of Community law additionally in the hands of private individuals, who often have more reason to bring actions. Danny might therefore consider an action before the national courts to get his machines released without too much delay.

Individuals may benefit as well as helping to bring about the compliance with Art 226 (ex 169) actions, as shown in *Commission* v *France* (advertising of alcoholic beverages) (152/78). It was held that a French ban on advertising foreign spirits was discriminatory and contrary to Community law. France failed to remove its legislation and prosecuted an importer for advertising. Waterkeyn the advertiser referred to the previous judgment as a defence. In *Procureur de la République* v *Waterkeyn* (314–16/81) it was held that individuals could rely on such past judgments as a defence to protect their rights.

Alternatively an individual may attempt to obtain damages from the Member State where the breach by the Member State is claimed to have caused damage to individuals who then make a claim against the Member State to recover. This form of action is now well established and proving to be extremely effective in encouraging Member States to comply with

Community law obligations if they find themselves having to pay out significant damages in an increasing number of cases.

It was tried in the case of the French turkey producers who, following the Commission Art 169 (now 226) action against the UK in the *Poultry Meat* case (40/82) which held that a British ban was contrary to Community law, sought an action for damages against the Ministry of Agriculture which applied the ban. The claim was dismissed as showing no good cause of action unless it could be shown that the Ministry acted in bad faith in which case the proper action is for judicial review and not a tort action for damages. However, in *Bourgoin SA* v *Ministry of Agriculture* ([1987] 1 CMLR 169), the case was settled out of court and the government paid £3.5 million compensation to the French farmers.

The case of *Francovich* (C-6 & 9/90) had the result that the Italian government was obliged to pay the claimants as a result of government failure to implement Community legislation. There are three conditions to such an action. The Directive must provide an individual right which could be determined by the provisions of the Directive alone, and there must be a link between the breach and the damage caused. It is not necessary to show that the Member State has already been held in breach of its Community obligations in an Art 226 (ex 169) action by the Commission (*Hedley Lomas* (C-5/94)). In fact, it was held in *Dillenkofer* (C-178, 179, 188 & 90/94) that a failure by a State to take any measure to transpose a Directive in the prescribed time constitutes a sufficiently serious breach of Community law in order to found liability, as long as the other two conditions are also met.

In *Brasserie du Pêcheur* v *Germany*; *Factortame* v *UK* (C-46 & 48/93), the ECJ extended the principle of state liability to all violations whatever organ of the state causes the infringement. The Court equated the criteria of *Francovich* liability to those which are applied in the case of liability of the Community institutions to pay damages for their wrongful legislative acts under Arts 235 and 288(2) (ex 178 and 215(2)). These are that (a) there must have been a serious breach by the Community law-making institution of a superior rule of law for the protection of the individual; (b) the law-making institution has manifestly and gravely disregarded the limits of its powers; and (c) there must be a causal link between the breach and the damage suffered. In considering this, the ECJ would take into account:

(i)   Whether the scope of the Community provision was clear and precise.

(ii)   The extent of the margin of appreciation left to the Member States.

(iii)   The intentional or voluntary character of the infringement.

(iv)   Whether the error of law was excusable or inexcusable.

(v)   Whether the attitude of the Community institutions had contributed to the breach.

In the *Factortame* case the Court considered that the UK government was well aware of the Commission's attitude to the Merchant Shipping Act, as well as the views of national courts that these rules infringed Community law. Moreover, the UK Government had failed to implement the judgment of the ECJ of 10 October 1989.

Given the facts of the case to hand it is likely there would be a similar result and the UK would be liable for any damage suffered by Danny as a result of the breach by the UK.

QUESTION 3

Natural and legal persons face substantial obstacles under Art 230. Outline the requirements which must be met by an individual seeking to challenge:

(a)   a Decision addressed to him;

(b)   a Decision addressed to another person or to a Member State;

(c)   a Regulation.

Do you consider the requirements of Art 230 to be unduly restrictive to individuals?

Commentary

This question concentrates on the admissibility element or otherwise known as the '*locus standi*' requirements of an Art 230 (ex 173) action and the particular difficulties encountered by the so called non-privileged applicants. In order to put your answer in context you must briefly outline the purpose and procedure of an Art 230 (ex 173) action. You are then required to address the requirements which must be met by an individual seeking to challenge acts in the given circumstances in the question, giving examples from the case law of the Court of Justice where you consider it appropriate. Finally, you are asked to consider whether the requirements as outlined are unnecessarily restrictive for individuals. This requires you to engage in a more general discussion of the purposes of such an action and will only be possible if you have undertaken wider reading than just from textbooks on the topic.

Note now that applications by legal and natural persons under Art 230 will be heard by the CFI rather than the ECJ itself, although there are limited grounds of appeal to the ECJ.

Suggested Answer

Article 230 (ex 173) provides for the action brought before the Court of Justice to review the validity of acts of the institutions of the Community. If those acts are found to be invalid, the Court of Justice has the sole right to declare acts void. There are two elements in respect of the action: admissibility and the merits or substance of the action. The first presents the greatest barrier to applicants in practice.

The article names the Member States, the Council and the Commission as privileged applicants, who have the right to attack any act. It further names the European Parliament and the European Central Bank as institutions which may invoke Art 230 (ex 173) as a matter of course but only to protect their own prerogative powers. All other persons are termed non-privileged applicants. Article 230 (ex 173) states that any natural or legal person may institute proceedings against a Decision addressed to that person or against a Decision which, although in the form of a Regulation or a Decision addressed to another person, is of direct and individual concern to the former.

(a) To challenge an act addressed specifically to the applicant automatically gives standing according to Art 230 (ex 173). This has been confirmed in numerous cases, for example, any case concerned with a challenge by an individual to a Decision issued by the Commission under its powers granted under competition policy in Arts 81 and 82 (ex 85 and 86) EC and Regulation 17.

(b) In order to challenge a decision addressed to someone else or a Member State, it must be shown to be of direct and individual concern to the applicant.

(c) In the case of challenging Regulations, it has been held that true Regulations are normative acts and not open to individual challenge, see *KSH* v *Council and Commission* (101/76) in which a challenge to a glucose levy Regulation in respect of certain producers was held not to be admissible. In addition to showing direct and individual concern, an individual must also show that in substance the Regulation is really a Decision or a bundle of Decisions, although in the exceptional case of *Codorniu SA* v *Commission* (C-309/89) it would seem that the Court of Justice confirmed the act's true status of a Regulation but nevertheless allowed a challenge from an individual.

In order to consider what precisely an individual must do in order to determine whether they are able to gain *locus standi* in the cases above, a number of questions can be posed to determine the various stages of admissibility which have to be considered before an action can proceed to the merits of the challenge.

Is the act in substance a Regulation? If the answer is yes, then there will be no *locus standi,* see the *Fruit and Vegetable Confederation* v *Commission* case (16 & 17/62). If the answer is no, then it must be asked whether the act is a decision? If the answer is again no, then the act is not one subject to review under Art 230 (ex 173). However, whilst the jurisdiction of the Court is limited to the legal binding acts of the Council and the Commission, it was held in the *Noordwijks Cement Accord* case (8–11/66) that other acts may be subject to review. The test to apply to a particular act is whether it has binding legal effects or changes the legal position of the applicant. Further, in *Commission* v *Council* (ERTA) (22/70) it was held that Art 249 (ex 189) is not exhaustive and special acts such as the minuted discussions of the Council, for the European Road Transport Agreement, could also be challenged. Thus the true nature of the measure is the determining factor, although the ability to challenge acts outside those listed under Art 249 (ex 189) would be rare.

If the answer to the second question in the previous paragraph is yes, the act is in substance a Decision, and the question next is whether it is addressed to the plaintiff. If the answer is yes, then the plaintiff has *locus standi.* If the answer is no, and the act is addressed to someone else, is the act of direct and individual concern? If yes, the applicant has *locus standi.* If no, there is no *locus standi.*

According to the case law many applicants fail, either trying to show that a Regulation was really a Decision or that it was of direct or individual concern to them. One of the difficulties in looking at problems in this area and trying to apply the available case law is that the Court of Justice has not always taken the same route in answering these questions. Sometimes it can be shown that if something is of individual concern, it logically follows that if it is a Regulation which is challenged, this Regulation must be, in substance, a Decision for the applicant although not necessarily for others. Therefore establishing *locus standi* can sometimes be done by considering direct and individual concern first. For example, in the *CAM* case (100/74), the Regulation was able to be challenged because of its direct and individual concern. Additionally in the *UNICME* case (123/77), it was held that if the act is of direct and individual concern there is no need to consider whether the measure is a Decision or a Regulation. However, in *Codorniu* v *Commission* (C-309/89), despite the ECJ confirming that the Regulation was a legislative measure applying to traders in general, it could still be of individual concern to one of them. Codorniu had distinguished themselves by the ownership of a trademark for the term Crement from the year 1924, which the Community had tried to reserve for French and Luxembourg producers. It must be noted, however, that since the *Cordorniu* judgment, the CFI has not shown any willingness to relax the *locus standi* requirements and open the floodgates to litigation nor the ECJ to do the same on appeal.

In looking at direct and individual concern the Court of Justice often defines 'individual' first. Individual concern has been very hard to demonstrate. In *Plaumann* v *Commission* (25/62), a Decision was addressed to the German Government refusing permission to reduce duties on Clementines. The test was whether the decision affects the applicant by virtue of the fact that he is member of the abstractly defined class addressed by the rule, for example, because he is a importer of Clementines, or does it affect him because of attributes peculiar to him which differentiate him from all other persons. Plaumann was held to be one of a class of importers and not therefore individually concerned. See also the *Codorniu* (C-309/89) case where the company had clearly distinguished itself as individually concerned. 'Direct' has been held to mean that the effect of the decision on the interests of the applicant must not depend on the discretion of another person (see the *Alcan* case (69/69) and the *Zuckerfabrik Schöppenstedt* case (5/71)).

After the strict requirements of *locus standi* have been proved, the merits or substantive grounds of the action must be proved and these are contained in Art 230 (ex 173).

The second part of the question addresses the issue of whether the requirements are restrictive. They are certainly restrictive but are they too restrictive?

The Court of Justice is much more restrictive than national courts but these also impose a requirement to show an interest in seeking to challenge administrative and legislative acts, e.g., there are *locus standi* requirements in seeking judicial review in the UK.

The reasons for the difficulties in demonstrating *locus standi* have been subject to much debate as to whether it is the policy of the Court of Justice, using the 'floodgates' argument, to maintain that some sort of filter system is necessary, or whether the ECJ desires to promote the Court more as a supreme Court of the Member States and not as one which is directly accessible as a first instance court for individuals. To some extent this debate has been answered by the establishment of the Court of First Instance to handle these cases and which elevates the Court of Justice into the role of an appeal court in relation to these categories of cases.

Those cases held to be admissible often arise from the application of retroactive legislation. The applicants thus belonged to a fixed and identifiable group which could not be added to. Other arguments revolve around discussions about balancing the interests of the Community and individuals in the Community. The decision making procedure in the Community is a complex procedure and often the resulting compromise makes legislation more difficult to enact. The inevitable economic choices of the Community are likely to affect individuals and must be allowed to be made otherwise the ability of the Community, and within it the Commission and Council, to operate would be undermined. Individuals' actions should not hinder the institutions' ability to operate. Comparisons with the Member States may be made that such challenges are also subject to equally rigid *locus standi* requirements. In those areas which, by contrast, individuals find it easier to achieve standing such as in competition law, State aids and anti-dumping measures, it may be argued that the very often closer involvement of particular individuals make the difference. The applicants are likely to be the ones involved in the process by informing the Commission of certain situations or can be seen clearly to be affected by the measures complained about. This then sets them apart from the many other challenges arising most frequently against legislative decisions made under the Common Agricultural Policy. However, the overall picture remains that of a restrictive *locus standi* for applicants.

Arguments which justify the strict requirements are that the role of the Court of Justice, apart from competition law and anti-dumping cases, is not really a court for individuals. It is a Community court for the institutions and the

Member States. There should be no direct individual access. Furthermore there is the provision of indirect action via Art 234 (ex 177) for individuals in Community law as an alternative, which may also lead to Community law being challenged. This appears to be favoured by the Court and the Treaty by the provision of Art 234 (ex 177). Consequently, it may therefore be argued the requirements are not too restrictive.

QUESTION 4

There was a surplus of sweet lupins within the EC in 1998 and as a result, Council Regulation (2/99) was enacted on 20 January 1999. Exporters of sweet lupins during 1999 were entitled under the Regulation to incentives of £100 per ton of sweet lupins exported. On 21 January 1999, R Hood Ltd applied for a licence to export 1,000 tons of sweet lupins. The company was granted the licence on the payment of a deposit of £5,000 which would be forfeit if the company did not comply with the requirements of the licence.

In February 1999, there was a serious disruption in the sweet lupin crop which resulted in a shortage of sweet lupins in the EC and on 21 February 1999 the Commission enacted Regulation 4/99 which eliminated the refund subsidies of sweet lupins, making exporters liable instead for a levy of £5 per ton exported. The Regulation specifically includes those who have already exported sweet lupins in the 1999 marketing year but did not contain reasons for its issue.

R Hood Ltd exported 400 tons of its quota before 21 February 1999 and is presented with a levy of £2,000. It must export the remaining quantity of its quota (600 tons) or lose the deposit of £5,000. Exporting the 600 tons will however make it liable to a further levy of £3,000.

Advise R Hood Ltd on whether, and on what grounds, if any, it can successfully challenge the second Regulation.

Commentary

The question specifically requests you to advise the company as to whether they can challenge the second Regulation enacted by the Commission. Hence you are immediately taken to a consideration of an action under Art 230 (ex 173) EC and you will need to consider both the admissibility of an action and the merits, if found to be admissible. The biggest task in answering problems on Art 230 (ex 173) is trying to resolve the often conflicting case law of the Court of Justice in considering the challenges to Community Regulations because of the restrictive *locus standi* requirements. Although not always dealt with in this way by the ECJ it would be easier for you to address the question of whether the Regulation is a Decision first of all and then address the issue of whether it is of direct and individual concern to the applicant. Having considered the admissibility and if you have found it to be proved, you can then consider the merits or grounds of the action to determine whether R Hood Ltd will be successful in its challenge.

Whilst not specifically required by the question, you may consider whether there are other grounds by which the Regulation could be challenged, particularly if the challenge using Art 230 (ex 173) proves unsuccessful.

Suggested Answer

If the second Regulation goes unchallenged R Hood Ltd face the situation where they either export the remaining 600 tons and become subject to a further levy of £3,000, or do not export and lose the deposit of £5,000 for failing to comply with the earlier Regulation. Neither of these alternatives would be welcome. R Hood are therefore interested to establish that the second Regulation should not apply and that they can rely solely on the first Regulation.

Challenges to Community legislation can be undertaken but only if specific requirements are met, particularly in terms of individuals who seek to challenge Community acts. For the so-called non-privileged applicants, admissibility is the most difficult part of the action because of strict *locus standi* rules. There is, however, more than just one issue to consider in respect of admissibility. The institution challenged must be one envisaged by the Treaty. Here it is the Commission, clearly named in Art 230 (ex 173). The Act challenged must also be one within the scope of Art 230 (ex 173). In the present case it is a Regulation, which is one of the Acts of the Community institutions which is authorised under Art 249 (ex 189). However, because a Regulation is a normative act applicable generally, it carries greater requirements on the part of legal and natural applicants to challenge it. Art 230 (ex 173) provides that the applicant must show that although in the form of a Regulation it is of direct and individual concern to them.

The final consideration in respect of applicability which is of vital importance is the time limit. Art 230 (ex 173) states that the challenge must be made within two months of the publication of the measure challenged. In the present problem given no further information it is assumed that the challenge is made within the required two month period.

Therefore admissibility is dependent on the ability to challenge the Regulation. It has been held that Regulations are normative acts of general concern as provided by 249 (ex Art 189) and therefore cannot individually concern applicants. As a result the ECJ has held that true Regulations cannot be challenged (see *KSH* v *Council and Commission* (101/76)), as they apply to categories of persons and not to individuals, although in the so far exceptional case of *Codorniu SA* v *Commission* (C-309/89) it would seem that the Court of Justice confirmed the act's true status of a Regulation but nevertheless allowed a challenge from an individual. If, however, it can be shown that the Regulation is in effect a Decision or bundle of Decisions it can be challenged. In *Fruit and Vegetable Confederation* v *Commission* (16 & 17/62) it was held that it is the nature and content of a provision that is the determining factor and not the form or label it is given. In *International Fruit Company* v *Commission* (41–4/70), a group of fruit importers was held entitled to challenge a Regulation where the identity of the natural or legal persons affected was already known and thus fixed and identifiable. The Regulation was thus the equivalent of a bundle of Decisions addressed to each applicant. Therefore if you can demonstrate that the Regulation has in mind or indeed has named, either in the Regulation or in the annex, a number of individuals to whom it applies, it will be considered by the ECJ to be a bundle of Decisions rather than a Regulation (see the case of *Roquette Frères and Maizena* v *Council* (138 & 139/79)). In the particular area of anti-dumping measures, the Court of Justice has held that despite Regulations being a measure of general application, certain individuals may challenge Regulations as if they were Decisions, especially when one of the Articles of the Regulation specifically referred to the applicant companies (see the *Japanese Ball-Bearings* cases (113, 118–21/77)). In the present case the Regulation under challenge 'specifically includes those who have already exported in 1999', thus demonstrating that the Regulation was really a bundle of Decisions.

The applicant is now required to satisfy the tests of direct and individual concern. In order for the application to be admissible the Decision must be of direct and individual concern to the applicant. The order in which these tests have been considered by the ECJ has varied and it can be case that if one is demonstrated the other follows almost automatically. In this case, 'direct' will be considered first. Direct concern will be demonstrated if there is no intervening action by the Member State agencies or any other discretion. In this case there is not, therefore it is of direct concern (see the *Alcan* case (69/69)).

Individual concern, on the other hand, has been very hard to demonstrate and has often been tested by the Court of Justice first or at the same time as direct concern to decide admissibility, as in *Plaumann* v *Commission* (25/62). A Decision was addressed to the German government refusing permission to reduce duties on clementines. The test was whether the decision affects the applicant by virtue of the fact that he is a member of the abstractly defined class addressed by the rule, for example, because he is an importer of clementines, or whether it affects him because of attributes peculiar to him which differentiate him from all other persons. Plaumann was held to be one of a class of importers and so not individually concerned. It is therefore a question of an open or closed and fixed class, although in the *Codorniu* case the lack of a fixed or closed class was no barrier to the ECJ in determining that the company was individually concerned and could thus challenge the Regulation. Can Hood be identified individually or as a part of a fixed and identifiable class? Furthermore, cases often revolve round retroactive regulations thus identifying certain persons (e.g., the *Toepfer* case (106 & 107/63)). As a result of the fact that specifically included in the Regulation are those who have already exported, Hood is directly and individually concerned. The company is in the named group of companies which have already exported sweet lupins in 1999 and the new Regulation also applies retroactively to exports already made.

Therefore if this is admissible, the merits or substance of the action can now be considered. The grounds of challenge are exhaustively but widely listed in Art 230 (ex 173). Two which appear applicable in this case are an infringement of an essential procedural requirement, or an infringement of the Treaty.

In response to the first one, specific requirements are laid down by Art 253 (ex 190) that all Community secondary law must give reasons and refer to any proposals and opinions made in respect of the provisions. The Court of Justice has held that insufficient or vague or inconsistent reasoning would constitute a breach of this ground. It was held in *Germany* v *Commission* (wine tariff quotas) (24/62) that reasons must contain sufficient details of the facts and figures on which they are based. Although Art 253 (ex 190) requires the reasons for legislation to be stated and the opinions on which they are based to be stated, there is no express requirement to state the legal base. However, it was held in *France* v *Commission* (C-325/91) that there is a requirement to state the Treaty base, without which the measure is void.

In the present case there are no reasons stated, hence the Regulation will be held to be in breach of the essential procedural requirement of Art 230 (ex 173). Whilst this is a clear breach it may be worthwhile suggesting that other, less certain grounds might be raised in respect of fundamental rights breaches amounting to a breach of a rule of law relating to the application of Community law, also considered by Art 230 (ex 173).

The grounds then might include general principles of legitimate expectation to be able to export all of the sweet lupins without penalty and that there should be no retroactive law or double jeopardy of sanction.

The conclusion is that R Hood Ltd will be successful in the challenge to the second Regulation.

Other challenges, which may be possible but not necessary in view of the above conclusion, may include a damages action under Art 288 (ex 215) against the Community, which is likely to be considered on the same substantive grounds; national proceedings; and an Art 234 (ex 177) reference to ask the ECJ to rule on the validity of the Community act, providing there is a national element to the case, e.g., if the firm concerned were being fined or prosecuted by the national authorities in the national courts, the legality of their basis in Community law may be challenged.

QUESTION 5

The circumstances in which an individual can recover damages for loss suffered as a result of some legislative act of the Community institutions are unduly restrictive.

Discuss.

Commentary

The above question requires a discussion of the action for damages under Art 288 (ex 215) which comes under the jurisdiction of the ECJ by virtue of Art 235 (ex 178). In order to answer the question, the main aspects of the procedure should first of all be outlined with particular emphasis on the requirements demanded by the Court of Justice in actions involving the legislative acts of the Community. Then you should consider whether an action for damages is unduly restrictive to individuals. This is best done by reference to case law for examples. The Art 288 (ex 215) action can also be contrasted throughout to the actions under Arts 230 and 232 (ex 173 and 175) to demonstrate whether it is any more restrictive or not.

Suggested Answer

It may generally be stated that, in contrast to the challenge to Community acts under Art 230 (ex 173) and the action to establish an omission to act under Art 232 (ex 175), there are less restrictive *locus standi* requirements imposed by Art 288 (ex 215) (2). Instead, it would appear that any attempt to restrict the number of cases is made at the stage of the consideration of the merits or grounds of the case by the ECJ and not at the stage of admissibility.

An action under Art 288 (ex 215) (2) consists of the following requirements which have been identified as necessary to establish liability. There must be a wrongful act or omission on the part of the Community which has breached a duty, the applicant must have suffered damage and there must be a causal link between the act or omission and the damage.

With Art 288 (ex 215), admissibility is not really a problem. First of all there is a much more generous time limit than with Arts 230 or 232 (ex 173 or 175). Art 288 (ex 215) has a five year limitation period on actions which commences from the occurrence of the event causing the damage, as held in the *Schöppenstedt* case (5/71). Furthermore, in contrast to Arts 230 and 232 (ex 173 and 175), there is not a restrictive *locus standi* imposed by either Art 235 or 288(2) (ex 178 or 215) (2).

Initially it was considered to be a dependent action following a successful action under either Art 230 or 232 (ex 173 or 175). If this position had been maintained it would have severely restricted its use. However, in the *Lütticke* case (4/69), the Court of Justice rejected this argument and declared that 'the action for damages provided by Arts 235 and 288(2) (ex 178 and 215) (2) was established by the Treaty as an independent form of action and whose object was to compensate a party for damage sustained and not to secure the annulment of an illegal measure'. This ruling was confirmed in the *Schöppenstedt* case (5/71). Therefore little difficulty faces applicants in respect of admissibility, the problem lies in proving that an act of the Community caused damage.

The act or omission of the Community must be shown to be wrongful. In respect of actions claiming damage resulting from the wrongful adoption of legislative acts, stricter requirements are imposed on the breach of the duty. This is because the Court has decided that in challenging such acts, which involve the Community in making choices in economic policies, far more stringent requirements are necessary, otherwise the functioning of the Community would be hindered and the Community could not operate as it needs to. Thus the Court of Justice has laid down a strict test in *Zuckerfabrik Schöppenstedt* v *Council* (5/71), which has been repeated often. 'The Community does not incur liability on account of a legislative measure which involves choices of economic policy unless a sufficiently serious breach of a superior rule of law for the protection of the individual has occurred.'

It has proved to be extremely difficult to determine exactly how severe a breach must be and how serious the resulting damage must be, as can be observed from a review of the case law of the Court of Justice. It may be argued that the reasoning for this is very similar to the strict requirements for *locus standi* for Art 230 (ex 173), in that the high degree of discretion that the institutions need to carry out the economic tasks necessarily affects many persons. Therefore it is not just unlawful conduct that will attract liability, but it is the degree of conduct which is important under the formula developed by the Court of Justice.

This formula can then be divided into two parts although it is also suggested that it can be divided into three parts. The first element is that the rule of law must be one for the protection of the individual. This should be taken together and not separated into component parts of a 'superior rule of law' which is 'for the protection of the individual'. The rules of law which are accepted as coming within the formulation include general principles of law. The principles of equality, non-discrimination and legitimate expectation seem most often to be raised.

The protection of the individual has been interpreted to include the protection of classes of persons as with the importers in the *Kampffmeyer* case (5, 7, 13-24/66).

Thus in the *CNTA* case (74/74) the Commission was held liable to pay compensation for losses incurred as a result of a Regulation which abolished with immediate effect and without warning the application of compensatory amounts. It was held to be a serious breach of the principle of legitimate expectation. In the *Gritz* and *Quellmehl (Dumortier Frères)* cases (64 *et al./76*), the ending of a subsidy was held to be a breach because it was retained on starch which was direct competition, and hence discriminatory.

Secondly, the breach must be sufficiently serious. In *HNL* v *Council and Commission* (83/76) this was required to be 'manifest and grave'. This was interpreted later in *KSH* v *Council and Commission* (143/77) as conduct verging on the arbitrary. Factors which influence the Court of Justice in its determination of whether the breach is sufficiently serious are the effect of the measure and the nature of the breach.

The effect of the measure relates to its scope, the number of people affected and the damage caused. For example, in *HNL* (83/76) there was little damage and thus the action was not successful. The damage must be over and above the risks of loss or damage normally inherent in business but, in the *KSH Isoglucose* case (143/77), even though the damage was so extensive, the action was not successful because the breach of the law was not held to be verging on the arbitrary. See the *Dumortier Frères* v *Council* (*Gritz* and *Quellmehl* cases) (64 and 113/76), and *Sofrimport* (C-152/88) in respect of the fact that the Court requires that only a small defined and closed group of applicants is affected. However, in the more recent case of *Mulder* (C-104/89 & 37/90) the presence of a large group of claimants did not defeat a claim, although a serious breach still had to be demonstrated and that there was no higher public interest of the Community involved.

The nature of the breach relates to its seriousness. In the *Isoglucose* case (143/77) the damage was extensive causing the insolvency of one company but the action was not successful because the breach of the law was not verging on the arbitrary although in the later case of *Stahlwerke Peine-Salzgitter* v *Commission* (C-220/91P) the ECJ held that it was no longer necessary to show that the conduct was verging on the arbitrary. The applicants in the *Sofrimport* case were successful because of the complete failure of the Commission to take into account the interests of the applicants, despite prior knowledge.

Other actions which do not challenge the legislative acts themselves, but only seek to show that the wrongful act was a failure of the administration in the implementation of law, do not need to satisfy the formula under *Schöppen-stedt* (5/71), hence a higher standard is imposed when individuals seek to obtain damages as a result of loss suffered from legislative acts of the Community.

Having established the existence of an act or omission attributable to the Community, damage to the applicant must be proved. Damage can be purely economic as in the *Kampffmeyer* case (5, 7 & 13–24/66) involving a cancellation fee and loss of profits but this must be specified and not speculative, or it can be moral damage and anxiety (*Willame* v *Commission* (110/63)).

Finally it must be shown that the act of the Community caused the damage. There must be a sufficiently direct connection between the act and the injury. The damages must be ascertainable *(Kampffmeyer* case (5, 7 & 13–24/66)). It cannot, however, be too remote, as held in the *Lütticke* case (4/69) but without further specification. In *Dumortier Frères* v *Council* (*Gritz* and *Quellmehl*) (64 & 113/76) it was held no need to make good every harmful consequence especially where remote. Damage must be a sufficiently direct consequence of the unlawful conduct of the institution concerned. In *Compagnie Continentale France* (169/73) it was held that the causal link was only established if, in the case, the misleading information given would have caused an error in the mind of a reasonable person.

The conclusion is that whilst Art 288 (ex 215) does allow wider access to commence an action, the actions seeking damages as the result of the adoption of a wrongful legislative act impose equally severe restrictions. The result of this combination is that applicants rarely succeed.

QUESTION 6

A Welsh company, Welsh Foods, has invented a substance known as 'Isolactic', which can be used as a substitute for milk in the manufacture of butter, cheese and ice cream. Isolactic is also significantly cheaper than milk. A few months after Welsh Foods has begun commercial production of Isolactic, with encouraging results, the EC Council, alarmed at the probable adverse consequences of Isolactic production for EC milk producers, adopts a Regulation imposing a production levy on Isolactic producers. The effect of the levy, which is to be collected by the national authorities of the Member States on behalf of the Commission, is to make Isolactic significantly more expensive than milk.

Welsh Foods, which is one of only three firms in the EC making Isolactic, feels that the Regulation is discriminatory and that its effect will be to make production of Isolactic uneconomic, thus causing Welsh Foods to cease Isolactic production, without having recovered its research and development costs. Its losses are such that the company expects to be forced into liquidation within six months unless something is done.

Advise Welsh Foods whether it could recover damages from the Council for any losses it may suffer.

Commentary

This is a problem type question which deals with the application of much of the discussion which arose in the answer to the last question.

The action under Art 288 (ex 215) which might be contemplated for Welsh Foods concerns the adoption by the Community of a legislative act which is allegedly wrongful. Apart from admissibility, the problem raises the difficulty of demonstrating that the alleged breach is serious enough for an action to be successful.

The material facts and issues arising in this problem can be identified easily. Welsh Foods considers the Regulation which imposes a levy on its production to be extremely damaging to it and that the Regulation was unlawfully enacted on the grounds that it is discriminatory. As a consequence, the company seeks damages and under Community law it would turn to the action under Art 288 (ex 215) (2).

It would be useful to set out the main considerations for an Art 288 (ex 215) action in an introductory paragraph. The question also involves a choice of court issue which should be considered.

Suggested Answer

An action under Art 288 (ex 215) (2) should be undertaken by Welsh Foods to recover losses already incurred.

First of all, it may be stated that for Art 288 (ex 215) (2) the *locus standi* requirements are much more relaxed and success is not so dependent on admissibility, as with Arts 230 and 232 (ex 173 and 175). There is also a much more generous five year time limit in which to make an application.

From case law it has been established that for a successful claim under Art 288 (ex 215) (2), an applicant must demonstrate: a duty, a breach of that duty by an action or inaction and damage which is caused as a result of the act or omission.

Before the action may commence a further issue arises in this case regarding the choice of court. It is stated that the levy is collected by national authorities. If there is an intervention by national authorities, the action should take place in the national courts with a reference to the Court of Justice if necessary (see *Haegemann* (181/73) and *Kampffmeyer* (5, 7 & 13–24/66) cases). However, it also depends on the discretion given to the Member States. If none is given and they merely act as agents for the Community then the action can also commence in the Court of Justice. In case of doubt, it would be advisable to go to the national courts and ask for a reference rather than have the case dismissed by the Court of Justice.

In this case the applicant is seeking to challenge a legislative Act of the Communities. It has been held (in the *Schöppenstedt* case (5/71)) that where actions concern legislative measures involving a choice of economic policy it is necessary to demonstrate in respect of the breach that it is a sufficiently serious breach of a superior rule of law for the protection of individuals. This then enhances the requirements to show both a breach of a duty and the level of damage suffered. The breach is now required to be sufficiently serious.

The consideration of this can be divided into two parts, i.e., the breach of the superior rule of law for the protection of the individual and, whether it was sufficiently serious.

The breach of a superior rule includes breach of general principles (*CNTA* case (74/74)). Equality and non-discrimination have been held to be recognised general principles. Non-discrimination is one covered specifically by Art 34(2) (ex 40(3)) and thus more likely to be regarded as a superior rule of law. There are many cases in which the Court of Justice has recognised general principles as superior rules of law (see the *HNL* (83/76), *Isoglucose* (143/77), *RSH* (103 & 145/77) and *Sofrimport* (C-152/88) cases).

In the *Gritz* and *Quellmehl (Dumortier Frères)* cases (64 and 113/76), the ending of the subsidy was held to be a breach of the principle of non-discrimination, because the subsidy was retained on starch which was direct competition.

Turning to the requirement that the breach must be sufficiently serious, this has been further defined as 'manifest and grave' in the *HNL* case, and as 'verging on the arbitrary' in the *Isoglucose* cases although in the later case of *Stahlwerke Peine-Salzgitter* v *Commission* (C-220/91P) suggests this latter requirement is not necessary. A breach of the rule on its own is not enough. In order to determine whether the breach was sufficiently serious a number of criteria must be considered and the nature and the effect of the breach must be examined. In the *Gritz* and *Quellmehl* cases the Court of Justice looked at the numbers affected, the extent of the loss suffered and the seriousness of the damage caused, i.e., is it far beyond the risks normally associated with business?

In the *HNL* case, which concerned the requirement to buy milk products rather than soya products, the increase in production costs was limited. The Court of Justice considered whether the company could pass on the increases with little loss of profit. If the company could not pass on the increases, then this suggested that the breach was serious, but if the company could pass on the increase then it was not sufficiently serious to found an action.

The damage must go beyond the risks normally associated with business. In the *Isoglucose* case (143/77), however, the damage was beyond what was normal, including causing the liquidation of some of the companies involved, but the breach was not flagrant and therefore not verging on the arbitrary.

The Court of Justice will look at the number of people affected, the degree of loss and most importantly whether there is a Community interest involved. The *Sofrimport* case (C-152/88) involved the import of Chilean apples which were on the high seas when the Regulation took effect. It was held that this involved a closed group because no other group could be similarly affected after the date of the Regulation. However, in the more recent case of *Mulder* (C-104/89 & 37/90) the presence of a large group of claimants did not defeat a claim although a serious breach still had to be demonstrated and that there was no higher public interest of the Community involved.

In applying all these considerations to the above problem it must first be determined whether there is an act which caused damage. The damage would be the losses caused by the Regulation imposing the levy. However, since a Regulation involves a choice of economic policy, the action is subject to the *Schöppenstedt* (5/71) formula and it must be considered further whether a superior rule of law has been breached.

The superior rule of law alleged to have been breached in the case of Welsh Foods is that of non-discrimination which has been clearly acknowledged as superior in previous case law. This can be proved by showing that equal or similar products have not been similarly affected. Factors in this consideration are, e.g., whether they are substitutable products. In the *Isoglucose* (143/77) and *Gritz* and *Quellmehl* (64 and 113/76) cases the alternative products of sugar and starch were held to be in competition or substitutable and therefore the rule had been breached. However, in the *Walter Rau* case (261/81), where equality of treatment was pleaded for margarine and butter, it was held the products were not substitutable and so there was no breach of the superior rule.

On balance in the case of Welsh Foods there is a likely breach as the product is in direct competition and can be used as a substitute for milk.

The attention then turns to whether the breach was sufficiently serious. As noted a number of criteria can be considered, including the nature and the effect of the breach, the numbers affected and whether it was a closed group and the seriousness of the damage. On the basis of the *Isoglucose* case, where companies were driven out of business, it would not be sufficiently serious but on the basis of the *Gritz* and *Quellmehl* cases (64 and 113/76) and the *Sofrimport* case (C-152/88), where it was considered that the risk went beyond that normally inherent in business, and also in view of the small numbers involved, then it would be sufficiently serious. It is not, however, predictable with certainty. Whilst the group is not entirely fixed it is unlikely that others would join at this stage and the losses are enough to drive Welsh Foods out of business. Thus according to the information given in this case, it is likely but not certain that Welsh Foods will succeed with its action however, the EC Council of Ministers does have a legitimate aim in preventing the re-establishment of the milk lakes and this may well weigh heavily in the decision of the ECJ.

QUESTION 7

Define the circumstances in which the ECJ would refuse to accept a reference under the Art 234 preliminary ruling procedure, and outline the guidelines for courts of last instance and other national courts in determining whether a reference should be made to the ECJ on:

(a) the interpretation of Community law

(b) the validity of Community laws.

Commentary

This is a two part question, clearly concentrating on the preliminary ruling procedure introduced under Art 234 (ex 177) of the EC Treaty. First, you should state the basic purpose of Art 234 (ex 177) and outline the procedure involved in national courts making references.

Secondly, you should discuss the right or ability of the Court of Justice to refuse to accept a reference, referring to established case law to assist your answer and then outline the guidelines for the national courts in making references.

Suggested Answer

The purpose of Art 234 (ex 177) is to act as a bridge or a link between the Community and national legal systems. It is to ensure the uniform interpretation of Community law throughout the Member States and thus provide consistency in Community law. It provides the national courts with assistance in cases concerning Community law by obtaining rulings on the interpretation and validity of Community law.

It should be pointed out that Art 234 (ex 177) is a judicial device and not part of an appeal system, nor is it a remedy of the individual, therefore the decision to refer remains that of the court of the Member State.

Article 234 (ex 177) basically provides that where a question of interpretation of the Treaty or a question of the validity and interpretation of Acts of the institutions arises, any court or tribunal in a Member State may request the Court of Justice to give a ruling on it. The national court should determine the facts of the case and decide whether a question of Community law arises which it considers must be resolved in order to decide the case before it. When the ruling of the Court of Justice is received the national court must faithfully apply that ruling to the case. Generally, references should not be made until the facts have been determined.

Initially, the Court of Justice stated that it was up to the Member States to decide whether a reference was necessary (see the case of *Da Costa* (28–30/62)). As the number of cases before the Court of Justice increased and a considerable backlog developed, the Court of Justice may well have been prompted to start considering whether all the references were entirely necessary. The Court has considered the validity of some of the references and has on occasion refused references which in its opinion are an abuse of the system. There may be genuine circumstances, particularly where Community law proves not to be relevant, when the Court of Justice is right to refuse the reference. Thus in a limited number of cases the Court of Justice has decided that there are reasons not to accept and has refused a reference. It has decided that cases which do not involve a real dispute and only concern a theoretical consideration which will not give an answer to a case before a court or tribunal, will not be accepted. In *SPUC* v *Grogan* (C-159/90), the case had been terminated at the national level, therefore the Court of Justice held there was no question left to be resolved. In *Mattheus* v *Doego* (93/78) a contract's continuation was determinable by the entry of Spain, Portugal and Greece to the Community. The Court of Justice held it had no jurisdiction as this was a matter to be determined by the Member States and the potential new states and refused jurisdiction.

The case of *Foglia* v *Novello* (104/79) is of special importance. It concerned a contract for wine between a French buyer, Novello and an Italian supplier, Foglia. Clauses stipulated that the buyer and the carrier (Danzas) should not be responsible for French import duties which were contrary to Community law. These were charged on the French border and reimbursed by Foglia. Foglia sought to recover the charges from Novello who denied responsibility to pay them on the basis that they were illegally charged by the French authorities. The Italian judge made a reference to the Court of Justice asking whether the French tax was compatible with the Treaty.

The Court of Justice rejected the reference on the grounds that there was no genuine dispute between the parties and that the action had simply been concocted to challenge French legislation. The Court of Justice considered this to be an abuse of the Art 234 (ex 177) procedure.

Not satisfied by this, the Italian judge made a further reference, *Foglia* v *Novello (No. 2)* (244/80), in which he specifically pointed out that the previous case marked a radical change in the attitude of the Court of Justice to a national court's decision to refer. He requested the Court of Justice to give guidelines on the respective powers and functions of the referring court. The Court of Justice held that its role was not to give abstract or advisory opinions under Art 177 (now 234) but to contribute to actual decisions and that although discretion was given to the national courts the limits of that discretion were determinable only by reference to Community law.

A further case in which the Court has refused jurisdiction is *Meilicke* v *ADV/ORGA* (C-83/91). The Court of Justice held that the questions raised in the reference concerned could not be answered by reference to the limited information provided in the file, and that the Court would be exceeding its jurisdiction in answering what was really a hypothetical question. A refusal of jurisdiction also occurred in *TWD Textilwerke* (C-188/92). A Commission Decision addressed to Germany was not challenged within the two-month time limit under Art 230 (old 173) but instead via the national court and Art 234 (ex 177). The ECJ held this to be an abuse of the procedure for not acting within the time limit, although the previous case of *Walter Rau* (133/85) and subsequent case of *Eurotunnel SA* (C-408/95) seem to suggest that this is an acceptable way to proceed.

However, if the Court of Justice goes too far, it may be infringing the discretion of the Member States. It has been argued that the case of *Foglia* v *Novello* may have gone too far in that direction. The Court of Justice may have, understandably, not wished to become involved in a clear dispute between Member States which should have been pursued by either the offended Member State under Art 227 (ex 170) or by the Commission under Art 226 (ex 169). It should, however, be stressed that the Court of Justice has refused jurisdiction in only a small minority of cases referred to it. It is not therefore a major problem. The Court has, however, issued guidelines in 1996 to the national courts to help them to decide whether a reference should be made.

Turning to the second part of the question, guidelines for national courts are contained both in Art 234 (ex 177) itself and in the pronouncements of the Court of Justice.

The obligation for courts of last instance to refer on points of interpretation is covered by Art 234 (ex 177) (3). As they are courts from which there is no further judicial remedy they are obliged to refer, subject to the view of the Court of Justice in the *Da Costa* (28-30/62), *Costa* v *ENEL* (6/64) and *CILFIT* (283/81) cases which essentially require there to be a materially identical question to be resolved before a national court of last instance can be relieved of the obligation to refer. The guidelines which the Court of Justice laid down in *CILFIT*, which would relieve the national court of the obligation to make a reference, suggest that national courts have a great deal more discretion than that given by Art 234 (ex 177). The French principle of law *acte clair* is often quoted in this respect, so that national courts need not make a reference where the application of Community law is so clear that the outcome of the case is not in doubt. Although this point is confirmed in the 1996 Guidelines, the Court of Justice also provided that before the obligation to refer was relieved, the national court should be sure that the outcome would be equally obvious to the courts in other Member States; something which in practice would be close to impossible to achieve. Hence the view that only materially identical cases would not require a reference to be made.

Courts of last instance which require a ruling on validity are also governed by Art 234 (ex 177) (3) and the Court of Justice has confirmed that a declaration of validity must be referred, but if a decision on validity has already been made on the same provision, this has a general effect which all courts may follow (see the *ICC* case (66/80)).

Lower national courts requiring interpretation have a discretion to refer but would also be able to apply previous judgments of the Court of Justice. Whilst it is not expressly stated, the application of the *Da Costa* principle would clearly be logical.

Finally, lower courts with questions of validity also have the discretion to refer or to allow an appeal to a higher court to decide the matter. They may not themselves rule on validity, and it was held in *Foto-Frost* (314/85) that they have an express obligation to refer where an answer to a question on validity is considered necessary to decide the case at hand. The 1996 Guidelines and the *Zuckerfabrik* case (C-143/88 and C-92/89), however, provided an exception where an urgent matter required interim measures suspending the application of Community measure whilst a preliminary ruling was sought.

QUESTION 8

The EC Commission addresses a Directive to the Italian government requiring it to ensure that paid holiday schemes and sickness schemes are equalised for male and female workers. The Italian Dentists' Association, a professional body to which 90% of Italian dentists belong, has, with the approval of the government, constituted its own professional arbitration tribunal to settle disputes relating to pay and conditions of work. Decisions of the tribunal are legally binding and there is no appeal. Angelo, a trainee dentist, claims to have received unfair treatment by comparison with female trainees and brings a case before the tribunal.

The tribunal dismisses his claim to protection by the EC Directive on the grounds that he is not a worker but a trainee, despite the fact that the ECJ had recently held that the term 'worker' included trainees.

The tribunal does not want to make a reference under Art 234, whereas Angelo insists that it must do so.

Consider whether there is a duty, ability or right for this tribunal or Angelo to have a question referred to the Court of Justice.

Commentary

The basic question is whether this tribunal can make a reference to the ECJ under Art 234 (ex 177), but first of all you have to consider whether this is a court or tribunal for the purposes of Art 234 (ex 177) and thus entitled to make references to the Court of Justice, because not all bodies have been so recognised. You should also consider the relevance of the fact that the question arising in the case has already been decided on by the Court of Justice and whether Angelo can insist that a reference be made.

Suggested Answer

The ability of a national court or tribunal to make a reference to the ECJ depends on whether it is a court or tribunal recognised by the ECJ for the purposes of Art 234 (ex 177). If it is, then it has a right to refer a question. A duty to refer arises when it is a court or tribunal of last instance and the obligation to refer is not relieved under the criteria outlined by the Court of Justice in case law.

The Court of Justice has accepted references from a varied number of bodies including administrative tribunals, arbitration panels and insurance officers. The determination of what is an acceptable court or tribunal is a question for the Court of Justice and is not dependant on national concepts. Certain criteria have, however, now been established by which it may reasonably be determined whether a particular body may refer to the Court of Justice for guidance under Art 234 (ex 177). For example, it was clear from *Van Gend en Loos* (26/62) that administrative tribunals were acceptable for the purposes of Art 234 (ex 177). Whilst the majority of bodies which decide legal matters in the Member States pose no problem, it is the bodies which lie either partially or entirely outside the state legal system which raise the question of whether it is suitable for the Court of Justice to accept a reference from them. A few examples will highlight some of the considerations taken into account by the Court of Justice.

The *Vaassen* case (61/65) concerned a reference from the arbitration tribunal of a private mine employees' social security fund. The Court of Justice held that because the powers to nominate members, to give approval to the panel and to facilitate rule changes were in the hands of a Government minister and because the panel was a permanent body operating under national law and rules of procedure, it qualified as a court or tribunal in the eyes of Community law.

Broekmeulen v *HRC* (246/80) concerned a reference made by the appeal committee of the Dutch medical profession's organisation. This was held by the Court of Justice to be acceptable because it was approved and had the assistance and considerable involvement of the Dutch public authorities, its decisions were arrived at after full legal procedure, the decisions affected the right to work under Community law, they were final and there was no appeal to Dutch courts, despite the fact that a legal remedy was in private hands.

In the next two cases jurisdiction was refused. In the case of *Borker* (138/80), a reference from the Paris Bar Association Council on the right of a French lawyer to appear as of right before German courts was refused on the ground that there was no lawsuit in progress and the council was therefore not acting as a court or tribunal called upon to give judgment in proceedings intended to lead to a decision of a judicial nature. In *Nordsee* v *Nordstern* (102/81) there was no involvement by national authorities in the case. Despite the fact that there was a legally binding decision and there was no appeal, the Court of Justice held that because there was no involvement of national authorities in the process there was not a sufficiently close link to national organisation of legal remedies and thus the arbitrator could not come under Art 177 (now 234).

Thus, it is not an essential factor whether the body is private or public or that there is no appeal from its decision. A strong indicator is the level of involvement by national authorities. However, the lack of an appeal may lead to instances where the national body itself has to interpret Community law without guidance if the Court of Justice is unwilling to accept jurisdiction, something which must be less desirable from a Community point of view. In *Dorsch* (Case C-54/96), the ECJ provided guideline questions for national courts to pose. These are: whether the body is established by law, whether it is permanent, whether its procedure is *inter partes*, whether it applies rules of law and whether it is independent. The ECJ also issued a guideline statement in 1996.

It must therefore be decided on a balance of factors whether the arbitration tribunal in the above problem is one which is acceptable for the purposes of Art 234 (ex 177). The factors in the present case are: the governmental approval; the fact that 90% of all potential members are included; and the legally binding decisions with no appeal. The membership figure could be used as evidence to decide either way in that it would suggest that this is not the only way in which dentists can have disputes resolved. The other 10% must presumably be able to avail themselves of the ordinary national courts. On the other hand, since this body clearly is involved with Community legislation, it would defeat the uniformity of Community law if it cannot refer and must decide matters of Community law itself. Individuals such as Angelo may thus be deprived of their true rights. This, in the end, may be the most important consideration and is certainly one which the Court of Justice would consider.

It is probable, therefore, that it is a tribunal for the purposes of Art 234 (ex 177).

The next question is whether it is obliged to refer or whether it has a discretion to refer. It can be stated immediately that whatever the answer to that question it is clear that Angelo has no right under Art 234 (ex 177) to a reference and that this matter comes within the discretion of the tribunal where it has a discretion. As a tribunal against which there is not a judicial remedy under Art 234 (ex 177) (3), the tribunal is obliged to make a reference. This obligation will only be relieved if the question has already been decided and the case thus comes within the guidelines of the *Da Costa* (28–30/62) or the *CILFIT* (283/81) cases.

The tribunal is not obliged to refer where the provision in question has already been interpreted by the Court of Justice or the correct application is so obvious as to leave no scope for any reasonable doubt and therefore no question to be decided arises. The *Da Costa* case raised the same question as had previously been asked in the *Van Gend en Loos* case (26/62). The Court of Justice referred to its previous judgment in *Van Gend en Loos* as the basis for deciding the issue and advised that such a situation might, if the national court wished, excuse the obligation to refer.

The *CILFIT* (283/81) judgment expanded the decision of *Da Costa* (28–30/62). In *CILFIT* the Italian Supreme Court asked the Court of Justice directly in what circumstances it need not refer. The Court of Justice replied that in addition to the reason given in *Da Costa* a court might not refer if the correct application, but not interpretation, may be so obvious as to leave no scope for any reasonable doubt that the question raised will be solved. However the Court of Justice qualified this by stating that the national court must be convinced that the matter is equally obvious to courts of other Member States, that it is sure language differences will not result in inconsistent decisions in Member States, and Community law will be applied in light of the application of it as a whole with regard to the objectives of the Community. These criteria would be extremely difficult to fulfil if properly followed.

In the case of Angelo, the identical question has already been resolved by the Court of Justice which has given a ruling on the interpretation of the relevant provision, that, a trainee is considered a worker under Community law and is thus subject to Community rules in respect of non-discrimination. Therefore, there would be no need to refer and the tribunal could simply apply the previous ruling of the Court of Justice. However, the national court retains its discretion to refer if it so wishes.

The only problem left is that caused if the tribunal, despite its obligation to apply Community law, still followed its own decision in considering a trainee not to be a worker and did not make a reference. In such circumstances it could not be prevented by the Court of Justice, although following recent Community case law such as *Francovich* (C-6 & 9/90) and *Factortame III* (C-46 & 48/93), the State may be held liable for damages provided the criteria for such a claim are satisfied.

QUESTION 9

Has Article 232 proved to be of any benefit to those capable of invoking it?

Commentary

This question concerns actions against the Council or the Commission for a failure to act. It is the remedy where the unlawfulness of the institution in question is the wrongful failure to act in violation of the Treaty. It can be divided into a discussion of those who are capable of invoking it and whether it has helped those who have got past the stage of admissibility. A description of the process itself should be given at the start.

Suggested Answer

Article 232 (ex 175) concerns actions against the Council or the Commission for a failure to act. It is the remedy where the unlawfulness of the institution in question is the wrongful failure to act in violation of the Treaty. This presupposes that there was a clear duty imposed on the institution to act in the first place. It complements an Art 230 (ex 173) action and can be pleaded in the same action. In *Chevalley* v *Commission* (15/70) the Court of Justice held that it was not necessary to state which action was the subject of the application. Art 232 (ex 175) is thus designed to cover illegal inaction. Both provisions, however, have as their objective the ending of a situation of illegality. Both actions are also similar in respect of the institutions which may be challenged, originally only the Commission and the Council, but Art 232 (ex 175) has been extended under the Treaty on European Union to include the European Parliament and the ECB within its field of competence.

Those who are capable of invoking it are defined initially by Art 232 (ex 175). Case law has then subsequently had the effect of excluding individuals in certain circumstances from having an application admitted.

The Community institutions and Member States have, under Art 232 (ex 175) (1), a privileged right of action which is not subject to restrictions on admissibility. Although not expressly stated, it is implicit that the European Parliament is a privileged applicant, as confirmed by the *Transport policy* case (13/83). The privileged applicants can request general legislative acts as well as decisions to be acted upon without having to show any special interest (the *Transport policy* case). The ECB was given the right to take action by the TEU in areas falling within its field of competence.

Individuals, on the other hand, have a restricted right of *locus standi* under Art 232 (ex 175) (3), more so than under Art 230 (ex 173), because there is no equivalent of the requirement of 'direct and individual concern' under Art 230 (ex 173). Article 232 (ex 175) provides:

> Any natural or legal person may, under the conditions laid down in the preceding paragraphs, complain to the Court of Justice that an institution of the Community has failed to address to that person any act other than a recommendation or an opinion.

It was established by case law that to challenge under Art 232 (ex 175) an individual must have been legally entitled to claim as a potential addressee (see *Lord Bethell* v *EC Commission* (246/81), involving a complaint of a failure to act on price fixing by the airlines. Any potential act would be addressed to the airlines and not Lord Bethell). This strict view on the *locus standi* requirements has been tempered by the ECJ in subsequent cases and now the requirements are analogous to the direct and individual concern of Art 230 (ex 173) (see the case of *T. Port* v *Bundesanstalt für Landeswirtschaft und Ernährung* (C-68/95)).

The Court has in many cases rejected applications by individuals requesting measures of general legislative content (see *Chevalley* v *Commission* (15/70) and *Nordgetreide* v *Commission* (42/71) in which it was held that applications are restricted to Decisions to be addressed to individuals). Regulations cannot be demanded by individuals because by their very nature they are not capable of being addressed to specific individuals.

Furthermore, Art 232 (ex 175) cannot be used to get around the restrictive time limits of an action to annul under Art 230 (ex 173) see the case of *Eridania* v *Commission* (10 and 18/68).

The action consists of a preliminary procedural step which must be taken before court action can ensue. Art 232 (ex 175) (2) provides 'The action shall be admissible only if the institution concerned has first been called upon to act'. The applicant must request the institution to take a specific action as legally required, and advise that the failure to take the action will result in a court action under Art 232 (ex 175). The invitation to act need not follow any precise form to qualify for the purposes of Art 232 (ex 175). Only if the institution fails to define its position within a two month period can the matter be brought before the Court. The application to the Court of Justice must be made within a further two month period from the end of the initial two month period.

If the institution complies with the request to act, as in *EP* v *Council* (13/83), the Court of Justice will not allow the action to proceed.

The definition of position has also been seen to defeat actions because where the institution has explained its refusal to act, the action is inadmissible. In *Lütticke* v *Commission* (48/65) the applicants had requested the Commission to take action against the German Federal Republic regarding a breach of Community law. The Commission was of the opinion that there had been no breach so therefore refused to take action but also notified the applicant of this. The Court of Justice declared the application inadmissible on the grounds that the notification of the refusal was a definition of position. Thus a refusal to act is not actionable.

In *Deutscher Komponistenverband* v *Commission* (8/71), a complaint that a decision taken by the Commission was wrong does not allow an applicant to proceed under Art 232 (ex 175) on the basis that the right decision was not taken by Commission, i.e., that it had failed to act in the right way.

In the *GEMA* v *Commission* case (125/78), a complaint was made to the Commission under Regulation 17 about Radio Luxembourg. When the Commission failed to take any action GEMA attempted an Art 232 (ex 175) action against the Commission. It was held that the letter from the Commission to GEMA stating its decision not to take action was a sufficient definition of position to defeat GEMA's action.

Until the *Transport policy* case (13/83) a declaration by an institution of its unwillingness to act was regarded by some as constituting a sufficient definition of position for the purposes of the Court of Justice. However, the Court in the *Transport policy* case stated that:

> In the absence of taking a formal act, the institution called upon to define its position must do more than reply stating its current position which in effect neither denies or admits the alleged failure nor reveals the attitude of the defendant institution to the demanded measures.

If it can be invoked successfully, and the case is proved, the institution is required under Art 233 (ex 176) (1) to take the necessary measures to comply with the judgment of the Court of Justice, within a reasonable time. A continued failure to act would of course be actionable under Art 232 (ex 175).

In the *Transport policy* case the European Parliament had complained that the Council had failed in its Treaty obligations under Arts 3, 61, 74, 75 and 84 (now 3, 51, 70, 71 and 80) to introduce a common policy for transport, lay down a framework for this policy and act on 16 specific proposals of the Commission.

The Court held with regard to the first claim that because the Treaty requirements were so vague, there could not be said to exist sufficiently specific obligations as to amount to a failure to act despite the fact that even as such obligations should have been completed long ago. The Court held that the obligation of Art 61 (now 51) of the Treaty could be identified with sufficient preciseness as to constitute a failure on the part of the Council to lay down a framework.

The second claim of failure to act on 16 proposals of the Commission was only successful in respect of the proposals and freedom to provide services. The other measures were within the greater margin of discretion left to Council by the Treaty.

Apart from the *Transport policy* case (13/83), admissible cases and those succeeding are extremely rare and despite the theoretical possibility that both privileged and non-privileged applicants may invoke, it has proved to be of very limited benefit to non-privileged applicants because of the other grounds on which its use has been restricted by the Court of Justice.

QUESTION 10

In what circumstances will the 'plea of illegality' under Art 241 be available to litigants seeking to obtain benefit from it?

Commentary

Whilst it would be rare for a question to concentrate entirely on this less familiar, and certainly less employed, article of the Treaty, it might never-theless be the subject of a question. It is more likely that you will have to consider an action using Art 241 (ex 184) within the answer to another question, as can be seen already in some of the questions above, which have asked you to consider the possible alternative actions which an individual challenging Community law might consider. It can also be seen in further questions on the jurisdiction of the Court of Justice in chapter 10 on mixed questions. However, it will do no harm to concentrate on this action so as to become familiar with it. It might even be the case that your particular course has not considered this action at all given the constraints on time whereby topics have to be considered according to priority and not all of them make it into the course.

To provide therefore an answer to this question a full explanation of the action and its availability to litigants needs to be given. The answer is straightforward and your only likely problem, given that the Article itself is not the subject of extensive treatment in textbooks, is finding enough to say about it. Hence the reason it is less likely to appear as a complete question in its own right.

Suggested Answer

The action under Art 241 (ex 184) provides an alternative right to plead the illegality of a Community Regulation but it is not a right to plead this directly before the Court of Justice as in the action under Art 230 (ex 173).

Article 241 (ex 184) reads:

Notwithstanding the expiry of the period laid down in the fifth paragraph of Article 230, any party may, in proceedings in which a regulation adopted jointly by the European Parliament and the Council, or a regulation of the Council, of the Commission, or of the ECB [European

Central Bank] is at issue, plead the grounds specified in the second paragraph of Article 230 in order to invoke before the Court of Justice the inapplicability of that regulation.

The action appears, at least at first sight, to be more easily available to litigants because it is not subject to the very restrictive *locus standi* requirements of Art 230 (ex 173) and is available to any party including Member States, the institutions and individuals. It is more likely to benefit individuals who are unable to scale the *locus standi* requirements of Art 230 (ex 173).

It is to be stressed that Art 241 (ex 184) is not an independent or direct cause of action to the Court of Justice, i.e., it cannot be the sole basis for an action before the Court of Justice. In *Wöhrmann* v *Commission* (31 & 33/62), the Court of Justice held that Art 241 (ex 184) was only available in proceedings brought before the Court of Justice under some other action and only as an incidental or indirect action. This means that some other action must be taking place in which the validity of a Community Regulation is questioned and which may have a bearing on the outcome of the case (see *Italy* v *Council* (32/65)). There must be a connection with the plea of illegality and the main action, it cannot be self standing.

The circumstances in which these criteria are likely to be met, so that the illegality of a Regulation could be challenged, would be where a challenge to some other form of Community law which is based on a Community Regulation is being made. Whilst Art 241 (ex 184) only refers specifically to Regulations, it has been held by the Court of Justice that other measures can be challenged. In *Simmenthal* v *Commission* (92/78), a Decision was challenged which was based on prior Regulations and Notices. The Regulations themselves could not be challenged under Art 230 (ex 173) because of the time limits, but could be indirectly challenged, via the Decision based on it, under Art 241 (ex 184). The Court of Justice held that it was not the form of the act which is important but the substance, therefore other acts which were normative in effect should be regarded as general measures that produced similar effects to a Regulation for the purposes of Art 241 (ex 184) and could therefore be challenged under Art 241 (ex 184). This clearly applies to Notices and Decisions.

However, Art 241 (ex 184) is not designed or intended to provide a backdoor for those who have failed to commence an action under Art 230 (ex 173), particularly after the two month time limit has expired, but who could have done. For example, in *Commission* v *Belgium* (156/77) a Community Decision was challenged directly before the Court of Justice. The Court of Justice refused the Belgian state the ability to plead under Art 241 (ex 184) because it had allowed its right under Art 230 (ex 173) to expire. It is argued this is a denial of Member State *locus standi,* but the real basis for the Court of Justice not admitting the case was that to allow it would make a nonsense of Art 230 (ex 173) time limits. Instead, it provides relief for those who are unable to get standing to bring an action under Art 230 (ex 170) but who are nevertheless affected by Decision based on an allegedly unlawful regulation as in *Simmental.*

So, whilst a challenge merely to try to circumvent the time limits for a direct challenge under Art 230 (ex 173) will fail, Art 241 (ex 184) nevertheless allows a challenge to be made providing it is incidental to some other form of action before the Court of Justice. This would include actions under Arts 230, 232 or 288 (ex 173, 175 or 215) (2).

The substantive grounds of the action are precisely the same as those listed for Art 230 (ex 173). The *Simmenthal* case (92/78), for example, succeeded on the grounds that the general measure had been used for purposes other than those for which it was intended.

The result of such an action is that the Regulation, or other general measure, is declared inapplicable in that case and that case alone and not generally void (*Meroni* v *High Authority* (9/56)). Any acts based on a voidable Regulation, however, will also be void and will be withdrawn. However, in practice the consequences will be that the Regulation will not be applied in subsequent cases, as in the case of Art 234 (ex 177) references which result in a declaration of invalidity being made in the case by the Court of Justice (for example the *ICC* case (66/80)).

Further questions on the jurisdiction of the Court of Justice appear in chapter 10 on mixed questions at the end of the book. As might be expected, these are concerned with two or more of the actions considered above, as it might be in such a format that questions may be posed on your course or in an examination.

6 The Free Movement of Goods

INTRODUCTION

This substantive area of Community law is likely to be included in most courses on EU/EC law. The area of law is regulated in the EC Treaty under Part Three, Title 1, Arts 23–31 (ex 9–37). Whilst this title includes the Common Customs Tariff in Arts 26–27 (ex 18–29), questions are more likely to be concentrated on the elimination of customs duties and measures having equivalent effect, Arts 25 (ex 12–17) and the elimination of quantitative restriction and measures having equivalent effect under Arts 28–30 (ex 30–37).

As with other substantive areas of Community law, questions can be posed both in the form of essay type questions and problem type questions. One particular topic of difficulty in this area, on which questions of either type are very likely, is concerned with the Court of Justice decision and statements in the case of *Cassis de Dijon* (120/78). One of the two emergent rules from this case, the rule of reason, continues to cause difficulties, not only for students of the subject but also for those who write about it. The questions in this chapter concentrate on charges and measures having equivalent effect, the restrictions allowed under Art 30 (ex 36) and the principles of law which have emerged from the case of *Cassis de Dijon*.

Although apt to cause difficulties in any part of the course, the renumbering of the EC Treaty by the Treaty of Amsterdam is even more problematic in this area as old Art 30 is now Art 28 and old Art 36 is now Art 30! Make sure you make it clear whether you are referring to the old or new Art 30.

QUESTION 1

'In spite of the aims of the EC Treaty, there is still not at the present time absolute freedom for a person in one Member State to import or export goods from or to another Member State.'

Discuss, explaining in particular the circumstances in which a Member State can lawfully restrict or prohibit the free movement of goods from another Member State.

Commentary

The first reference in this question is to the aims of the EC Treaty. You must therefore state the aims as contained in the preamble and Arts 2 and 3 of the Treaty and generally introduce the provisions of the Treaty concerned with the free movement of goods, i.e., Arts 25–28 (ex 12–30), and the restrictions allowed the Member States in Art 30 (ex 36). Outline then the rights provided by those Articles and the restrictions which are allowed the Member States by virtue of the Treaty. The further reasons for which Member States can lawfully restrict the free movement of goods arising from the *Cassis de Dijon* case (120/78) should also be discussed.

Suggested Answer

The internal market is defined in Art 14(2) (ex 7a) of the EC Treaty in the following terms:

The internal market shall comprise an area without internal frontiers in which the free movement of goods, persons, services and capital is ensured in accordance with the provisions of this Treaty.

The aim is to achieve the circulation of goods without customs duties, charges or other financial or other restrictions; to promote unlimited trade and to remove from the Member States the control over export and import matters. The Community is to be solely responsible for the latter.

The preamble of the Treaty has proved instrumental in the ECJ's rulings in reaching a decision on cases involving the free movement of goods, as have Arts 2 and 3 and the fidelity clause Art 10 (ex 5) and the prohibition of discrimination in Art 12 (ex 6).

There are four main groups of provisions in the EC Treaty connected with the free movement of goods: first, customs duties and charges having equivalent effect, Arts 23–25 (ex 9–17); secondly, the Common Customs Tariff, Arts 26–27 (ex 18–29); thirdly, the use of national taxation systems to discriminate against goods imported from other Member States, Art 90 (ex 95); and finally, quantitative restrictions or measures having an equivalent effect on imports and exports, Arts 28–30 (ex 30–36).

Articles 23 and 25 (ex 9, 12, 13 and 16) are aimed at the abolition of customs duties and charges having equivalent effect and at prohibiting the introduction of any such measures.

Article 23 (ex 9) states that the Community shall be based on a customs union, with a common customs tariff, involving the prohibition of all customs duties on imports and charges having equivalent effect. This provision covers 'all trade in goods', goods being defined by the Court of Justice in *Commission* v *Italy* (art treasures case) (7/68) as 'products which can be valued in money and which are capable, as such, of forming the subject of commercial transactions'. The definition has been extended in *Commission* v *Ireland* (Dundalk water supply) (45/87) to include the provision of goods within a contract for the provision of services. Article 25 (ex 12) prohibits the introduction of new customs duties or charges having equivalent effect, and equally prohibits the increase of those which are already in existence. The prohibition applies both to imports and exports and was held to be directly effective in the leading case of *Van Gend en Loos* (26/62). The Treaty of Amsterdam has amended this by adding a second sentence to make it expressly clear that the prohibition also applies to customs duties of a fiscal nature.

Article 28 (ex 30) provides a general prohibition on quantitative restrictions and measures having equivalent effect. This Article and Art 30 (ex 36) are those most closely concerned with the freedom to import and export goods and thus the answer to this question.

The concept of measures having equivalent effect has been defined by secondary legislation (Directive 70/50) and by the jurisprudence of the Court of Justice.

Directive 70/50 Art 2, defines 'measures having equivalent effect' to include those which 'make imports, or the disposal at any marketing stage of imported products, subject to a condition, other than a formality, which is required in respect of imported products only'. They also include any measures which subject imported products or their disposal to a condition which differs from that required for domestic products and which is more difficult to satisfy.

In *Procureur du Roi* v *Dassonville* (8/74) the term 'measures having equivalent effect' was held to include 'all trading rules enacted by a Member State which are capable of hindering, directly or indirectly, actually or potentially, intracommunity trade'.

Basically, therefore, any measure which makes import or export unnecessarily difficult and so discriminates between the two, would clearly fall within the definition.

Thus, the basic regime promotes free movement but within the Treaty, Art 30 (ex 36) provides exceptions to the general prohibition of Art 28 (ex 30). It states that Arts 28 and 29 (ex 30–34) shall not apply to prohibitions on imports, exports or goods in transit which are justified on any of the following four sets of grounds:

(a) public morality, public policy or public security;

(b) the protection of health and life of humans animals or plants;

(c) the protection of national treasures possessing artistic, historic or archaeological value; or

(d) the protection of industrial and commercial property.

Therefore, Art 30 (ex 36) allows Member States to enact measures which can impede the free movement of goods but this does not take account of the Court of Justice's restrictive interpretation or the fact that the application of these exceptions is subject to the limitation, set out in the second sentence of Art 30 (ex 36), that they may not be used as a means of arbitrary discrimination or a disguised restriction on trade between Member States. The ECJ has refused many attempts to widen the scope of Art 30 (ex 36) or to allow the Member States to define the scope of it themselves. Very few cases have thus survived the strict application of the second sentence of Art 30 (ex 36) to justify measures taken by Member States. Examples are, amongst others, *Commission* v *Ireland* (metal objects) (113/80), *Campus Oil* (72/83) and the *Prantl* case (16/83). In the *Prantl* case, the attempt by the

Member State to classify any criminal restriction as coming within the scope of public policy under Art 36 (now 30), failed. The argument based on public security in the *Campus Oil* case (72/83) however succeeded, by which Irish laws insisting that 35% of petrol supplies be purchased from the State refinery were held to be acceptable. Another successful use of Art 30 (ex 36) was in the case of R v *Henn and Darby* (34/79) in which a ban on the import of pornographic materials was upheld. It was, however, held to be necessary that similar domestic products were also prohibited.

The case of *Cassis de Dijon* (120/78) has added to the grounds on which Member States may restrict the free movement but only on an equal footing with domestic products. In this case, the Court of Justice stated that, in the absence of harmonising Community rules, obstacles to the free movement of goods, which are indistinctly applicable in that they apply or appear to apply to both domestic and imported goods, may be allowed only as far as these mandatory provisions are justified by an objective of public interest taking precedence over the free movement of goods. Mandatory requirements of the Member State could be imposed to relate in particular to: the effectiveness of fiscal supervision, the protection of public health, or, the fairness of commercial transactions and the defence of the consumer. However, the measures are subjected to further requirements, that they must be justified and proportional, i.e., necessary to achieve the result, that there is no Community system of rules and they must be neither an arbitrary discrimination nor a disguised restriction on trade.

The case of *Cassis de Dijon* had started to cause the ECJ problems because it was seized on both by Member States to justify restrictions and traders to attack virtually any nationally imposed restriction on trade practices or commercial freedom, particularly where rules were not just aimed directly at imports. The Court of Justice has therefore re-defined its position in the *Keck* case (C-267 & 268/91). The Court considered that certain equally applicable or non-discriminatory provisions restricting selling arrangements are not to be considered a hindrance on trade according to the *Dassonville* case (8/74) provided that they affect all traders and all products domestic and imports in the national territory, in the same manner and do not impose additional requirements (*Vereinigte Familiapress* C-368/95). Therefore such rules fall outside Art 28 (ex 30).

Thus, if measures which are adopted by a Member State satisfy either the provisions of Art 30 (ex 36) or the requirements laid down in the case of *Cassis de Dijon* for mandatory requirements, the Member State will be able, lawfully, to restrict the free movement of goods and thus there is not absolute freedom to import or export goods.

QUESTION 2

'However wide the field of application of Article 28 may be, it nevertheless does not include obstacles to trade covered by other provisions of the Treaty. Thus, obstacles which are of a fiscal nature or have equivalent effect and are covered by Articles 23–25 and 90 of the Treaty do not fall within the prohibition of Article 28.'

Discuss.

Commentary

This quotation is taken from the Court of Justice judgment in the case of *Iannelli & Volpi* v *Meroni* (74/76) as amended to take account of the renumbering of the Treaty but it is not necessary to know that, or even that it is a quotation from the Court of Justice, to be able discuss the meaning of the quotation. Instead, however, you will need to consider the scope of the application of Art 28 (ex 30) by considering the provision itself and by giving examples from the case law of the Court of Justice. The first sentence of the question suggests that the scope of application of Art 28 (ex 30) does not extend to prohibiting obstacles which are covered by other Treaty Articles. The question proceeds in the second sentence to spell out which other Treaty Articles serve to cover the obstacle that lie outside the scope of Art 28 (ex 30). It suggests that the Treaty Articles create mutually exclusive categories.

Essentially, the question seeks to determine whether Arts 23–25 and 90 (ex 9–16 and 95) apply only to charges or measures with an equivalent effect or to fiscal measures and Art 28 (ex 30) applies only to physical measures and that there is no overlap.

Suggested Answer

Article 28 (ex 30) provides a general prohibition on quantitative restrictions and measures having equivalent effect. Its scope has been determined both by legislation and case law. In *Geddo* v *Ente Nationale Risi* (2/73), the Court of Justice held that a prohibition on quantitative restrictions covers measures which amount to a total or partial restraint of imports, exports or goods in transit. The most obvious examples of quantitative restrictions on imports and exports are complete bans or quotas restricting the import or export of a given product by amount or by value. These are clearly in contravention of Art 28 (ex 30) and prohibited. The cases of *Commission* v *France* (import of lamb) (232/78) and *Commission* v *UK* (import of potatoes) (231/78) are straightforward examples.

The concept of measures having equivalent effect was defined by Directive 70/50 Art 2, which provides 'measures having equivalent effect' to include those which 'make imports, or the disposal at any marketing stage of imported products, subject to a condition, other than a formality, which is required in respect of imported products only'. They also include any measures which subject imported products or their disposal to a condition which differs from that required for domestic products and which is more difficult to satisfy.

In *Procureur du Roi* v *Dassonville* (8/74) the term 'measures having equivalent effect' was held to include 'all trading rules enacted by a Member State which are capable of hindering, directly or indirectly, actually or potentially, intracommunity trade'.

Basically, therefore, any measure which makes import or export unnecessarily difficult and thus discriminates between the two, would clearly fall within the definition.

Article 28 (ex 30) has been held to apply widely to a number of indirect measures including a government sponsored advertising campaign in *Commission* v *Ireland* (buy Irish campaign) (249/81), national marketing rules in *Commission* v *Belgium* (packaging of margarine) (314/82 and 189/83). Import bans on health grounds on food additives have been held to be in breach of Art 28 (ex 30) in two cases against Germany, *Commission* v *Germany* (beer purity) (178/84) and *Commission* v *Germany* (sausage purity) (274/87). In *R* v *Pharmaceutical Society of Great Britain* (267/87) the rule of the Pharmaceutical Society prohibiting dispensing pharmacists from substituting for the product named on a doctor's prescription, any other with identical therapeutical effect except under certain exceptional conditions. was also held to be capable of coming within the operation of Art 28 (ex 30).

Moreover, the scope of Art 28 (ex 30) applies not just to measures which are directly discriminatory but also to measures affecting both imports and domestic goods, termed equally or indistinctly applicable measures. Directive 70/50, Art 3 provides that measures which are equally applicable to domestic and imported goods will breach Art 28 (ex 30) where the restrictive effect on the free movement of goods exceeds the effects necessary for the trade rules, i.e., they would be disproportionate to the aim and would thus tend to protect domestic products at the expense of the imports. See, for example, cases concerned with health checks and spot checks, *Commission v UK* (UHT milk) (124/81) and *Commission v France* (Italian table wines) (42/82).

Thus, the scope of Art 28 (ex 30) is extremely wide, covering physical trade barriers, government assistance and measures which are applicable to both imports and domestic products. The scope of Arts 23–25 and 90 (ex 9–16 and 95) will now be outlined to compare with Art 28 (ex 30).

Articles 23 and 25 (ex 9, 12, 13 and 16) are aimed at the abolition of customs duties and charges having equivalent effect and at prohibiting the introduction of any such measures.

Article 23 (ex 9) states that the Community shall be based on a customs union, with a common customs tariff, involving the prohibition of all customs duties on imports and charges having equivalent effect.

Article 25 (ex 12) prohibits the introduction of new customs duties or charges having equivalent effect, and equally prohibits the increase of those which are already in existence. The prohibition applies both to imports and exports. A customs duty is usually clear to recognise but a charge having an equivalent effect is more difficult and has been the subject of a considerable body of case law. In *Commission v Luxembourg and Belgium* (gingerbread) (2 & 3/62), the Court of Justice held that:

a duty, whatever it is called, and whatever its mode of application, may be considered a charge having equivalent effect to a customs duty, provided that it meets the following three criteria:

(a) it must be imposed unilaterally at the time of importation or subsequently;

(b) it must be imposed specifically upon a product imported from a Member State to the exclusion of a similar national product; and

(c) it must result in an alteration of price and thus have the same effect as a customs duty on the free movement of products.

Furthermore, charges which are argued to be fees for services rendered, have also been classified as contrary to Art 25 (ex 12) unless they meet specific criteria including that they have been sanctioned under either Community or international law. The Treaty of Amsterdam has amended Art 25 (ex 12) by adding a second sentence to make it expressly clear that the prohibition also applies to customs duties of a fiscal nature which are applied when goods cross the border.

However, if a fee imposed by a Member State on imported goods is a measure of internal taxation, it cannot be a charge having equivalent effect, and cannot be caught by Arts 23–25 (ex 12–16). It is instead governed by Art 90 (ex 95) on taxation but Art 90 (ex 95) is designed to prevent circumvention of the customs rules by the substitution of discriminatory internal taxes.

Article 90 (ex 95) (1) prevents Member States from imposing on imports internal taxation of any kind in excess of that imposed directly or indirectly on similar domestic products. This prohibits discrimination in favour of the domestic products. Article 90 (ex 95) (2) prohibits Member States from imposing on the products of other Member States any internal taxation of such a nature as to afford indirect protection to other products. This serves to cover products that may be different but are nevertheless in competition with the domestic products.

Taxation was defined in *Commission v France* (reprographic machines) (90/79) as a general system of internal dues applied systematically to categories of products in accordance with objective criteria irrespective of the origin of the products. In *Molkerei-Zentrale* (28/67) the Court of Justice ruled that the words 'directly or indirectly' were to be construed broadly and embraced all taxation which was actually and specifically imposed on the domestic product at earlier stages of the manufacturing and marketing process.

Article 90 (ex 95) is therefore complementary to Arts 23–25 (ex 9–16) in that it is also concerned with outlawing fiscal measures which are discriminatory. Article 25 (ex 12) applies to charges which occur as goods pass a frontier and Art 90 (ex 95) should apply only internally within the importing state. Articles 25 and 90 (ex 12 and 95) were held to be mutually exclusive by the Court of Justice in the case of *Deutschmann v Germany* (10/65).

The final part of the answer must address the issue of whether Arts 25 and 90 (ex 12 and 95) overlap in any way with Art 28 (ex 30). The area of fees charged for inspection has emerged as the situation where all of the Articles under examination may come into play. The imposition of charges or alleged taxes may occur at the same time or following an inspection of goods. Thus a consideration of measures having equivalent effect may be undertaken, the result of which may be that the inspection proves to be a breach of Art 28 (ex 30) and not excused by Art 30 (ex 36). If a fee is charged, it will still have to be considered either as a measure of taxation under Art 90 (ex 95) or under Arts 23–25 (ex 9–12) because it may not be acceptable as a tax, see *Dansk Denkavit* (29/87). However, if it is the case that a Member State claims that a charge made on import inspection is a tax and there is not a fee levied at a similar stage internally on a counterpart domestic product, it may be held to be a charge having equivalent effect, as in the cases of *Commission* v *Belgium* (314/82) and *Commission* v *Denmark* (C-47/88). The distinction, however, between the physical barrier of the inspection and the fee charged remains quite distinct. The Court of Justice has considered in the case of *Iannelli & Volpi* v *Meroni* (74/76) that Arts 23–25 and 90 (ex 9–16 and 95) do not overlap with Art 28 (ex 30). It is possible that inspections may be lawful, but the fees for them may not, see, for example, the *Marimex* case (29/72). Therefore, the conclusions to be drawn from observing the scope of the articles are that there is no overlap of Arts 23–25 or 90 (ex 9–16 or 95) with Art 28 (ex 30).

QUESTION 3

Healthy-eat Ltd is a manufacturer of fruit-flavoured yoghurt and breakfast muesli. It has recently decided to try to export to the Continental market. In order to ensure the products are in good condition when they reach the shops in the Member States, certain measures are taken by Healthy-eat Ltd in the marketing of three special Continental product lines. The first is frozen yoghurt containing only natural ingredients. The second is unfrozen yoghurt to which preservatives are added. The third is muesli in sealed cellophane bags. All the ingredients of the products are listed on the packaging.

Healthy-eat Ltd found that the products were particularly popular in Germany and for four months sales boomed until Germany imposed a ban, justified on 'public health grounds', on the importation of any dairy product containing preservatives. A new German consumer protection law also forbids the application of the description yoghurt to all frozen yoghurts. Following this, consignments of yoghurt were turned back at the frontier.

Meanwhile, consignments of muesli were subject to long delays at the German ferry port whilst spot checks for health reasons were carried out.

These involved opening half the packets in every fifth case of muesli. Payment was required for the inspections and parking fees were imposed on the trucks.

When Healthy-eat Ltd challenged the parking fees and charges for the health checks, they were told that they were the equivalent of an internal tax imposed on domestic food products to finance a system of factory inspection in the German food industry.

Advise Healthy-eat Ltd as to its rights under Community law.

Commentary

This problem is concerned with the free movement of goods including aspects of charges having equivalent effect, measures having equivalent effect and internal taxation measures. A brief introduction to the area of law and the attitude of the Court of Justice would help to set the scene before answering the specific points in the question.

The material facts to be considered are the yoghurts containing additives, frozen yoghurts and the checks and payments for the muesli. The issues thus arising are whether the bans breach Art 28 (ex 30) or whether the measures introduced by the German government are justified under Community law by Art 30 (ex 36) or justified under the rule of reason from the case of *Cassis de Dijon* (120/78). Furthermore it must be considered whether the charges are in fact non-discriminatory taxation or charges contrary to the Treaty. As there are a number of issues a good structure to your answer is vital.

Suggested Answer

The applicable legal regime is that of the free movement of goods contained in the Treaty under Arts 23–25, 28–30 and 90 (ex 12–16, 30–36 and 95) concerned with taxation. Free movement of goods is one of the fundamental freedoms guaranteed by the EC Treaty and is a cornerstone or one of the foundations of the Community. Hence, the Court of Justice has interpreted the provisions widely and the exceptions allowed the Member States restrictively. Furthermore, Art 90 (ex 95) may be applicable, because a claim has been made that the charges are equivalent to a domestic tax.

The problems that have been identified are those concerned with the additives in yoghurts, the frozen yoghurts and the checks and payments for the muesli.

First of all, in relation to the yoghurt with preservatives, Art 28 (ex 30) prohibits all quantitative restrictions or measures having equivalent effect. Measures which are in breach of Art 28 (ex 30) are those which meet formulae provided by the provisions of Directive 70/50 or the Court of Justice in the *Dassonville* case (8/74) in that they impose measures to hinder imports. The imposed ban would appear to come within this category. However, Art 30 (ex 36) allows exceptions on public health grounds and this is what Germany pleads in respect of the ban on preservatives. There is considerable case law now dealing with bans on health grounds to the effect that any measure must be reasonable and proportional to the aim; see the *UHT Milk* case (124/81) and the German Beer Purity Law case, *Commission v Germany* (178/84). In the latter case it was not contested that the prohibition on the marketing of beers containing additives fell within the definition of a measure having equivalent effect to a quantitative restriction in Art 28 (ex 30), but the German government argued instead that it was justified under Art 30 (ex 36) on public health grounds. The Court of Justice held that, the use of a given additive which is permitted in another Member State and having regard to the results of international scientific research, in particular the work of the World Health Organisation, amongst others, and to eating habits in the country of importation, it must be concluded that the additive does not constitute a danger to public health. Certain of the additives used in beers from other Member States, were permitted in Germany in the manufacture of almost all drinks other than beer. Therefore, there must be a real danger to human health, the alleged harmful effects must be proved and the additives must be banned in all products. It is thus unlikely that this ban will be acceptable, unless it meets those strict requirements laid down by the Court of Justice.

The second problem concerns the ban on the grounds that the term 'yoghurt' cannot be used to describe frozen yoghurt. If not excused or justified this will also be a breach of Art 28 (ex 30). This time, however, the justification for the prohibition is not made on the basis of Art 30 (ex 36) but based on the new consumer protection law. As the rules appear to apply to both imports and domestic products and the ground given of consumer protection lies outside Art 30 (ex 36), the case law of the Court of Justice, notably the case of *Cassis de Dijon* (120/78) must be considered. The Court held that Member States are allowed to impose restrictive mandatory rules provided they apply to both imports and domestic products and that certain criteria were met. This rule has become known as the rule of reason. The criteria are that the measure must not be covered by a Community system of rules, it must be proportionate and it must not be an arbitrary restriction or a disguised discrimination.

Thus, the question that must be asked is whether the measure applies to all frozen products equally and whether a more appropriate measure could protect the consumer. The German Beer Purity Law case, *Commission* v *Germany* (178/84) and the Italian Pasta Purity Law case, *Drei Glocken GmbH* v *USL Centro-sud* (407/85) would be applicable here. It was held that protection would be equally, if not better served by appropriate labelling together with an indication of the sell by date, to guarantee consumer information. Hence, unless the measures meet the above, they will not be acceptable. In fact, there is a case concerned with deep-frozen yoghurt in which the insistence of the French authorities that it be given a description different from yoghurt was held by the Court of Justice to be capable of infringing Art 28 (ex 30); see *Smanor* (298/87).

The aspects concerned with the muesli involve a consideration of measures and charges having equivalent effect. Are these 'spot checks' for health reasons prohibited under Art 28 (ex 30) or permitted under Art 30 (ex 36)? Provided they are only spot checks and they take place with the same frequency as checks on the equivalent domestic product, they will be acceptable. They must not be an arbitrary discrimination nor a disguised restriction on trade. They are also subject to the principle of proportionality, see *Commission* v *France* (Italian table wines) (42/82) and *Commission* v *UK* (UHT Milk) (124/81). The checks in this case appear disproportionate and discriminatory because they are systematic.

The charges for the checks are argued to be an equivalent tax and it must first be considered whether they are. If the charges are not an acceptable tax, it then needs to be considered whether they are an acceptable or unacceptable charge prohibited by Arts 23–25 (ex 9–16).

Article 90 (ex 95) allows internal taxes to be imposed on imports as long as they are the equivalent of an internal tax and not discriminatory in their application. In *Denkavit* v *France* (132/78), it was held that the tax to which an imported product is subject, must be imposed at the same rate on the same product, be imposed at the same marketing stage and the chargeable event giving rise to the duty must be the same for both products. The chargeable event here is different because if it is a tax it would be on distribution, whereas the domestic product would be taxed pre-production, and thus would not come within the provisions of Art 90 (ex 95).

It must now be considered whether the fee imposed is an unlawful charge. The statistical levy case (*Commission* v *Italy* (24/68)) defined a charge having equivalent effect to include: 'any pecuniary charge, however small and whatever its designation and mode of application, which is imposed unilaterally on domestic or foreign goods by virtue of the fact that they cross a frontier, and which is not a customs duty in the strict sense'. The Court held that, such a charge is a charge having equivalent effect even if it is not imposed for the benefit of the Member State concerned, even if it is not discriminatory or protective in effect and even if the product on which it is imposed is not in competition with any domestic product.'

Under certain conditions charges may be acceptable. If they are health checks with a legal basis in Community law, they may be charged for; see *Commission* v *Germany* (health inspections) (18/87). They cannot be regarded as charges having effect equivalent to customs duties if the fees do not exceed the cost of the actual inspections in respect of which they are charged; the inspections in question are mandatory and uniform for all the products in question in the Community; the inspections are provided for by Community law in the interests of the Community; and the inspections promote the free movement of goods. It would seem unlikely that Community law would be the basis of these inspections, particularly as the inspections appear to be breaching Art 28 (ex 30), and therefore the charges in this case do not meet the criteria and would appear to breach Art 25 (ex 12).

The parking fees will also be held to be charges having equivalent effect to customs duties and prohibited by Art 25 (ex 12); see two cases concerned with customs warehouses, *Commission* v *Belgium* (314/82) and the *Marimex* case (29/72).

In conclusion, none of the products could be restricted lawfully under Community law.

QUESTION 4

The UK government has banned the import from France of nitrate fertilisers on the grounds that excessive nitrates in the soil are a danger to animal and human health. There is no ban on the production of this type of fertiliser in the UK but there is a government issued code of practice advising that other types of fertiliser must be used.

The UK government has also banned the import from Germany of all types of aerosol sprays which contain CFC propellants on the grounds that CFCs constitute a danger to the environment. In the UK, a law which phases out the manufacture of CFC aerosols, over the next two years, has come into effect on the same day as the ban. Other CFC products are not banned domestically.

The French and German governments are considering asking the Commission to take action and need to know whether these bans are a breach of Community provisions on the free movement of goods. You are asked to advise them.

Commentary

You are asked to comment on the two bans on the import of goods coming under Community law provisions on the free movement of goods. As an introduction, you should briefly outline the free movement of goods as one of the fundamental areas of Community law and that the Court of Justice, if it considered these bans, would interpret the provisions with the aims of the Community in mind and any derogations allowed the Member States, restrictively. The principal provision to consider is Art 28 (ex 30) which prohibits quantitative restrictions on imports. Article 30 (ex 36), however, allows the Member States to restrict imports for specific reasons and these include the protection on health grounds of humans and animals. You should therefore consider whether the bans come within Art 28 (ex 30). Then you should determine whether the reasons given by the UK will be held to be justified under Community law. Not all the grounds stated by the UK government are mentioned in Art 30 (ex 36), only the health grounds in respect of the nitrate fertilisers are contained in that Article. The ban on the grounds of the protection of the environment are not contained in Art 30 (ex 36) and the case of *Cassis de Dijon* (120/78) must therefore be considered.

Hence, you should identify the material facts, and outline the applicable law to discuss the issues that arise and the likely outcome of the case.

Suggested Answer

The free movement of goods has been declared to be one the fundamental policies of the Common Market and so of the Community. As a result, the Court of Justice has adopted a liberal interpretation of the freedoms to allow goods to circulate freely in the Community and at the same time has adopted a restrictive approach to measures enacted by a Member State which impinge on these freedoms. This problem question is concerned generally with the ban on import quotas and measures having equivalent effect under Art 28 (ex 30) of the Treaty and the grounds by which the measure may be justified under Art 30 (ex 36), which provides a number of grounds by which a Member State can lawfully restrict imports, including the protection of life and health of humans and animals. Additionally there is the prospect that the ban may be excused under reasons recognised by the Court of Justice in case law.

There are two issues to be decided in this answer. The first one concerns a ban on the import of fertilisers and the second one the ban on imports of CFC propellants.

The ban on the import of fertilisers is a clear prohibition on imports and thus comes within the terms of Art 28 (ex 30), as confirmed both by Directive 70/50 and the case of *Dassonville* (8/74), in that it directly hinders the import of goods. The ban is therefore contrary to Community law. The only question remaining would be whether the ban can be justified by the grounds cited by the UK. The measure can be justified on the grounds that it is protecting the health and life of humans and animals as stated in Art 30 (ex 36). However, the second sentence of Art 30 (ex 36) does not allow a health ban to be an arbitrary discrimination or a disguised restriction. In the case of the fertilisers, discrimination is still present because domestic products are not similarly banned and the UK would therefore not be justified in preventing imports, see *Commission* v *UK* (UHT milk) (124/81) or *Commission* v *UK* (turkey imports) (40/82). Yet, it may be argued by the UK that there is a government code of practice which acts as the equivalent of a ban on domestic products and therefore there is no discrimination. Such an argument, that non-legally enforceable means of preventing discrimination exist, has not previously been accepted by the European Court of Justice; see the case of *Commission* v *France* (merchant seamen) (167/73). Additionally, it must be proved by those relying on the ban that a threat to life and health exists and that the fertilisers banned from import are banned domestically as well. This case is therefore similar to the bans on imports on health grounds in the purity cases; see *Commission* v *Germany* (beer and sausage purity) (178/84 and 274/87). The ban appears not to conform with the second sentence of Art 30 (ex 36) and so is a breach of Art 28 (ex 30).

The second ban relating to the CFC aerosol products from Germany also applies in respect of domestic CFCs and is thus equally or indistinctly applicable. Directive 70/50, Art 3, provides that bans which apply both to imports and domestic products may also infringe Art 28 (ex 30). Such measures can, however, also be justified under Art 30 (ex 36), except that in this case the grounds given, environmental grounds, are not covered by Art 30 (ex 36). However, although the measure may be in breach of Art 28 (ex 30) it may nevertheless be excused if it meets criteria established by the Court of Justice in case law. The case of *Cassis de Dijon* (120/78) and subsequent case laws have added to the grounds by which the Member States may lawfully restrict the free movement of goods. The measure taken must, however, apply on an equal footing with domestic products. In the case of *Cassis de Dijon*, the Court of Justice stated that, in the absence of harmonising Community rules, obstacles to the free movement of goods may be allowed as far as these provisions are justified by an objective of public interest taking precedence over the free movement of goods. Mandatory requirements of the Member State could be imposed to relate in particular to: the effectiveness of fiscal supervision; the protection of public health; the fairness of commercial transactions; and the defence of the consumer. However, the measures are subjected to further requirements: that they must be justified and proportional, i.e., necessary to achieve results and not arbitrary; that there is no Community system of rules; and that they must be neither an arbitrary discrimination nor a disguised restriction on trade. The Court of Justice has further defined its position in the *Keck* case (C-267 & 268/91) in which it considered that certain equally applicable, i.e., non-discriminatory provisions which restrict marketing arrangements are not to be considered a hindrance on trade according to the *Dassonville* (8/74) case and thus should not be considered contrary to Arts 28–30 (ex 30–6), provided that they affect all traders and all products domestic and imports in the national territory, in the same manner. Such rules would be held to fall outside Art 28 (ex 30).

Thus, if measures which are adopted by a Member State satisfy either the provisions of Art 30 (ex 36) or the requirements laid down in the case of *Cassis de Dijon* for mandatory requirements, the Member State will be able, lawfully, to restrict the free movement of goods.

It must therefore be established that the interest cited by the Member State as the ground for preventing imports comes within the reasons acceptable to the Court of Justice. The ground stated of environmental protection was recognised by the Court of Justice in *Commission v Denmark* (disposable beer cans) (302/86) as an interest which comes within the scope of the ruling in the *Cassis de Dijon* case (120/78) and the principle of the rule of reason.

It must then be established whether it satisfies the criteria established by the Court of Justice in the *Cassis de Dijon* case. It must apply to both imports and domestic products, there must not be an applicable Community system in force, the measure must not be a disguised restriction on trade or an arbitrary discrimination and it must meet the requirements of proportionality.

From the facts of the present case, it is not stated that there is a Community regime on the matter, and so it may be concluded that this aspect is satisfied. However, the national rule will only apply to imports and domestic products after the expiry of the two year phasing in period and not all CFC products are covered by the ban, which, according to the case of *Keck*, they should be. At the present time it would seem to fail on the fact that it does not apply immediately to all domestic CFC products. The rule would more likely be justified if it applied to all CFCs and there was no delay in phasing in the requirements of the domestic ban. It is likely to be concluded that, whilst probably satisfying the requirements of proportionality, the ban is acting as a disguised restriction on imports and thus contrary to Art 28 (ex 30).

QUESTION 5

The *Cassis de Dijon* case (120/78) has helped clarify the complicated mass of case law on Articles 28–30 EC and has done this in a sense notably favourable to the basic Community objective of creating a unified market.

Discuss.

Commentary

The answer to this question requires a discussion of the case law on Arts 28–30 (ex 30–36) and the ruling of the Court of Justice in the *Cassis de Dijon* case. It would be best to deal with the material by considering the Treaty Articles first, then the case law arising from Arts 28–30 (ex 30–36) and finally considering the *Cassis de Dijon* case.

To do this, provide a basic outline of Arts 28–30 (ex 30–36) and explain why you consider the emergent body of case law from these articles to be complicated, if this is your opinion. Then consider the *Cassis de Dijon* case itself. Finally, the particular issues to be answered are whether it is considered that the *Cassis de Dijon* ruling has clarified the complicated mass of case law and whether it has helped achieve the creation of a unified market. It is important for the answer to this question to be aware of, and to address the fact that the *Cassis de Dijon* case is important for two principles of law.

A further part of the answer would include considering the approach of the ECJ, i.e., that Art 30 (ex 36) is an exception to the general principle of the free movement of goods and is therefore to be construed narrowly, and to consider any refinements of the *Cassis de Dijon* case which have taken place as a result of the misunderstandings as to the application of *Cassis* in some instances and the further attempts of the ECJ to clarify its scope, for example, notably in the *Keck* and *Mithouard* case (C-267 & 268/91).

Suggested Answer

The main provisions of Arts 28–30 (ex 30–36) will first be considered. Article 28 (ex 30) lays down a general prohibition on quantitative restrictions and measures having equivalent effect. In *Geddo* v *Ente Nationale Risi* (2/73), the Court of Justice held that a prohibition on quantitative restrictions covers measures which amount to a total or partial restraint of imports, exports or goods in transit. The concept of measures having equivalent effect has also been defined by secondary legislation (Directive 70/50) and by the jurisprudence of the Court of Justice. Directive 70/50 Art 2, defines 'measures having equivalent effect' to include those which 'make imports, or the disposal at any marketing stage of imported products, subject to a condition, other than a formality, which is required in respect of imported products only'. They also include any measures which subject imported products or their disposal to a condition which differs from that required for domestic products and which is more difficult to satisfy. Therefore any measure which makes import or export unnecessarily difficult and thus discriminates between the two, would clearly fall within the definition.

In *Procureur du Roi* v *Dassonville* (8/74) the term 'measures having equivalent effect' was held to include 'all trading rules enacted by a Member State which are capable of hindering, directly or indirectly, actually or potentially, intracommunity trade'.

Article 30 (ex 36) provides exceptions to the general prohibition of Art 28 (ex 30). It states that Arts 28 and 29 (ex 30–34) shall not apply to prohibitions on imports, exports or goods in transit which are justified on any of the following four sets of grounds:

    (a)   public morality, public policy or public security;

    (b)   the protection of health and life of humans animals or plants;

(c)   the protection of national treasures possessing artistic, historic or archaeological value; or

(d)   the protection of industrial and commercial property.

The application of these exceptions is subject to the limitation, set out in the second sentence of Art 30 (ex 36), that they may not be used as a means of arbitrary discrimination or a disguised restriction on trade between Member States.

The cases arising from Arts 28–30 (ex 30–36) are considered complex because of the difficulties which have arisen from cases in which there is no apparent discrimination. These are cases where the Member State has adopted measures restricting imports which apply equally to imports and domestic products. Whilst Directive 70/50, Art 3 provides that such measures are capable of infringing Art 28 (ex 30), they could also be justified under the grounds given in Art 30 (ex 36). For example, the protection of the health or life of humans or animals is a frequently argued ground for import restrictions and virtually all types of goods, especially foodstuffs, have been subjected to restrictions on health grounds and other rules applicable to both imports and domestic products. The Court of Justice has developed two main principles of law to deal with such situations. First, the principle of equivalence, often referred to also as the principle of mutual equivalence, which provides that if a product meets the equivalent standards of another Member State, that product should be regarded as meeting the standards of the state of import. Furthermore, all measures seeking to prevent or restrict the import of goods should be proportionate. Thus, if any less drastic method of protecting health existed, short of a ban, this should be employed. Hence, the systematic opening of sealed milk cartons for health checks amounted to import restriction in the UHT milk case, *Commission* v UK (124/81) (confirmed in the *Cassis de Dijon* case (120/78)). The health of consumers would be adequately protected by the necessary controls being carried out in the country of production to meet all the reasonable requirements of the country of import.

A further complication has arisen because it was previously considered to be the case, and confirmed by the Court of Justice, that the grounds under Art 30 (ex 36) are exhaustive. However, Member States were looking and still look for grounds by which they may lawfully restrict the import of non-domestic goods. Many new grounds to justify a restriction on imports were claimed by the Member States. It was in the case of *Cassis de Dijon* that the Court of Justice stated that obstacles to the free movement of goods resulting from disparities in the national laws on the marketing of products must be accepted, as far as these provisions are necessary to satisfy mandatory requirements relating in particular to: the effectiveness of fiscal supervision; the protection of public health; the fairness of commercial transactions; and the defence of the consumer. The rules which hinder trade may be acceptable if they are in pursuit of a special interest which the Member State has the right to protect. However, the Court of Justice narrowed the scope of the possible exceptions by adding to this so-called 'rule of reason', the requirements that measures taken to satisfy such mandatory requirements must apply to imported and domestic products, (i.e., indistinctly applicable) there can be no applicable Community regime, they must be proportionate and must be neither an arbitrary discrimination nor a disguised restriction on trade.

The case of *Cassis de Dijon* had started to cause the ECJ problems because it was seized on by Member States to justify restrictions and by traders to attack virtually any nationally imposed restriction on trade practices or commercial freedom, particularly where rules were not just aimed directly at imports. Complex litigation has arisen from this area of law. The Sunday trading case law serves as a good example of the confusion that can arise as a result of the seemingly more relaxed regime introduced. A ban on Sunday trading is a restriction on trade, so traders claimed it breached Art 28 (ex 30). It was not overtly discriminatory but applied to imported goods and domestic goods. The grounds given to justify the ban by the Member State were not contained in Art 30 (ex 36). Earlier case law before the Court of Justice led to contradictory decisions depending on whether the UK courts took into account the protection of workers, which would appear to justify a ban on Sunday trading, and the attempt to keep Sunday special which appeared not to justify a ban; see *Torfaen BC* v *B & Q* ([1990] 3 CMLR 455) and *B & Q Ltd* v *Shrewsbury BC* ([1990] 3 CMLR 535). However, the Court of Justice held in *Stoke City Council* v *B & Q* (C-169/91) that the UK's restrictions on Sunday trading do not conflict with Community law. It held that such rules reflected 'choices relating to particular national or regional socio-cultural characteristics'. The Member States have the discretion to make such choices. Thus, there is no breach of Art 28 (ex 30) by Sunday trading rules. The Court of Justice has re-defined its position in the *Keck* case (C-267 & 268/91) and held that certain equally applicable provisions restricting selling arrangements are not to be considered a hindrance on trade according to the *Dassonville* case and thus conform to Art 28 (ex 30), provided that they affect all traders and all products domestic and imports in the national territory in the same manner. Or, looked at in another way, an impediment to trade is acceptable where the rule in question impedes both the trade in domestic products and imported products equally. It was an attempt to remove many national rules which were introduced for reasons other than those which were a restriction on imports. Thus, providing national rules do not impede access to markets but merely regulate them without discrimination, either direct or indirect, they will be acceptable. Subsequent cases have accepted Dutch laws concerning the times and places at which petrol could be sold (*Tankstation't Heukste* (C-401 & 402/92)), Belgian laws prohibiting offering products for sale at a loss of profit (*Belgapom* (C-63/94), but *Vereinigte Familiapress Zeitungsverlags v Bauer Verlag* (C-368/95) witnessed a return to pre *Keck* considerations. An Austrian law prohibiting the offering of free gifts linked to the sale of goods was the basis for an Austrian publishers suit against a German magazine containing a prize crossword puzzle. The ECJ repeated its position established since *Keck* that certain national rules would not breach Art 28 (ex 30) unless imposing additional requirements. Austrian rules would constitute a hindrance to free movement if the content of the magazine had to be altered for the Austrian Market. However, maintaining the diversity of the press was the legitimate public interest objective given by the authorities and accepted by the ECJ. It remains up to the national judge to determine whether the ban is proportionate, or whether less restrictive aims to reach the objective are available. Thus, this case does not involve a rule falling outside of Art 28 (ex 30) but a restriction which could nevertheless be justified under the *Cassis de Dijon* rule of reason.

In summary two principles of law arising from *Cassis de Dijon* (120/78) are the principle of equivalence and the rule of reason. Whilst the rule of reason appears to have widened the grounds by which Member States can justify import restrictions and complicated matters by providing an extra set of rules to consider, the national interests claimed must nevertheless comply with strict criteria. In combination with the principle of equivalence, which combats technical rules imposed by the Member States, the criteria make it more restrictive for the Member States to impose restrictions; see as examples the beer and sausage purity cases, *Commission v Germany* (178/84 and 274/87). Furthermore, with the refinement of the *Keck* case, it can be concluded that the *Cassis de Dijon* line of case law is essentially favourable to the Community objective of the unified market by encouraging the free movement of other Member State products, which may have no direct equivalent in the host market and thus be subject to a ban which would not apply to any of the host state's products. The principle of equivalence in

Cassis is most important in this respect because it allows national rules to survive in the host state and thus provides more choice for the Community consumer and does not as a result encourage the same or common minimum or maximum Eurostandard to be established for every product.

7 The Free Movement of Persons

INTRODUCTION

In this area of substantive Community law both essay type questions and problem type questions are possible, although it is likely that problem type questions will be more frequent. The area of law straddles three main subdivisions, comprising the free movement of workers, involving most of the secondary legislation and case law, and then the freedom of establishment and the freedom to provide services. Questions can concentrate on any one of the topics or involve a combination of any two or all three. It may be that in your course only the free movement of workers is covered or that questions will only arise on the free movement of workers. Consultation of your course syllabus, past exams and current teaching staff will reveal whether you need to cover all three for the purposes of question answering or whether only one topic in this area of law will be examined.

This chapter includes all types of questions mentioned above: combination essay type questions, combination problem type questions, problem questions concerned only with the free movement of workers and an essay type question concentrating on the free movement of professionals.

QUESTION 1

The Court of Justice has interpreted the provisions of Articles 39–55 EC and the secondary legislation, in a more liberal manner than would be dictated by a purely functional view of the Treaty based on its economic motives.

Discuss.

Commentary

This is a very wide question and covers the topics of the free movement of workers, the freedom of establishment and the freedom to provide services. You must therefore plan carefully to make sure you are covering relevant material.

Two statements are made in the question which must be discussed: the view that the Court of Justice has been liberal in its interpretation of the provisions and the fact that this leads to quite different consequences from those that would follow from the Court of Justice taking a purely functional view of the economic motives of the Treaty.

The answer could be structured in two ways. The first would be to consider the functional economic view and then give examples of the Court's liberal interpretations. In this way, a form of control or basic position is established first which can be used to compare with the later case law. Alternatively, and also valid, would be first to give the examples from case law of the liberal interpretations and compare these with how a purely functional view would look. Both methods of answering achieve a correct end result.

The range of legislation noted in the question is very wide covering a number of Treaty Articles and secondary legislation. It would be too time consuming to go through every provision. The liberal interpretation could be demonstrated by an overview and then by explaining selective examples. The functional view, on the other hand, appears to be restricted to considering Treaty Articles and secondary provisions and it would seem best to take an overview of the Treaty objectives and then select examples from the provisions.

You might make a general mental note to help frame your mind in answering the question or indeed even incorporate into the answer the statement that the free movement of persons is one of the fundamental principles or foundations of the Community. But is this because (a) it assists the economic goals of the Community; or (b) it improves the opportunities and working conditions of the work force; or possibly (c) a combination of both of these?

Suggested Answer

Articles 39–55 (ex 48–66) cover the areas of the free movement of workers, freedom of establishment and the freedom to provide services. The free movement of persons has been described as one of the fundamental foundations of the Community but the reason why it may so be described is not obvious. Two main grounds might be given. One, that it is fundamental because these areas assist the economic goals of the Community in establishing an internal market in which all factors of production can freely circulate. Alternatively, the view might be taken that the aims for these areas of Community law are to improve the opportunities and working conditions of the work force of the Member States.

Essentially, the Treaty Articles provide that workers and the self employed can take up employment opportunities in the other Member States without discrimination on the grounds of nationality. Furthermore they should enjoy the same rights and benefits granted in such circumstances to nationals, but certain restrictions may be made in respect of employment in the public service. These basic rights can be viewed then in two ways.

A purely functional view might be that the economic motives are paramount and therefore it is only the economies of the Community and the Member State that are important. The granting of individual rights is incidental and just a way of ensuring that the commodity of labour can be imported and exported to suit the demands of European capital so that it can take advantage of the free market and can compete equally in attracting and securing labour. The personal rights given to workers are then secondary to the prime objectives in setting up the internal market and ensuring that business in the Member States is operating under the same rules. Under this view, it would be expected that the rights would be subject to the minimum interpretation possible to give effect to the rights granted. For example, there would be no right to be in other Member States whilst unemployed and looking for work; the Member States would have complete freedom to discriminate in the public service; or rights would not be extended to members of the family or to students.

The contrasting view is that of the liberal interpretation. The Court of Justice clearly interprets all parts of the Treaty in a distinct style using the so-called teleological approach. This means that specific measures are interpreted in the light of the objectives and goals of the Community and are not just subject to a literal interpretation of the words.

It is clear that in respect of the free movement of persons the Court of Justice has gone far beyond a literal or functional interpretation of the provisions and has, in its judgments, sought to give the widest possible scope to the rights provided. The following are examples and are not exhaustive.

Article 39 (ex 48) and the secondary legislation have been held to provide the status of worker to those who are not employed in the host state and have entered for the express reason to search for work; see the *Antonnisson* (C-292/89) and *Lebon* (316/85) cases. The term worker for the purposes of EC law also applies to those in part-time work and those who have worked only a few hours per week or were paid largely in kind. See, e.g., the cases of *Kempf* v *Staatssecretaria van Justitie* (139/85), *Lawrie-Blum* v *Land Baden-Württemberg* (66/85) and *Steymann* v *Staatssecretaris van Justitie* (196/87).

The general prohibition of discrimination on the grounds of nationality contained in Art 39 (ex 48) was considered in *Alluè and Coonan* v *University of Venice* (33/88) concerning two non-national language teachers employed by the University of Venice. It was held that discrimination in circumstances where a rule was being applied to both nationals and other Community citizens would still be present but affected the non-nationals indirectly; i.e., indirect discrimination is covered by Art 39 (ex 48).

The exception allowed to the Member States under the public service provision in Art 39 (ex 48) (4) has been restricted in two ways. First, once a worker is employed in the public service, there can be no discrimination in respect of the conditions of work and employment. Furthermore, entry is not restricted to levels of the public service which do not exercise power conferred by public law or safeguard the interests of the state. See the cases of *Sotgui* v *Deutsche Bundespost* (152/73) and *Commission* v *Belgium* (149/79). Such restrictions on the Member States are not readily construed from a functional view of the provision.

When we turn to the secondary legislation, even more surprising interpreta-tions can be cited as examples. Whilst it may be possible to perceive that a non-community national spouse has the right to stay in a Member State after separation from the Community worker, as in *Diatta* (267/83), it is unlikely that one would realise from the legislation that the rights to the same treatment in social matters would include the right to the companionship of a co-habitee; see *Netherlands* v *Reed* (59/85). The case law on Art 7(2) of Regulation 1612/68 has certainly demonstrated the very liberal interpretation that can be achieved by the Court of Justice. These include the right of members of the workers family, regardless of nationality, to join the worker but also to claim various types of social security benefit to financially help them stay in the host state. See, e.g., *Fiorini aka Christini* v *SNCF* (32/75), *ONE* v *Deak* (94/84).

Finally, by way of example, is the extension of the term 'worker' to apply in specific circumstances to students, an interpretation which is not obvious from a reading of the appropriate provisions and which took place even before the Directives granting general rights of residence were passed by the Council in 1990. See the cases of *Lair* v *Universität Hannover* (39/86) and *Bernini* v *Netherlands Ministry of Education and Science* (C-3/90).

Furthermore, in respect of establishment and services, the Court of Justice ruled that Arts 43 and 49 (ex 52 and 59) were capable of giving rise to direct effects, an interpretation which could not be expressly derived from the Articles. The fact that the Court of Justice did not see the need for completing legislation to achieve this is, a liberal interpretation; see the cases of *Reyners* (2/74) and *Van Binsbergen* (33/74).

With regard to the free movement of services, there is nothing in the Treaty or in the secondary legislation to suggest its application to education or the receivers of services; but this has been achieved in a number of cases. For example, *Luisi* v *Ministero del Tesauro* (286/82) concerned a prosecution under Italian currency regulations for taking money out to pay for tourist and medical provisions abroad. These were held by the Court of Justice to be payments for services and thus under the provisions of the EEC Treaty, payments being a fundamental freedom of the Community (Arts 49 and 50 (ex 59 and 60) and 12 (ex 7 EEC)). *Gravier* v *City of Liège* (293/83) concerned the decision that the fee charged for vocational training courses to foreign students but not to nationals was contrary to Community law.

It can be seen from the above cases that there are good examples that the Court of Justice has interpreted Articles and secondary legislation in a far more liberal manner than a functional view would dictate.

QUESTION 2

After a number of incidents involving minor offences of public order, which led to convictions for disturbing the peace, the founding member of the Tooting Popular Front, a self-proclaimed neo-communist revolutionary party, Wolfie Smith, and his girlfriend Shirley, both of whom had been unemployed in the UK for many months, decided to seek opportunities for work in Germany.

They were accompanied by Shirley's retired father, Charles, and mother, Florence, who is mentally disturbed.

Shirley obtained work but Wolfie did not and after seven months the immigration authorities, who now had details of Wolfie's convictions and political associations, ordered the expulsion of Wolfie from Germany as a threat to public security and as a person whose presence was contrary to public policy.

Charles had claimed retirement pension and Florence had made a claim for a special benefit to attend a mental health clinic. Both were refused on the grounds that they had not contributed to the German social security system and were not German citizens and were thus not entitled to benefits. In addition a deportation order was issued against Florence on the ground that her mental illness was a threat to public policy and public security.

Wolfie appealed against his deportation on the grounds that he was a worker and entitled to remain in Germany as a result of his street busking (playing guitar in the street for donations of money from the passing public). Wolfie had also joined a local band and played a series of gigs (about 80 hours in total) before ideological differences led the band to split. Afterwards he applied for a grant to attend Music College but was turned down by the German Authorities.

Shirley's parents also appealed against the refusal of benefit and Florence's deportation.

In order to help them in their appeals before the local administrative tribunal, before which representation is not compulsory, they obtained the services of Ken, a qualified UK solicitor with a practice in Tooting, who visited them in Germany. The tribunal, however, refused to recognise his right to represent them unless he works in conjunction with a local lawyer and rents and maintains local chambers as a professional base whilst in Germany. Ken's protest that the provision of services should not be subject to the same restrictive rules is rejected by the German authorities because they argue he has established in Germany and hence they can impose their rules on him.

You are asked to consider the position of Wolfie, Shirley's parents and Ken under Community law.

Commentary

This long and involved problem question concerns a number of aspects of the free movement of workers including their rights in the host state, the rights of their relatives and the free movement of professionals. As with many problem questions on this topic, it can be difficult to answer because there are often a considerable number of points to be considered. These include procedural points, rights and benefits to be claimed, rights of members of the family and reasons why deportation would not be appropriate.

A good plan is essential in order to structure this answer.

You should commence by outlining the general approach of the ECJ in this area of law before noting the issues that should be tackled in the answer. Then, identify the problems which must be considered. These can be listed person by person. Wolfie is concerned about the deportation, whether he is a worker or has the status of a worker for other reasons, and then whether there are substantive grounds for the deportation order. Florence and Charles need to know their rights as relatives of a worker to claim benefits and Florence is concerned about the deportation order issued. Ken wishes to know about his ability to provide services.

The order in which these points are tackled is also important and the procedural points should be dealt with first because these are of first relevance for the persons concerned. This should be done even if you have not yet decided whether there are grounds for the deportation. Then you can deal with each person in turn or combine the treatment of persons where the issues are the same. Given that Wolfie is so complex you might provide a list of the items you need to tackle in respect of him in the answer or maybe just to put these down in your plan. I have provided them here as it might be valid to say that such a list would not be appropriate in the answer itself.

Wolfie's concerns are: Deportation; Worker in own right?; Providing services?; Established?; Student?; Seeking work?; Member of family?; Co-
habitee?; Right to be deported and past convictions and personal conduct.

Suggested Answer

The free movement of persons is catered for in the EC Treaty under Arts
39–55 (ex 48–66), in secondary Community law and the case law of the
Court of Justice. In this area of law, the Court of Justice has taken a line
which has sought to promote and protect the freedoms available to individual
workers and to restrict, where possible, the reasons for which the Member
States can restrict those freedoms.

Wolfie and Florence are facing deportation. Community citizens in such
circumstances are provided with rights under Directive 64/221 not to be
deported immediately but to be allowed to stay for at least a month if they
have already taken up residence in the host state; see Art 7 of that Directive.
Whether they can stay longer depends on the facts of the case, for example,
whether they can stay to argue the substantive grounds of the deportation
decision through the courts, which may take longer; see Art 9 of the
Directive and the cases of *Adoui* and *Cornaille* (115 & 116/81) and
Pecastaing (98/79). However, they cannot be subject to immediate deportation.

The answer can now consider the substantive grounds in respect of Wolfie.
His right to remain in the host state must be considered in the light of the
grounds for deportation. If he has no right to stay, then deportation will be
within the right of the host state. First of all, it should be considered whether
he has the right to stay because he is a worker. Is a busker a worker? A
busker does not seem to satisfy the criteria of a worker laid down in the case
of *Lawrie Blum* (66/85). His busking is not at the direction or remuneration
of an employer, therefore he is not a worker.

Does the 80 hours membership of the band and playing gigs qualify him as
a worker? Although the case of *Raulin v Netherlands Ministry of Education
and Science* (C-357/89) would seem to support this suggestion, again the
criteria of Lawrie Blum seem not to be satisfied. If he is not classified as a
worker, it may then be questioned whether he can be considered as
self-employed, either as providing services or establishing himself in the host
state. In order to establish or provide services in a host state, a self-employed
person must first be established in another Member State. Wolfie was not.

A definition for establishment has been given in *Factortame* (C-221/89) by the ECJ, which considered that it was the actual pursuit of an economic activity through a fixed establishment in another Member State for an indefinite period. Wolfie has no fixed establishment, therefore the status of a self-employed person is denied him. The conclusion must be that he has no status as a self employed person, especially as he plays no part in the tax and social security systems of the host state. So, he has no right to stay unless it can be argued that he is *seeking work* as considered by the ECJ in the case of *Antonisson* (C-292/89). The guidelines in that case are that, if he is actively seeking and there are genuine chances of him finding work, he should be accorded the status of a worker for that purpose. Given the limited facts, it would seem that he is not seeking work, apart from his busking which does not appear to constitute work, therefore on the basis of *Antonisson* he has no right to stay.

The final ground which might be argued to provide Wolfie with a right to stay would be the right as a co-habitee of Shirley, as in the *Netherlands* v *Reed* (59/85) case. Shirley has obtained work and is therefore a worker. It must be stressed that if this were accepted he does not have the right to stay in his own right but as one of the social advantages which Shirley must be allowed to enjoy under Art 7(2) of Regulation 1612/68. Finally, the following considerations in respect of the grounds for the Member State to deport him, must be considered in the light of this tenuous right to stay.

The grounds for deportation of public policy and public security stated by Germany are those allowed by Art 39 (ex 48) (3) of the Treaty. These are further defined in Directive 64/221, Art 3(1) which states that, they must be based exclusively on the personal conduct of the person concerned. So, simple membership of the Tooting Popular Front should not justify deportation. However, the ECJ in the case of *Van Duyn* (41/74) held that association with the aims of an organisation may be sufficient, even if the organisation or its activities are not illegal. Given that Wolfie is the founding member it may be possible to deport him for this reason depending on the view of the state of the threat posed by the organisation.

Article 3(2) of the same Directive further provides that the state authorities cannot use past convictions as grounds in themselves to warrant deportation. However, the ECJ held in the case of *Bouchereau* (30/77) that where they are a present threat and point to a future threat, they can be employed as evidence. In Wolfie's case there are only past convictions and no present problems so it is unlikely that this ground would be upheld as acceptable.

On balance, whilst an unequivocal answer is difficult, deportation may be possible on the basis of the *Van Duyn* case and because Wolfie's right to stay is weak. However, a reference to the ECJ may reveal a change on this point.

Florence and Charles's rights to remain in the host state are based on their status as ascendants of a worker under Art 10(1)(b) of Regulation 1612/68. However, Florence is also facing deportation. The Member State may argue that the annex to Directive 64/221 provides that profound mental disturbance is a disability which might threaten public security or public policy. Whether Florence's mental disturbance is sufficient to satisfy this requirement would depend on her medical condition which would arguably have to be quite severe. Her mental condition is unlikely, therefore, to justify deportation.

The claim for retirement pension for Charles is straightforward and the case of *Castelli* (261/83) can be cited in support, which provides that benefits in respect of members of the family of a worker are also social advantages under Art 7(2) of Regulation 1612/68 which must be enjoyed by the worker.

As far as the special benefit for Florence to attend the mental health clinic is concerned, there is the case of *Michel S* (76/72) which may be argued but this is only applicable to children of workers under Art 12 of Regulation 1612/68. Arguably the ECJ would also hold this to be a social advantage under Art 7(2).

Finally the situation with regard to Ken must be considered. It is to be assumed that Ken is seeking the freedom to provide services rather than establishment, as there appears no intention to settle permanently or on a long time basis. Article 49 (ex 59) is the applicable Treaty Article which is directly effective but Directive 77/249 specifically concerns the freedom of lawyers to provide services. Whilst under Art 5 of this Directive a Member State may require a lawyer providing services to work in conjunction with a national lawyer, the ECJ has held in the cases of *Commission* v *France* (C-294/89) and *Commission* v *Germany* (427/85) that this may be imposed only if compulsory representation of clients is required before the court concerned. In Ken's case this is not the position, so he cannot be required to work in conjunction with a national lawyer.

The requirement to rent and maintain a local office are excluded by Art 4(1) of the Directive and the ECJ confirmed in the cases of *Van Binsbergen* (33/74) and *Klopp* (107/83) that local residence requirements cannot be required of lawyers merely wishing to provide services.

As a result of the more recent *Gebhard* case (C-55/94), the German authorities may be correct in describing Ken as established in Germany, but this can only be judged on the facts. A one-off visit would not qualify, but continuing to keep chambers in Germany might. In any event as a result of the *Säger* (C-76/90) and *Gebhard* cases, now, and almost regardless of whether the provision of services or establishment is involved, any rules which hinder or make less attractive the exercise of the fundamental freedoms will be subject to four conditions. The rules must be:

(a) non-discriminatory application;

(b) justified by imperative reason relating to the public interest;

(c) suitable to secure the objective sought; and

(d) proportional.

Whilst this is a matter for the national courts to decide, it is arguable the requirements do not meet the criteria but a reference to the ECJ might be necessary to settle the matter.

QUESTION 3

François, a French national, moved to Belgium several years ago when he obtained work in a shipyard. Some months ago, due to a down turn in shipbuilding, he was put on short time working, as a result of which his wages fell below subsistence level.

His application for social security assistance was refused on the grounds that he was not a 'worker' within the meaning of Community law, and that, in any case, foreign nationals were not entitled to such assistance. François appealed against the decision. Before his appeal could be heard, the shipyard where he worked was taken into public ownership. The social security tribunal dismissed his appeal, holding that François's original contentions were invalid, and in any case he would now be excluded from assistance because of Art 39 (ex 48) (4) of the EC Treaty.

He has subsequently been issued with a deportation order on the grounds that he possesses no documentation for residence and because his ID card is now out of date.

François's wife, Bella, a Bulgarian national, moved to Belgium with François. A few months ago that marriage broke down and Bella is now living on her own in another part of Belgium. She has recently received a deportation notice from the Belgian authorities on the grounds that she is not a Community national. The notice also referred to Bella's conviction two years ago for possession of a small quantity of cannabis (for which she was given a small fine).

Advise François and Bella of their rights under Community law in the light of the above events.

Commentary

This is a typical problem question in the area of the free movement of workers. It requires you to consider a number of issues of both substantive law and procedural law. You should start by outlining the general approach of the ECJ in this area of law before noting the issues that should be tackled in the answer.

The structure of the answer is also very important. The issue of first importance to consider would be the impending deportations and when this has been resolved, the substantive issues arising in respect of each person can be considered.

Suggested Answer

The free movement of workers is catered for in the EC Treaty under Arts 39–42 (ex 48–51), secondary Community law and in the case law of the Court of Justice. In this area of law, the Court of Justice has taken a line which has sought to promote and protect the freedoms available to individual workers and to restrict, where possible, the reasons for which the Member States can restrict those freedoms.

The problems thus arising are the deportation orders issued in respect of François and Bella, the continuing status of François as a worker and his claim for social assistance, the change of status of employer, the grounds for deportation, the residence of Bella and the grounds given for her deportation.

In this case both François and Bella face deportation but for different reasons. The rights of those facing deportation should be considered before moving on to consider the substantive rights at issue in the problem, as this is their immediate concern and other rights may be prejudiced if deportation takes place. Community citizens and non-Community national family members in such circumstances are provided with rights under Directive 64/221 not to be deported immediately but to be allowed to stay for at least a month if they have already taken up residence in the host state; see Arts 1 & 7. Whether they can stay longer depends on the facts of the case, for example, whether they can stay to argue the substantive grounds of the deportation decision through the courts, which may take longer, see Art 9 of the Directive and the cases of *Adoui* and *Cornaille* (115 & 116/81) and *Pecastaing* (98/79). However, they cannot be subject to immediate deportation. The grounds for deportation can be discussed later now that the immediate threat of deportation has been diverted.

The first substantive aspect is to determine whether François continues to enjoy the status of a worker, which he previously would have obtained by reason of his full time employment in a shipyard. He has since been put on short time work and has had to claim financial assistance from the state in order to obtain a minimum subsistence level. Case law has shown that neither the short time work nor the need for his wages to be supplemented lawfully from other means would deprive a person of the status as a Community worker. In *Kempf* v *Staatssecret-aris van Justitie* (139/85), it was held that despite only teaching for 12 hours per week and the fact that supplementary benefit was being claimed and received to support himself, Kempf qualified as a worker. The 'effective and genuine activity' as an employed person on a part-time basis qualified Kempf as a worker. This is not defeated by the fact that income was augmented lawfully from other means. François is thus a worker. As a worker, therefore, his entitlement to benefit would be secured under Art 39 (ex 48(2)) of the Treaty and Art 7(2) of Regulation 1612/68, as confirmed in the case of *Hoeckx* (249/83).

The second substantive aspect in respect of François is the change of status of employer to a public employer. Whilst this arguably might affect his chances of obtaining work in the first place, he is already employed and it was held in the case of *Sotgui* v *Deutsche Bundespost* (152/73) that Art 48(4) (now 39(4)) of the Treaty applies to entry and not to conditions of employment. It is most likely, therefore, that this ground will not be accepted by the ECJ.

Finally, in respect of François, the grounds for deportation remain to be considered. These were stated to be that he possesses no documentation for residence and that his ID card has expired. Directive 68/360 provides that entry into a state may require an ID card, but rights of residence must not be weakened by disproportionate penalties which hinder free movement when the worker has failed to comply with national legal requirements demanded of him. For example, in *R* v *Pieck* (159/79), Pieck, a Dutch national, re-entered the UK after his original six-month entry permit had expired and he had failed to renew it. The authorities sought to deport him. The Court of Justice held that Art 4 of Directive 64/221 means that a failure to obtain a permit could only result in penalties for minor offences. The residence permit is not a precondition for residence, it is merely evidence of the entitlement to enter and reside, i.e., not the right itself but merely the proof of it. Furthermore, Directive 64/221, Art 3(3) provides that the expiry of an ID or a passport is no justification for expulsion. Therefore he could not be deported for these reasons.

The substantive issues affecting Bella concern first of all the fact that she is a non-community national spouse of a Community national who is now separated from the Community worker and is living on her own. Additionally, the fact that she was previously convicted for the possession of a small quantity of cannabis is cited as a ground for deportation. In answer to the first point, it was held in *Diatta* v *Land Berlin* (267/83) that the rights of a spouse are not dependent on residence with the entitled worker. In the case, Mrs Diatta, a Senegalese citizen, was married to a Frenchman living and working in Berlin. She obtained work in Berlin, but shortly after the couple separated to live apart. Upon her application to extend her residence permit, the German authorities refused on the ground that she was no longer a member of the family for the purposes of Regulation 1612/68. The Court of Justice ruled that the rights under 1612/68 were not dependent on the requirements as to how or where members of the family lived. Therefore a permanent common family dwelling cannot be implied as a condition of the rights granted under Regulation 1612/68. Bella has the right to stay in the host state.

It now remains to be seen whether she could be deported for the previous conviction for possession of a small quantity of cannabis. As far as the criminal conviction is concerned, Directive 64/221, Art 3(2), provides that previous criminal convictions shall not of themselves constitute grounds for expulsion. In *R* v *Bouchereau* (30/77), a Frenchman had been convicted in the UK on a number of occasions for drugs possession. The UK magistrate asked the Court of Justice whether Bouchereau could be deported to stop him committing such acts in the future. The Court of Justice held that it was not possible to look at past record to decide future conduct unless it constituted a present threat and 'a sufficiently serious threat to the fundamental interests of society'. Hence the reason given in the question for deportation would not be acceptable under Community law and Bella would be entitled to remain whilst still married to François.

QUESTION 4

Lister, a UK citizen, has moved to Denmark to take up employment in the Virtual Reality Computer Company (VRCC) as a technician. He is accompanied by his girlfriend Kristine, also a UK national, who is an expectant mother of twins. The claims she has made for unemployment benefit and maternity payments have been rejected by the authorities in Skive, where they have settled. The grounds given are that she is not a national and has not been resident for the required six months. Her claim that she is dependent on Lister is also rejected as she is not married to him.

Another UK national, Rimmer, has also obtained work as a technician in VRCC. Once settled he is joined by his cousin, Cat, who is not a Community national. Cat attempts to claim unemployment benefit but is refused. The authorities, now aware of his presence, have issued him with a deportation order which only states that he has no right to remain in Denmark. On a visit to Rimmer's home, a quantity of drugs brought in by Cat were discovered. As a result, Rimmer is also issued with a deportation order, stating that the presence of persons in the possession of drugs is considered to be contrary to public policy.

Advise the parties as to their rights under Community law.

Commentary

This problem question on the free movement of persons concentrates this time not so much on the rights of the workers themselves but to a large extent on the rights of persons connected to and dependent on the worker. You have to consider the rights of Kristine, the girlfriend of Lister, to stay and claim benefits, and the right of Cat to stay and claim benefits. It would be better to start the answer with a general introduction to the area of law, before moving on to consider the issue of the threatened deportations and thus the procedural rights of Rimmer and Cat. You can then consider the substantive issues in the problem. Do not, however, spend an inordinate amount of time proving that Lister or Rimmer are workers, as it is the rights of the others that are more problematic. You should, of course, state that they are workers but only briefly as this point is not contentious. Avoid also entering into a discussion about how criminal law and procedure would regard the discovery of drugs in the home of Rimmer. Stick to the Community law issues at hand.

Suggested Answer

The free movement of workers is provided for in the EC Treaty under Arts 39–42 (ex 48–51), by secondary Community law and the case law of the Court of Justice. In this area of law, the Court of Justice has taken a line which has sought to promote and protect the freedoms available to individual workers and to restrict, where possible, the reasons for which the Member States can restrict those freedoms.

The issues arising in this question are the deportation orders issued against Kristine, Cat and Rimmer, the rights of Kristine to remain and claim benefits, the right of Cat to remain and claim benefits and the reasons given for the deportation of Kristine, Cat and Rimmer.

The rights of those facing deportation should be considered before considering the substantive rights at issue in the problem, as this is of immediate concern to them. Community citizens in such circumstances, and members of the family who are given rights under other Community legislation, are provided with rights under Directive 64/221 not to be deported immediately but to be allowed to stay for at least a month if they have already taken up residence in the host state; see Art 7. Whether they can stay longer depends on the facts of the case. For example, whether they can stay to argue the substantive grounds of the deportation decision through the courts, which may take longer; see Art 9 of the Directive and the cases of *Adoui* and *Cornaille* (115 & 116/81), and *Pecastaing* (98/79). However, they cannot be subject to immediate deportation. The grounds for deportation can be discussed later now that the immediate threat of deportation has been diverted.

The first substantive consideration is that of the right of Kristine to stay in Denmark and claim unemployment and maternity benefits. It should first be noted that, as it is stated in the question that Lister has taken up employment and is a Community national, it can safely be concluded that he is a worker for the purposes of Community law. This point is more important for Kristine.

First, however, it must be determined whether Kristine has any Community law rights of her own under the free movement of persons.

Kristine could be looking for work and would benefit from the rights provided under Art 39 (ex 48)(3)(b), confirmed in the case of *Antonnisson* (C-292/89), that Community nationals have the right to enter a host state and stay for a limited period providing they are actively seeking work and there is a genuine chance of being engaged. Given the facts of the case it is unlikely that this conclusion could be reached, however, if she could prove these requirements, she should be given the right to stay for six months at least.

A second possibility exists in the general Residence Directive 90/364. This is subject to the Community national being covered by adequate sickness insurance, which Lister could provide, but also to the proviso that they do not become a burden on the state (Art 1). The claims that she is making would seem to undermine the right to claim the protection of this Directive and it appears unlikely that it is applicable in her favour.

However, the Community free movement of workers' provisions provide not only rights for the worker but also rights for the worker's family. Regulation 1612/68 provides the details of those who can claim rights by virtue of their relationship to the worker. The spouse and other members of the family are defined in Art 10. The Regulation extends the rights available to the worker to the spouse and descendants and ascendants regardless of nationality. The descendants can be any nationality and include those under 21 and adult children over 21 where they are dependent on the worker. The Regulation does not, however, include non-married partners but this was considered by the Court of Justice in the case of *Netherlands* v *Reed* (59/85). Reed applied for a residence permit in Holland claiming her right to remain was based on her co-habitation with a UK national working in the Netherlands. The Dutch Government refused to recognise this. The Court of Justice was aware that provisions of national laws regarding co-habitees' legal rights could be quite varied. It was unable to overcome the clear intention of Art 10 which referred to a relationship based on marriage. The Court referred instead to the 'social advantages' guaranteed under Art 7(2) of the Regulation as being capable of including the companionship of a co-habitee which could contribute to integration in the host country. Where such relationships amongst nationals were accorded the legal advantages under national law, these could not be denied to nationals of other Member States without being discriminatory and thus breaching Arts 12 and 39 (ex 6 and 48) of the Treaty. The co-habitee does not have rights in their own right, but the companionship of a co-habitee is merely regarded as one of the advantages to which workers are entitled.

Therefore, as a co-habitee, Kristine would obtain residence rights to stay but can she claim benefits? There are a number of cases from the Court of Justice which have confirmed that a number of benefits may be claimed by members of the family. See, in respect of unemployment benefit, the case of *ONE* v *Deak* (94/84). Furthermore it has been held that Art 7(2) also applies to maternity and childbirth allowances without discrimination, see *Commission* v *Luxembourg* (C-111/91). Her rights therefore depend on how a national cohabitee would be treated because, as she has the right to stay, the general prohibition of discrimination under Art 12 (ex 6) EC would ensure that she should be treated the same. Providing that unemployment benefit and maternity rights were granted to the co-habitees of national workers, it is at least arguable that they would be extended to other Community co-habitees, but at the present time the position is unclear and a reference to the ECJ would be advisable.

A consideration of the legal position of Cat also involves a discussion of the rights provided in respect of non-immediate members of a worker's family. He is not a Community national and therefore cannot acquire his own rights to stay. Other members of the family who are not directly ascendants or descendants are subject to Art 10(2) which provides that Member States shall facilitate the entry of other members if they are dependant on or living under the roof of the worker in the home country. Cat is arguably dependant on Rimmer, but in the absence of supporting case law an Article 234 (ex 177) reference to the ECJ is the only way to clear this up. A generous ECJ would probably determine he has the right to stay because if not, Rimmer might be dissuaded from exerting his rights of free movement.

A further argument, which is admittedly slim, to find a right for him to stay is that he is the co-habitee of Rimmer. Quite whether the Court of Justice would entertain this and whether the facts would allow this conclusion to be drawn is speculative and would certainly need a reference to the Court of Justice under Art 234 (ex 177). Therefore, there is no clear and direct obligation to allow Cat to remain, let alone to claim benefits. In the case of *Lebon* (316/85), a dependant who had the right to stay to find work could be classed as a worker for this purpose but not to be able to claim benefits. Other members of the family have, however, been able to claim benefits when their right to stay was established; see *Deak* (94/84).

In this case, as the Member State is not obliged to let him stay, it is possibly the case that the possession of drugs would be sufficient excuse for the Member State to deport him, although the Member State has not given the reasons for the deportation which they are required to do under Art 6 of Directive 64/221. The Directive will only apply if Cat has a right to stay in the first place, if not then deportation cannot be prevented. The deportation for drugs may well depend on the nature of the drugs involved. On balance, his rights to avoid deportation and stay are very weak.

The right to deport Rimmer would be subject to other considerations. Directive 64/221, Art 3(1), provides that measures adopted on public policy or security must be based on personal conduct. See also *van Duyn* (41/74) in this respect. In this case it appears not to be the personal conduct of Rimmer but of Cat which has prompted the Member State to order deportation. Thus, as no other reasons are apparent, Denmark would not be justified under Community law in deporting Rimmer.

QUESTION 5

Discuss the view that recent case law concerning the freedoms of establishment and the right to provide services has blurred the distinction between these two concepts.

Commentary

This question is really asking you to consider the affect of the cases of *Säger* v *Dennemeyer* (C-76/90) and *Gebhard* v *Consiglio dell'Ordine degli Avvocati* (C-55/94). However, to make sense of this you must put these in context by defining the establishment and the provision of services and then outlining the original distinction between, indicating this by way of any case law relating to them. Finally you can then consider what affect, if any, the above cases have had.

You should therefore outline the Treaty applicable to the self employed. In particular you should consider the national rules, especially professional rules which may be considered acceptable for establishment but not for services and how the latest case law has affected this position.

Suggested Answer

The Community free movement policies are broadly outlined in Arts 2 and 3 of the EC Treaty. Free movement for the self employed is provided by the freedom of establishment (Arts 43–48 (ex 52–58) of the EC Treaty) and the freedom to provide services (Arts 49–55 (ex 59–66)). Both establishment and the provision of services have been held by the Court of Justice to be fundamental policies of the Community and thus to be strongly defended by the Court. A person wishing to take advantage of either must first be established in one of the Member States of the Community. These provisions, like those applying to workers, are in favour of nationals of the Members States. Article 12 (ex 6) provides the general legislative base to ensure there is no discrimination on the grounds of nationality for those establishing or providing services, rather than secondary legislation. Clear authority for the no discrimination rule is *Commission* v *UK (Re: Nationality of Fishermen) (Factortame)* (C-246/89).

What is meant by these two terms? The basic definitions are as follows:

Establishment includes the rights to enter another Member State and stay on a long term or permanent basis, to take up and pursue activities as self-employed persons and to set up and manage undertakings. The concept suggests either permanent residence in the host state or at least the establishment of a permanent professional base. A definition has been given in *Factortame* by the ECJ: 'the actual pursuit of an economic activity through a fixed establishment in another Member State for an indefinite period'.

The provision of services envisages a temporary state of affairs. Appearance in the host state would only be for a limited period to provide specific services and there would be no permanent personal or professional presence in the host state or a necessity to reside. The concept of services is defined by Art 50 (ex 60) (1) as those provided for remuneration, in so far as they are not governed by provisions relating to freedom of movement of goods, capital and persons, i.e. a distinct concept.

The provision of services can also be effected without having to leave the home country or enter the host country by either the provider or receiver of services as was the case of telephone sales in *Alpine Investments BV* v *Minister of Finance* (384/93). Thus far, it would seem that establishment and services could be distinguished by the duration of the activity and to some extent the type of activity. Even this was, however, undermined at an early stage by case law.

Originally, the Commission was empowered under Treaty Arts 53, 57 and 63 (now 47 and 52) to issue Directives to obtain the general objectives set for these two areas. This was addressed by the adoption of Directives to abolish national restrictions and provide for the mutual recognition of qualifications on an occupation by occupation basis, however, this process encouraged the view that the only way in which these rights could be promoted was by Directives and not directly from the Treaty, therefore progress was limited and slow.

Two leading cases, in which Arts 43 and 49 (ex 52 and 59) were held to create direct effects by the Court of Justice, radically changed the approach of the Commission in taking steps to achieve free movement. The case of *Reyners* v *Belgian State* (2/74) involved the attempt by a Dutchman to get access to the Belgium bar. The Government argued that Art 52 (now 43) was not directly effective because it was incomplete without the issue of Directives required by Art 57 (now 47). The Court of Justice held that the prohibition of discrimination under Art 52 (now 47) was directly effective and declared that nationality could be no barrier to appropriately qualified lawyers entering a country to practise. The Directives were simply to facilitate free movement and not to establish it, which had already been done by the end of the initial transition period of the Communities. The *Van Binsbergen* case (33/74) concerned a professionally qualified Dutchman, resident in Belgium, who was refused audience rights before the Dutch courts. The Court of Justice held Art 59 (now 49) was directly effective and was not conditional on the issue of a subsequent Directive in respect of the specific professions, nor on a residence requirement. Both establishment and services were therefore directly effective and did not therefore need any Directives to define the conditions upon which they could be taken up.

Distinguishing the concepts of Establishment and Services

A clear factual distinction is difficult to maintain. For example, the Court of Justice considered that the provision of services which included the setting up of offices on a long term basis and staffed by nationals of the host state could be held to be establishment even though the legal entity remained in the home state. See, *Commission* v *Germany (Re: Insurance Services)* (205/84). Whilst Art 50 (ex 60) (3) of the EC Treaty states that services may be provided under the same conditions as are imposed by the state on its own nationals, some rules may not be relevant to the temporary provision of services. However, not all home rules have been found by the Court of Justice to be suitable or acceptable for the provision of services. Hence the difficulty to maintain factual distinction has serious legal consequences.

In *Ministere Public* v *Van Wesemael* (110–111/78), a Belgian was prosecuted under a Belgian law for using a French employment agency and not one registered in Belgium, unless it operated in conjunction with a registered Belgian agency, to obtain the services of a variety artist in Belgium. The Court of Justice held that since the agency was registered in one Member State, it was contrary to EC law for another to restrict its right to provide services in that country.

In *Van Binsbergen* it was held that professional rules such as the requirement that advocates must be resident for professional purposes within the jurisdiction of certain courts for the provision of services was not objectively justified and proportionate to the aims.

In *Commission* v *Germany (Re: Insurance Services)* (205/84) the Court of Justice held that Member States were under a duty not only to eliminate all discrimination based on nationality but also all restrictions based on the free provision of services on the grounds that the provider is established in another Member State. It also emphasised that all those national rules which apply to the self employed permanently established in a Member State will not necessarily automatically apply to those 'activities of a temporary character which are carried out by enterprises established in other Member States'. Hence a further difference is introduced that not all national rules would apply to services even though they would still apply to nationals and Community nationals establishing in the host state.

In the case of *Säger* v *Dennemeyer* (C-76/90), the ECJ moved further in the development of a rule which prevents the restriction of services from other Member States but may still persist to limit activities of the home providers of services. Dennemeyer wished to provided patent services in Germany, something requiring a licence whose issue was restricted. His right to obtain a licence was challenged by a German Patent agent but Dennemeyer claimed a breach of Art 49 (old 59). The rule was non-discriminatory in that it applied to all patent agents regardless of residence. The ECJ held that not just discriminatory rules are prohibited, but any rules which are liable to prohibit or otherwise impede persons providing a service which they already lawfully do in the state of their establishment. To be allowed, such rules must satisfy the criteria that they be: justified, with no other rules already protecting the public interest and proportionate. It was suggested by the Court that Member States may not apply the same requirements for establishment as those providing services only, thus maintaining a distinction between these two forms of freedom.

However, when faced with a later case, the ECJ does appear now to have narrowed the difference. In *Gebhard* v *Consiglio dell'Ordine degli Avvocati*

(C-55/94), a German lawyer who had established a second chamber in Milan was prevented from using the title Avvocato. No Community law Directive was of help to him. The question was raised as to whether the Italian rules could be imposed on him. In principle and according to the general Treaty provision Art 43 (ex 52), he was required to comply with the rules. The ECJ characterised 'establishment' as the right of a community national to participate on a stable and continuous basis in the economic life of a Member State other than on his or her own and 'services' by the temporary, precarious and discontinuous nature of the services which is to be determined in the light of its duration, regularity, periodicity and continuity.

Hence, the setting up of chambers in Italy by a German lawyer, still practising in Stuttgart, was held to be establishment. So Gebhard, despite non-permanent presence, was deemed not to be providing services. However, the ECJ held that national measures which hinder or make less attractive the exercise of fundamental freedoms must fulfil four conditions. They must be:

(a) non-discriminatory in application;

(b) justified by imperative reason relating to the public interest;

(c) suitable to secure the objective sought; and

(d) proportional.

It is left to the national courts to determine whether national rules are applicable. The consequence of this decision is that establishment is now closer to services. It could be argued after this case that it doesn't matter where or how you practice, either on a temporary or permanent basis, provided qualifications are roughly equivalent. Rules which seek to prevent this must satisfy the criteria or be struck out, at least as far as EC citizens are concerned. Hence then some rules which can apply to nationals may not be appropriate for both services and establishment now. The distinction has arguably narrowed.

8 Competition and Merger Law

INTRODUCTION

Questions on competition law can vary considerably in EC courses depending on the approach of a particular course or lecturer in addressing this topic. It is unlikely that all aspects of competition law are addressed in depth on a general course on EC law, unless competition law is itself the subject of a particular course, half course or module in today's terms. If this is the case, then some of the questions in this chapter will be too general. Even if it is not, one of the problems in this area is the amount of material which it is necessary to cover to do justice to the subject. Some courses will not be concerned with the procedural aspects of competition law in any significant way, whilst others may simply provide an overview of the subject matter without going into detail on any aspect. Many courses will probably provide a discourse on the basic concepts and the main requirements of Arts 81 and 82 (ex 85 and 86) of the EC treaty. However, the exam questions set for your particular course should reflect the approach adopted by your course.

A variety of questions on competition law have been provided in this chapter, ranging from a general overview question, a question which surveys the basic concepts and requirements of Arts 81 and 82 (ex 85 and 86) and the Mergers Regulation, to questions concentrating on specific aspects of competition law including the procedure of competition law investigations and enforcement.

QUESTION 1

Why is competition law policy an integral and necessary part of the
European Community?

Commentary

This first question is one which concerns an overview of the topic and its
place in the Community legal order.

To answer this you must consider the main objectives of the European
Community which are outlined in the Preamble to the EC Treaty and in Arts
2 and 3. Then it is suggested you provide a brief overview to the main
provisions of competition law and the secondary legislation in order to
explain how it is to be pursued in the Community legal order.

Finally, you should consider its relations with other policies of the Community and the reasons why it is considered to be a necessary policy in the
Community.

Suggested Answer

The EC was aimed at the establishment of a common market and the
progressive approximation of the economic policies of the Member States.
The preamble to the Treaty and Arts 2 and 3 spell out these basic objectives.

The general aims include the creation of the Common Market which was to
be achieved by abolishing obstacles to the freedom of movement of all the
factors of production, namely goods, workers, providers of services, and
capital. The Treaty also provided for the abolition of customs duties between
the Member States and the application of a common customs tariff to imports
from third countries. There were to be common policies in the spheres of
agriculture and transport, and a system ensuring that competition in the
Common Market is not distorted by the activities of cartels or market
monopolists.

Community competition policy was based both on the American experience
of the concentration of power in the market place in too few hands and also,
to some extent, on the long German legislative experience with large
undertakings and cartels. Attitudes were also influenced by the desire to

protect emerging and expanding industries and companies and to encourage the re-birth of European industry after the devastation of the Second World War. Thus, one of the fundamental positions of competition law to be established was that there should be no barriers against the entry to the market of new companies and industries. The broad policy objective of competition law, therefore, which was formulated by the European Economic Community was to maintain and encourage competition for the benefit of the Community and its citizens.

Competition law was therefore constructed to ensure the maintenance of the Common Market. One of the aims of the internal market is to establish and maintain European wide competition to stimulate the entire economy of the Community for both the domestic and world markets and thus assist European capital in competing in the world market. Competition law is designed to help achieve a single market and the integration of the Community, to encourage economic activity amongst small and medium size enterprises and to maximise efficiency by allowing the free flow of goods and resources. At the same time it must be ensured that companies do not become too competitive and able to eliminate competition, thereby starting to dominate a market, or to cooperate in such a way as to act as one unit to the detriment of consumers and smaller firms in the Community. Competition law may also be regarded therefore as necessary to prevent these undesirable developments being realised. In order to retain fair competition, more so in a capitalist free market, some form of intervention on the part of the state is required. Action is concentrated on the larger players in the market rather than the small and medium business enterprises.

The specific EC competition rules are generally designed to intervene to prevent agreements which fix prices or conditions or the supply of products, to prohibit agreements which carve up territories, to prevent abuses of market power which have the effect of removing real competition and by controlling mergers which would also remove competition.

The Preamble to the EC Treaty states that the 'removal of existing obstacles calls for concerted action in order to guarantee steady expansion, balanced trade and fair competition'. Art 2 includes 'establishing a common market' and 'a harmonious and balanced development of economic activities' and Art 3(g) of the EC Treaty lists among the activities of the Community the institution of 'a system ensuring that competition in the internal market is not distorted'.

Art 10 (ex 5) has also been pleaded with Art 3(g) EC (previously 3(f) EEC) and Art 81 (ex 85) as a general principle of law supporting the argument that competition law also applies in respect of the Member States and not just undertakings, so that they are prohibited from encouraging or requiring acts or conduct by companies which may distort competition in the Community.

These basic rules are expanded in three sets of rules, one relating to the activities of legal persons, i.e., the business undertakings; one relating to anti dumping measures and the final one relating to the activities of the Member States.

The Commission is given the task under Art 85 (ex 89) EC and Regulation 17 of ensuring that competition in the Community is not distorted by companies setting up their own rules and obstacles to trade, thereby replacing the national rules and obstacles which the Community is trying to abolish by application of the free movement of goods provisions. These rules seek to prevent the creation of artificial barriers to trade on the national boundaries. Competition law is therefore inextricably linked to other Community policy areas especially to the free movement of goods, because it would prove to be impossible to have the one without ensuring you have the other. To have prevented the Member States on the one hand from restricting the movement of goods just to allow private companies to do it by their agreements and practices, would defeat the objectives of the first policy and, vice versa, to prevent companies from artificially dividing the markets but to allow the Member States to do so would undermine a competition policy. A further argument for having an effective competition policy is that some multinational companies are in a better position to divide the market than some Member States, because they have the same or greater turnover than the GNP of some of the EC Member States and so need to be subject to international control.

The application of the rules by the Commission and the interpretation of the rules of the Court of Justice has not been done in isolation by looking at the provisions alone, but in the light of the objectives of competition policy. The rules are also applied in the light of the general objectives of the Treaty. In *Commercial Solvents* v *Commission* (6 and 7/73), the Court of Justice held 'The prohibitions in Articles 85 and 86 (now 81 and 82) must be interpreted and applied in the light of Article 3(f) (now 3(g) EC) of the EEC Treaty which provides that the activities of the Community shall include the institution of a system ensuring that competition is not distorted, and Article 2 of the Treaty which gives the Community the task of promoting "throughout the Community harmonious development of economic activities"'. The case of *Metro* v *Commission* (26/76), is also a good example, whereby the

Commission, in pursuit of a goal, was forced to rely on Art 2 of the Treaty
to justify particular decisions reached. The agreements in question were
deemed to satisfy competition rules because they helped to maintain employment. This latter case serves as an example of the Commission, in carrying
out its tasks in relation to competition law, being required to balance the
competition policy with other policies such as regional development or
concern for unemployment, and this may cause it to modify its position on
the behaviour of companies. The general economic climate also influences
the Commission, particularly in respect of merger policy, in that in times of
poor economic growth, the Commission may treat mergers as being more
acceptable because of the efficiency gains to be achieved and the greater
ability the emerging company will have in the world market.

Competition law policy cannot, therefore be pursued alone and it is to be
concluded that the competition law policy is an inextricable part of the EC
and its policies.

QUESTION 2

The Clear Vision Company (CVC) is a manufacturer of camcorders. It
wishes to enter into an exclusive distribution agreement of unlimited duration
with two dealers of electrical equipment to distribute its products in the UK
and Germany. The German Company 'Foto GmbH' (F) and the UK company
'Video-camera Ltd' (V) are the chosen companies. There is no connection
between the two companies.

The Agreements between CVC and F and CVC and V contain the following
clauses:

1 CVC undertake not to supply any other distributor in the UK or Germany.

2 F and V shall follow the Advisory Retail Price structure and price
increases of CVC.

3 F and V shall not seek to sell outside of their respective areas and shall
pass on sales enquiries from the other area to the other party. They shall not
sell to other distributors.

4 F and V shall provide a sales display area according to the annex
attached and ensure that only CVC-trained staff are responsible for the sales
of CVC camcorders.

The parties to the agreement wish to know whether the terms of their agreement are ones which fall either within or outside a block exemption. If not, you are asked to advise whether the terms do then infringe Art 81 EC.

Commentary

This problem on competition law concentrates on distribution agreements and the block exemption Regulation.

The problem question itself sets out what issues it wants you to discuss. You are asked to determine whether the agreement reached between the parties is one which would, for special reasons, be exempted by a block exemption from the consequences of being contrary to Community competition law. This assumes that the agreement is already one likely to offend Community competition law provisions and it must be determined whether this is correct or incorrect.

It is not clear from a first sight whether the agreement is an exclusive or selective one, as it appears that it could be either.

This is certainly less important now following the enactment of single vertical agreement block exemption (Regulation 2790/1999) replacing three different vertical agreement Regulations (1483/83, 1984/83 and 4087/88). The only question here as to whether Regulation 2790/1999 may apply is whether we are dealing with a vertical agreement. As the problem concerns the agreement with a manufacturer and two distributors, this is clearly satisfied. Before this is considered in detail, a brief general introduction to the Competition law rules would put the issues into context.

Suggested Answer

EC competition law is one of the fundamental policies of the Community and is mentioned generally in the Preamble and Arts 2 and 3 of the Treaty. The principal provisions of the policy are contained in Arts 81 and 82 (ex 85 and 86) EC. Article 81 (ex 85) is the Article applicable to this problem because it concerns prohibited agreements and practices, and prohibits 'agreements between undertakings, decisions by associations of undertakings, and concerted practices which may affect trade between the Member States, and which have as their object or effect the prevention, restriction or distortion of competition within the Common Market'. Article 81 (ex 85) (2) provides that 'any agreements or decisions prohibited pursuant to this Article shall be automatically void'. However, there are ways in which an agreement may be considered to be acceptable.

Article 81 (ex 85) (3) provides that the provisions of Art 81 (ex 85) (1) may be declared inapplicable in the case of:

any agreement or category of agreements between undertakings;
any decision or category of decisions by associations of undertakings;
any concerted practice or category of concerted practices;

which contributes to improving the production or distribution of goods or to promoting technical or economic progress, while allowing consumers a fair share of the resulting benefit, and which does not: (a) impose on the undertakings concerned restrictions which are not indispensable to the attainment of these objectives; (b) afford such undertakings the possibility of eliminating competition in respect of a substantial part of the products in question.

Previously, the parties to such agreements were required to make an individual notification to the Commission under Art 81 (ex 85) (3), and Art 4 of Regulation 17/62. Failure to notify meant that the agreement would be void and the parties would be liable to fines. However, in order to avoid unnecessary work for all involved, common agreements may be exempted from the prohibition in Art 81 (ex 85) (1) by virtue of a block exemption for typical types of agreement, sometimes within certain industries or areas of trade. In such cases there is no need to apply for individual notification. Block exemptions set out types of restrictions or provisions which do not infringe Art 81 (ex 85) (1) or would be exempted and there is one for vertical distribution agreements under Art 2(1) of Regulation 2790/99. The main thrust of this Regulation is that there is a presumption of legality, i.e., compliance with Art 81 (ex 85), for agreements involving firms whose combined transaction counts for less than 30% of the relevant market share (Arts 3 and 9), unless the agreement itself or parts of it contain so-called 'hard-core restrictions' which would not qualify for exemption under Art 4. As we are not given market share information, we shall have to consider the agreement in further detail. Apart from the fact that the agreements have been entered into for an unlimited duration, which does not satisfy Art 5 of the block exemption and therefore the agreement will not benefit from an exemption, the individual clauses in the agreement would also appear to be unacceptable under the block exemption. Article 4 of Block Exemption Regulation 2790/99 states that it does not apply to vertical agreements which contain anti-competitive restrictions such as price fixing or territorial protection. Clauses 2 and 3 would appear to offend these prohibitions. Hence then it is very unlikely that a block exemption will save the agreements from the application of Art 81 (ex 85) (3). Each of the clauses will therefore have to be considered in turn in the light of Art 81 (ex 85) and the judgments of the ECJ as they appear to set up a distribution agreement which have been held by the Court of Justice to be acceptable where the restrictions are objectively necessary for the performance of a particular type of contract. Contracts relating to technical products requiring specialist sales staff would be ones which the ECJ has considered compatible with Art 81 (ex 85) (1), see for example the *Metro* cases of 1977 and 1986 (26/76 and 75/84). The actual agreements must not, however, contain clauses which go beyond what is strictly necessary to meet the objectives of a controlled distribution of the product.

Clauses which fix prices or which effect a partitioning of markets between manufacturer and distributor, and are capable of affecting trade between Member States, constitute restrictions on competition contrary to Art 81 (ex 85) (1). Therefore it is necessary to consider the present scheme by looking at the terms of the agreement on a clause by clause basis.

The first clause is a complete refusal to supply and is probably not acceptable; see the *Konica* decision (88/172). If other companies comply with the other terms there should be no reason to refuse to supply them.

The pricing clause is ambiguous. If it tries to fix prices rather than simply make recommendations, it will not be acceptable; see the *Pronuptia* case (161/84) in which advisory prices were considered by the Court of Justice to be acceptable.

The sales restriction in clause 3 of the agreement almost certainly amounts to an export ban and it will not be acceptable; see the case of *Consten* and *Grundig* (56 and 58/64), the *Bayer Dental* case (65/86) or the *Konica* decision (88/172).

The final clause appears to be an acceptable condition to ensure quality distribution of specialist products; see the *Metro* cases (26/76 and 75/84) and the *Perfume* cases (253/78 & 1–3/79).

Given that two of the clauses appear to offend Community law competition provisions, unless the companies are prepared to amend them to eradicate the aspects which infringe Art 81 (ex 85), it is unlikely the agreement will come within the terms for a block exemption or permitted selective distribution agreement according to case law.

A complete answer would then determine whether, in fact, an infringement of Art 81 (ex 85) (1) has taken place. To do this it would be necessary to determine whether there is an agreement between undertakings, decisions by associations of undertakings, or a concerted practice which may affect trade between the Member States, and which have as their object or effect the prevention, restriction or distortion of competition within the Common Market. The agreement reached between the companies is express and clauses 2 and 3 are specifically designed to restrict or distort competition. It is then necessary to demonstrate that the agreement has affected or will potentially affect trade between Member States; see the *Consten* and *Grundig* cases (56 and 58/64) which would indicate that an infringement is most likely. Therefore unless the parties apply for an individual exemption and negotiate the terms of it with the Commission to obtain approval, it will held to be in breach of Art 81 (ex 85) (1) and thus void under Art 81 (ex 85) (2). Further details on these more general aspects of the question can be studied in the answers to the questions below.

QUESTION 3

Branches of two non-EC Member State companies, the Red Dwarf Mining Corporation (RDMC) and Green Giant Mining (GGM) have moved into the EC to exploit the remaining European deposits of tin. In informal meetings of the management of the two companies, which took place before their move into the EC, they decided on a strategy to work the European market to their advantage. They have restricted supplies to customers in and outside the EC to drive up prices and thus profits for their parent companies. So far RDMC have secured 42% of the market and GGM have secured 23%.

Complaints have been made by competitors and customers which the Commission is investigating. The companies claim the investigations cannot apply to either companies or agreements from outside the EC.

(a)   Advise RDMC and GGM.

(b)   Would your answer be any different if RDMC and GGM formally merge prior to any action being taken?

Commentary

This problem question will involve you in a general consideration of the application of the principal provisions of both Arts 81 and 82 (ex 85 and 86).

After a general introduction to the area of competition law and highlighting the relevant issues in the case, you should briefly outline the scope of Arts 81 and 82 (ex 85 and 86) and determine whether the case concerns an agreement between the parties contrary to Community competition law, or whether it concerns the abuse of a dominant position by the parties. A particular issue which should be considered is the fact that the companies' head offices are based outside the EC and whether this will affect the ability of the Commission to investigate and prosecute a breach of Community law.

Finally, you are required to address the alternative situation in which the companies merge. Given that you are not supplied with any real facts to come to definitive conclusions on this aspect, all you can do is generally describe the Community concern and involvement in mergers.

Suggested Answer

Competition law is one of the fundamental policies of the Community and is generally mentioned in the Preamble to the Treaty and in Arts 2 and 3 of the Treaty. The Preamble refers to fair competition and Art 3(g) of the EC Treaty lists among the activities of the Community the institution of 'a system ensuring that competition in the internal market is not distorted'.

The relevant facts in this case are that the branches of two non-EC Member State companies are pursuing a strategy agreed on outside the EC which involves the restriction of supply to customers to drive up prices and profits. As a result it would seem that both companies have secured a sizable share of the Community market. The facts thus involve a consideration of the two principal provisions to combat anti-competitive behaviour, Arts 81 and 82 (ex 85 and 86).

Article 81 (ex 85) deals with restrictive practices. Article 81 (ex 85) (1) EC prohibits agreements between undertakings, decisions by associations of undertakings, and concerted practices which may affect trade between the Member States, and which have as their object or effect the prevention, restriction or distortion of competition within the Common Market. Article 81 (ex 85) (2) provides that any agreements or decisions prohibited pursuant to this Article shall be automatically void.

Article 82 (ex 86) applies where individual organisations have a near monopoly position or share an oligopolistic market with a small number of other companies and take unfair advantage of this position to the detriment of the market, other companies and the end consumers. Article 82 (ex 86) provides that the abuse by one or more undertakings of a dominant market position within the Common Market, or in a substantial part of it, which affects trade between Member States is prohibited.

First of all, the possible breach of Art 81 (ex 85) will be considered. In order for it to be breached, it must be shown that there is a form of agreement or concerted practice which may have affected trade between Member States. It has been demonstrated that no actual agreement is necessary to breach Art 81 (ex 85) and the Article allows for a concerted practice to suffice. In the case of *ICI* v *Commission* (dyestuffs) (48/69) general and uniform increases were witnessed from a small number of leading producers. The Court of Justice defined a concerted practice as a form of coordination between enterprises, that had not yet reached the point of true contract relationship but which had in practice substituted cooperation for the risks of competition. See also the *Sugar cartel* case (*Suiker Unie* v *Commission* (40–48/73)) in which the firms responsible for the alleged breach said there was no plan. The ECJ held that there did not have to be one. In the *Polypropylene* cases (T-7/89, T-9/89 and T-11/89) the CFI has held that expressions of intention, even if not in writing, of particular conduct could constitute an agreement or concerted practice. Countering these cases is the *Wood Pulp* case (C-89, 104 & 125–9/85), in which the ECJ held that parallel conduct could not be regarded as proof of a concerted practice unless there was the only plausible explanation for the conduct. In the present case, providing there is some indication that an an agreed practice is being pursued, it is likely that a concerted practice between undertakings will be established.

Next, it must be demonstrated that the agreement was one which had the object or effect of restricting competition which may affect trade between Member States. Article 81 (ex 85) (1) focuses on particular practices which would offend competition law. Amongst these are those listed under Art 81 (ex 85) (1)(b) and (c), which limit markets or supply. In the present case the agreement is clearly one which has this object. In fact, even a potential impact will do; see the *Consten* and *Grundig* case (56 and 58/64). However to infringe Art 81 (ex 85), the practice complained of must be capable of affecting trade between Member States. The cases of *Consten* and *Grundig* and the *Cement Association* (8/72) are examples of the simple requirements for this to be met. It has to be questioned whether it is probable in law or fact that the agreement in question may have an influence, direct or indirect, actual or potential, on the pattern of trade between Member States. If there is an impact on the pattern of trade then there is an effect on trade. The restrictions on supply and the consequent price increases would clearly fall into this category, therefore a breach of Art 81 (ex 85) (1) is probable.

Article 82 (ex 86) may also be breached if there is an abuse of a dominant position in the EC. Dominance must be established both in terms of the product and geographic market.

The product must be a unique product which is not interchangeable. In the absence of further facts it must be assumed that there is no substitute for the raw metal tin. Is there dominance? We are only told that RDMC has 42% and GGM has 23% of the market in the Community. In *United Brands* (27/76), the share of 45% was considered sufficient but the next competitor had 16% only, a greater difference from the position here with 42% and 23%. Thus considering each company alone, it would be arguable whether RDMC or GGM would be dominant. Whilst there is no clear word from either the Commission or the Court on this point, the Mergers Regulation states that concentrations whose market share does not exceed 25% would not be considered to impede competition. However, Art 82 (ex 86) applies to one or more companies and the combined share would be 67% which in a joint action would be a position of dominance.

The geographic market is also satisfied as it is the whole of the Community; see the *United Brands* (27/76) and *Tetra Pak* (T-51/89) cases.

It then has to be shown that there is an abuse of dominant position. Limiting production is one of the grounds listed in Art 82 (ex 86) and refusal to supply was held to be a ground in the *United Brands* case, therefore an abuse can be shown in the present case.

In fact, according to the recent case of *Compagnie Maritime Belge Transports* before the ECJ (C-395 & 396P/96) an agreement within the meaning of Art 85(1) (now 81) may result in undertakings being so linked that they become and act as a collective entity as far as their competitors and customers are concerned and as such a collective dominant position can arise, which can then be abused in the manner already noted.

Finally, trade between Member States must be affected. In the *Commercial Solvents v Commission* case (6 & 7/73) it was held that conduct which has the effect of altering the competitive structure within the Common Market will satisfy the requirement of effect on trade between the Member States. This would be the case with RDMC and GGM. Thus a breach of Art 82 (ex 86) is also likely to be established.

A significant objection of the two firms is that the companies and the agreements are from outside the EC and they would argue that they cannot be touched by the Community competition law rules. However, the basic position adopted by the Community is that the competition rules apply to all undertakings whose operations or agreements affect trade between Member States and have as their object or effect a restraint on competition in the Community. The ICI *Dyestuffs* case (48/69) considered that the unity of conduct in the market between the parent and the subsidiary was the decisive factor in the case. The *Woodpulp* case (C-89, 104 & 125–9/85) is also instructive. In this case the pricing agreements took place outside the EC but the implementation took place within the EC. So, if the agreements led to anti-competitive consequences through the activities of branches, they would infringe Art 81 (ex 85).

The fact that the breaches are committed in the Community puts the companies within the territorial jurisdiction of the Treaty and thus the Commission and Court of First Instance, even where the parent companies have no direct physical involvement and the agreements were outside the EC (ICI *Dyestuffs* case).

In the alternative, it is necessary to consider the effect merger would have. If the merger takes place outside the EC, as is assumed to be the case here, it may still be a concentration with a Community dimension as far as the Mergers Regulation 4064/89 is concerned; see the Decision of the Commission in *Matsushita/MCA* (IV/M37). Article 1 states that it applies where there is a world-wide turnover of more than 5,000 million ECU and an aggregate Community-wide turnover of each of at least two of the undertakings of more than 250 million ECU. A Community dimension may nevertheless pertain, if:

(a)   the combined aggregate worldwide turnover of all the undertakings is more than 2,500 million ECU;

(b)   in each of at least three Member States, the combined aggregate turnover of all the undertakings is more than 100 Million ECU;

(c)   in each of at least three Member States, the aggregate turnover of each of at least two of the undertakings concerned is more than 25 Million ECU; and

(d) the aggregate Community-wide turnover of each of at least two of the undertakings concerned is more than 100 Million ECU.

This information is not provided in the problem, but if the turnover does not reach these thresholds then the merger is not one of a Community dimension. If they do exceed the thresholds the companies are required under Art 4(1) to inform the Commission. Failure to do so will render them liable to a fine under Art 14. The Commission will determine under Art 2 whether the concentration is compatible with the Common Market with a view to declaring it compatible or suspending it. This may be difficult to enforce outside the EC and has not yet been tested before the courts. Hence recourse to Art 82 (ex 86) may still be necessary to combat the anti-competitive behaviour. However, it should be noted that a formal merger might not be required to be subject to the Mergers Regulation and that independent firms may be subject to its rules. In joined cases *France* v *Commission* (C-68/94) and *Société Commerciale des Potasses et de l'Azote (SCPA)* v *Commission* (C-30/95), the ECJ determined that the Mergers Regulation applies also to collective dominance, although as noted above collective dominance short of merger may also be caught under Art 82 (ex 86). A reference to the ECJ would be required, however, to be certain about this.

QUESTION 4

Widgets Ltd (W) is a UK manufacturer of the widgets which are fitted into beer cans to ensure that the drink has a frothy head. It holds 40% of the EC market. There are three other European manufacturers of this product, the largest of which is Krimskrams GmbH (K) in Germany, which holds 30% of the EC market. The rest of the EC market, valued at more than 1,000 million ECU, is made up by two other EC companies with less than 10% of the market between them and imports from the USA, Japan, Korea, and Hong Kong.

W and K are the only manufacturers of the machines which produce the widgets.

Press reports have noted that, following the twice yearly Convention of European Widget Manufacturers (CEWM), prices of the UK and German built widgets rise, followed shortly by the prices of other manufacturers. The companies stated, in a recent statement, that there was never any form of agreement between them in respect of pricing policy. However, W and K have now decided to merge to consolidate their position in the European and world market for widgets. They have also refused to supply spares for the machines to the non-Community manufacturers.

In the light of the developments, the Commission has commenced an investigation into the actions of the companies to determine whether a breach of Community law has been committed.

Advise the Commission as to the likelihood that the Court of Justice will uphold their claim:

(a)　that the companies have breached either Article 81 or 82;

(b)　that the companies have breached the Merger Regulation 4064/89.

Commentary

This is a general problem question on competition law covering aspects of Arts 81 and 82 (ex 85 and 86) and the Mergers Regulation 4064/89. It concentrates on the main principles of each of these areas rather than going into precise details of any provision in particular. As with other problem type questions, the issues to be tackled need to be identified. In this question, this is to some extent already done for you in the question because it asks you to consider whether the companies have breached either Art 81, 82 (ex 85, 86) or the Mergers Regulation 4064/89. Thus you can concentrate on whether the main requirements of these elements of Community law have been infringed by the actions of the parties.

Suggested Answer

Competition law in general is designed to ensure there is healthy competition in the Community which will benefit not only the Community market but also consumers. The Community competition law policy seeks to achieve this by outlawing any behaviour which is contrary to this credo. Competition law in the Community therefore attacks concerted action which is anticompetitive and individual actions which abuse market strengths to the detriment of competition. The Community has also enacted legislation to combat anti-competitive mergers of a European dimension.

The issues to be considered in the answer are: the price rises which occur after the meeting of CEWM, the decision to merge and the refusal to supply spares for the machines.

The law applicable to this answer is as follows. Article 81 (ex 85) (1) EC prohibits agreements between undertakings, decisions by associations of undertakings, and concerted practices which may affect trade between the Member States, and which have as their object or effect the prevention, restriction or distortion of competition within the Common Market. Article 81 (ex 85) (2) provides that any agreements or decisions prohibited pursuant to this Article shall be automatically void.

Article 82 (ex 86) provides that the abuse by one or more undertakings of a dominant market position within the Common Market or in a substantial part of it which affects trade between Member States is prohibited.

The Mergers Regulation 4064/89 establishes a division between large mergers with a European dimension, over which the Commission will exercise supervision, and smaller mergers which will fall under the jurisdiction of national authorities.

First of all, the possible breach of Art 81 (ex 85) will be considered. In order for it to be breached it must be shown that there is an agreement which may have affected trade between Member States.

Whilst the companies have declared that there was no formal agreement between them, it has been demonstrated that no actual agreement is necessary to breach Art 81 (ex 85) and the Article allows for a concerted practice to suffice. In the case of *ICI* v *Commission* (dyestuffs) (48/69) general and uniform increases were witnessed from a small number of leading producers. The Court of Justice defined a concerted practice as 'a form of co-ordination between enterprises. that had not yet reached the point of true contract relationship but which had in practice substituted co-operation for the risks of competition'.

In a particular instance there would be a need to show the similarity of rate and timing of increases and whilst not having to prove the existence of agreements, there is still a requirement to establish that some form of contact existed.

In our case it is the meeting of CEWM that should establish this. See also the *Sugar cartel* case (*Suiker Unie* v *Commission*) (40–8/73) in which the firms responsible for the alleged breach said there was no plan. The ECJ held there did not have to be one. The *Wood Pulp* cases (C-89, 104 & 125–9/85) would, however, increase the burden on the Commission to demonstrate that there were no plausible explanations for the parallel price increase other than by agreement or concerted action.

Thus, if it is considered that a concerted practice is in existence it must be shown that the object or effect of it was to restrict competition. A potential impact will be sufficient for the requirements of the Article, see *Consten* and *Grundig* (56 and 58/64). Price fixing, which was the object of the present activity, clearly offends as it is an example provided by Art 81 (ex 85) (1(a)), therefore this aspect is established in the present case.

To some extent the same question of an impact on trade is applied to determine whether there has been an effect on trade between Member States. The cases of *Consten* and *Grundig* (56 and 58/64) and the *Cement Association* (8/72) are examples of the simple requirements for this to be met. If there is an impact on the pattern of trade then there is an effect on trade. Clearly price increases will impact on the pattern of trade between Member States.

Article 82 (ex 86) will be breached if there is an abuse of a dominant position in the EC. Dominance must be established both in terms of the product and geographic market. The Commission has published a Notice on the Definition of the Relevant Market (OJ 1997 C372/5) which provides a summary of the case law and Commission methodology and hence then guidelines for determining the relevant markets. The product market is widgets for beer cans. In the *United Brands* case (27/76), it was held it must be a unique product which is not interchangeable. In the absence of any evidence to the contrary, this is the position in the present case. It then has to be considered whether there is dominance. We are informed that the two companies, Widgets and Krimskrams, have 40% and 30% respectively of the market in the Community. Taken individually, the market share of 40% held by Widgets might not, in view of the case of *United Brands,* be enough on its own to constitute dominance, especially where the next competitor has 30%. If this is uncertain, then it is even more unlikely that the 30% held by Krimskrams would be enough to constitute market dominance.

However, Art 82 (ex 86) also covers the situation of one or more undertakings which together occupy a dominant position. If the two parties were subject to a joint decision of the Commission, the resultant market share of the two companies of 70% would most probably be held to be a position of dominance.

In fact, according to the recent case of *Compagnie Maritime Belge Trans-ports* before the ECJ (C-395 & 396P/96) an agreement within the meaning of Art 85(1) (now 81) may result in undertakings being so linked that they become and act as a collective entity as far as their competitors and customers are concerned and as such a collective dominant position can arise under Art 82 (ex 86), which can then be abused.

The geographic market is also satisfied as it is the whole of the Community; see the *United Brands* and *Tetra Pak* (T-51/89) cases.

The supply of spares for the machines is a separate market. In the case at hand, the 100% share of the market by the two companies will establish complete dominance; see the *Hugin* case (22/78). It may, however, be argued that, in respect of the machines, the refusal to supply only has effects outside the EC, but in the *Commercial Solvents* case (6 & 7/73), where the supply was outside the EC market, the Court of Justice held that this fact did not remove its jurisdiction as the effect would still be prominent in the EC market. See also the *Woodpulp* case (C-89, 104 & 125–9/85) in this respect.

The abuse which offends the community regime is the price fixing in respect of the widgets and the refusal to supply in respect of the spares, specifically noted in Art 82 (ex 86) (a) and (b).

The *Continental Can* case (6/72) also suggested that a further form of abuse could be the merger itself but this point can now be addressed under the Merger Regulation 4064/89.

The next topic for consideration is the lawfulness of the merger. After merger the companies have 70% of a market for widgets estimated at over 1,000 million ECU and 100% of the machines and spares supply market.

Article 1 of the Mergers Regulation states that it applies where there is a world-wide turnover of more than 5,000 million ECU and an aggregate Community wide turnover of each of at least two of the undertakings of more than 250 million ECU. A new Art 1(3) provides that a Community dimension may nevertheless pertain, if:

   (a)   the combined aggregate world wide turnover of all the undertakings is more than 2,500 million ECU;

   (b)   in each of at least three member states, the combined aggregate turnover of all the undertakings is more than 100 Million ECU;

(c)   in each of at least three member states, the aggregate turnover of each
of at least two of the undertakings concerned is more than 25 Million ECU;
and

(d)   the aggregate Community-wide turnover of each of at least two of
the undertakings concerned is more than 100 Million ECU.

Whilst we know the share of the Community market, we do not know the
share of the world market. If not in excess of 5,000 million ECU, then the
merger is not one of a Community dimension. If they do exceed the limits
of Art 1, Regulation 4064/89 requires them to inform the Commission. By
failing to inform the Commission (Art 4(1)), they can be fined (Art 14).

The Commission will determine under Art 2 whether the concentration is
compatible with the Common Market. The facts do not reveal whether this
merger has taken place. If it has, the Commission may investigate with a
view to declaring it compatible or suspending it. If not, the abuse of a
collective dominance on the part of the two companies may still breach the
Mergers Regulation according to the ECJ in the cases of *France* v *Commission* (C-68/94) and *Société Commerciale des Potasses et de l'Azote (SCPA)*
v *Commission* (C-30/95) or Art 82 (ex 86) according to *Compagnie Maritime
Belge Transports* (C-395 & 396P/96), however, a reference to the CFI would
be necessary to determine this.

QUESTION 5

On the information of Adam, a former employee of 'Kidstuff' (K), a
manufacturer of children's toys, the EC Commission is investigating the
possibility that K has entered into forms of agreements with companies in
France, Italy and Germany which have resulted in price fixing and market
sharing. Suspecting that this is the case, EC Commission officials raid all of
the companies involved in an attempt to obtain further information.

When they arrived at the premises of K, they were refused entry for five
hours and when they were finally allowed in, company employees were
obstructive by not facilitating access to locked filing cabinets and computer
programs. The Commission officials returned later and seized a considerable
amount of correspondence. The company has later claimed that many of the
letters were subject to principles of professional secrecy and legal privilege
and should not have been taken and cannot be used in the investigation and
decision in respect of their activities.

As a result of the fact that Adam's new employer, a competitor of K, has learned from Commission documents that Adam had tipped off the Commission, he has been dismissed.

With reference to the case law of the Court of Justice, outline the rights and duties of the Commission and the company in the investigation of competition law infringements.

Commentary

This problem on competition law is largely concerned with the application of Council Regulation 17 which sets out the powers and duties of the Commission in investigating suspected competition law infringements and is thus concerned with the procedural law of investigations by the Commission. To answer the question you will need to identify the issues and then consider the power of the Commission to raid the premises of companies, the entry rights the Commission has, the ability or power it has to take documents, professional privacy, the duty of secrecy which is imposed on it and the rights of the employee who has lost his job.

Suggested Answer

Competition law policy in the EC seeks to maintain and encourage competition in the EC for the benefit of the whole Community and for its consumers and citizens. It aims to do this by preventing anti-competitive practices and the abuse of dominant positions by undertakings in the Community. In order to achieve this effectively, the competition rules enacted need to be enforced. In turn, an enforcement agency must be given adequate powers and sanctions by which it can operate to make the policy effective.

Within the EC Treaty, the Council was empowered under Art 87 (now 83) to enact secondary Community legislation to give effect to the principles of law set out in Arts 81 and 82 (ex 85 and 86), which are the principal provisions to combat anti-competitive behaviour. Article 85 (ex 89) empowers the Commission to ensure Arts 81 and 82 (ex 85 and 86) are applied and to carry out investigation of suspected infringements of the Treaty articles. This was substantially supplemented by Council Regulation 17 which was the first Regulation to be enacted implementing Arts 81 and 82 (ex 85 and 86) of the Treaty.

Regulation 17 sets out the powers and duties of the Commission in the conduct of investigations of competition law abuses. Articles 1–9 are mainly concerned with the notification of agreements, complaints to the Commission and with the procedure of the declarations by the Commission that the agreement either infringes the Treaty Articles or is exempt from the Treaty provisions. They are not, therefore, of direct concern in answering this question.

This question is more concerned with Arts 10–14 which concern the powers of the Commission in conducting investigations, and with Arts 15–19 which are concerned with sanctions available to the Commission in the case of established infringements and the rights of the parties under investigation.

Article 11 is concerned with requests for information. It generally empowers the Commission to request information to assist its investigations from both the authorities of the Member States and from the undertakings. The owners of undertakings or their representatives are obliged to supply the information requested. If this is not forthcoming the Commission can adopt a formal Decision requiring the information to be supplied (Art 11(5)). Penalties may then be imposed for non-compliance with the terms of the Decision.

Article 14 empowers the Commission to undertake all necessary investigations including the right of its officials to examine books, take copies of records and books, ask for oral explanations and enter the premises of undertakings. This can be undertaken without the consent of the undertaking involved providing it is specifically authorised in advance by the Commission; see Art 14(2) and the *National Panasonic* case (136/79). Alternatively, a formal Decision may be adopted for a mandatory investigation (Art 14(3)). There is no need to approach the company in advance and the Commission should not be subjected to a delay before the investigation can take place. The investigations authorised under this provision include the infamous 'Dawn Raids' on the premises of companies under investigation. In *Hoechst* (cases 46/87 & 227/88) the authority to raid was challenged on the ground that it lacked precision but the ECJ held that it was acceptable providing the Commission indicated clearly its suspicions rather than have to supply full information.

Therefore, in application to the case at hand, the Commission has the right to request information and be given it by the company. It can also obtain the right of entry to the premises of the company and K should not have refused entry, although it has been held that waiting a short time for a lawyer to arrive may be acceptable; see the *National Panasonic* case. Case law has, however, further determined that force cannot be used by Commission officials to gain entry and examine documents, but assistance to gain entry must be obtained via the national authorities, see the cases of *Hoechst* v *Commission* (46/87 and 227/88), *Dow* v *Commission* (85/87) and *Orkem* v *Commission* (374/87). In the latter case, it was held by the ECJ that the power to compel the production of information does not extend to requiring the company to admit breaches of the competition rules and thus incriminate itself. In effect a company can be obstructive but may suffer the penalty of fines being imposed on it under Art 15 which can range from 100 to 5,000 Euros, which can be levied additionally on a daily basis and fines can be much higher, up to 50,000 where a company has misled the Commission.

In the Decision *Fabbrica Pisana* (80/334) it was held that a duty of the company existed to assist the Commission to find documents and in a situation where the company is being obstructive, the Commission has a right to search, see the *Hoechst* case.

Thus, whilst the company may delay the entry to the building, the Commission, if sufficiently prepared with a Decision to enter and search and with the prior cooperation and assistance of the national authorities, will be able to obtain the information it requires. Any failure to comply with the Commission or not to cooperate will render the company liable to a fine under Arts 15(1)(c) and 16(1)(c) and (d); confirmed in the *Sugar* case (40–48/73). However, in respect of the rights over the documents, it is a right to take copies and not the documents themselves (Art 14). Therefore, in this case, the Commission may have overstepped the mark and rendered the Decision void. An appeal by the Company should be made to the Court of First Instance, under Art 230 (ex 173) EC.

In the present case the company has also claimed that certain documents are subject to professional secrecy and legal privilege. The types of documents which are subject to legal privilege and professional secrecy have been the subject of case law. Legal privilege is recognised and covers correspondence between the company and an independent lawyer; see the *AM & S* case (155/79). Inhouse lawyers do not enjoy such privilege, so it depends on the nature of the correspondence. The *Hilti* case (T-30/89) decided that the privilege extends to in-house lawyers' reports of the independent lawyers findings. In the *Samenwerkende* case (C-36/92 P), a refusal to hand over documents considered to be confidential was held to be unjustified in the light of the existing protections in Community law under which the Commission is required to notify undertakings of the documents they intend to release to the national authorities and thus give the undertakings the chance to seek judicial review to protect these documents. Therefore refusal to supply would be unjustified. In the end the Court of First Instance and European Court of Justice must be the arbiters of what is privileged.

The principle of professional secrecy does not apply to allow a company to protect documents from the Commission but to ensure that information received by the Commission in an investigation is not disclosed to competitors, Arts 19 and 20 and the case of *Dow Benelux, Van Landewyck* (209–15 & 218/78) and *AKZO* (53/85).

Finally, the Commission owes a duty of care to Adam not to disclose his name. An action for damages may be successful under Art 288 (ex 215) EC. Here the case of *Adams* v *Commission* (145/83) is clearly relevant. It may be that, as in the Adams case, Adam had a duty to ensure he could not be identified, in which case the damages payable may be reduced.

QUESTION 6

Even though Art 81 is meant to cover concerted actions as opposed to abusive conduct covered by Art 82, both provisions need to be interpreted in conjunction with each other (*Van Bael and Bellis*).

Discuss.

Commentary

This question requires you to consider the relationship of Arts 81 and 82 (ex 85 and 86) to each other. First of all, you should outline the basic legislative regime under the Treaty and then briefly outline the specific area covered by Arts 81 and 82 (ex 85 and 86). Then you should address the quotation and consider whether the provisions do need to be interpreted in conjunction with each other, or whether they can be regarded as mutually exclusive.

Suggested Answer

EC competition law is one of the fundamental policies of the Community and is generally mentioned in the Preamble and Arts 2 and 3 of the Treaty. Its aims are to prevent anti-competitive behaviour which will distort the competitive balance of the Community market. EC competition rules are generally designed to intervene to prevent agreements which fix prices or conditions or the supply of products, to prohibit agreements which carve up territories, to prevent abuses of market power which have the effect of removing real competition and by controlling mergers which would also remove competition.

The Preamble states that the 'removal of existing obstacles calls for concerted action in order to guarantee steady expansion, balanced trade and fair competition'. Article 2 includes 'establishing a common market and an economic and monetary union' and 'a harmonious and balanced development of economic activities' and Art 3(g) of the EC Treaty lists among the activities of the Community the institution of a 'system ensuring that competition in the internal market is not distorted'.

Two main provisions have been enacted to tackle two different situations. Article 81 (ex 85) deals with anti-competitive practices arising as a result of agreements or concerted actions of two or more undertakings and Art 82 (ex 86) concerns the abuse of a position of dominance by one or more undertakings.

Article 81 (ex 85) (1) deals with restrictive practices. It sets out the prohibitions and details of the consequences of the failure to observe the prohibition and provides a framework by which exemptions from the prohibitions can be obtained.

Article 81 (ex 85) (1) EC prohibits agreements between undertakings, decisions by associations of undertakings, and concerted practices which may affect trade between the Member States, and which have as their object or effect the prevention, restriction or distortion of competition within the Common Market.

Article 81 (ex 85) (2) provides that any agreements or decisions prohibited pursuant to this Article shall be automatically void, although there are ways in which an agreement may be held to be acceptable. An individual exemption may be granted by application to the Commission. The terms of an agreement may be accepted as being consistent with one of the block exemptions provided by one of a number of Regulations issued by the Community.

Article 82 (ex 86) applies where individual organisations have a near monopoly position or share an oligopolistic market with a small number of other companies, and take unfair advantage of this position to the detriment of the market, other companies and to the end consumers. Article 82 (ex 86) provides that the abuse by one or more undertakings of a dominant market position within the Common Market, or in a substantial part of it which affects trade between Member States, is prohibited. The requirements are therefore a dominant position, abuse of it and the effect between Member States.

At first sight, therefore, there seems to be at least a different focus of the two Articles, with Art 81 (ex 85) aimed at two or more undertakings in collusion, and Art 82 (ex 86) aimed at just a single entity. However, it can be observed in the case of *Ford* v *Commission* (25 and 26/84) that the unilateral action of one undertaking may still fall foul of Art 81 (ex 85), whereas Art 82 (ex 86) expressly provides that it also applies to the activities of one or more undertakings.

The relationship of Arts 81 and 82 (ex 85 and 86) is highlighted in a case concerned with the difficulties in dealing with the realities of complex commercial cross holdings. In *BAT* v *Commission* (142 and 156/84), the Court of Justice had to determine whether the Commission decision was correct that the acquisition of a minority holding in a competing company was not an infringement of Arts 81 and 82 (ex 85 and 86). Two applicant and competitive companies had objected to the decision. The companies whose activities were the subject of complaint, had remained independent after their agreement to establish cross holdings, so Art 81 (ex 85) was considered first. The Commission's decision that no anti-competitive object or effect had been established was upheld by the Court. Furthermore no control by a particular company had been proved, and so there was no case under Art 82 (ex 86) either. However, the Court of Justice did consider that, although the acquisition itself might not restrict competition, it may subsequently lead to a restriction or distortion of competition. Thus, it becomes necessary to consider the application of both Articles in such complex situations.

Prior to the Mergers Regulation 4064/89 coming into effect, it was in the area of mergers and acquisitions, or, in Community jargon, concentrations, that the relationship of Arts 81 and 82 (ex 85 and 86) with each other had come under closest scrutiny.

Originally the Commission was of the view that Art 81 (ex 85) would not apply to concentrations. Thus, if competition was restricted or distorted by a concentration of companies, Art 82 (ex 86) was the appropriate measure with which to tackle it. This policy was pursued by the Commission in the case of *Continental Can* (6/72) when the Commission tried to remedy an abuse of a dominant position which had been achieved by takeovers and substantial holdings in European companies by an American company. It was the first attempt at merger control in this way by the Commission. It was not successful, mainly because the Commission failed to establish the relevant markets, rather than failed to show abuses by the concentration.

The view of the Court of Justice in the case was, however, instructive in respect of the relationship of Arts 81 and 82 (ex 85 and 86) and the restrictive approach to the problem adopted by the Commission. The Court of Justice considered that, by refusing to consider the use of Art 81 (ex 85) as well, the Commission had handicapped itself.

The Court of Justice held that 'Arts 85 and 86 [now 81 and 82] seek to achieve the same aim on different levels, *viz.*, the maintenance of effective competition within the Common Market. The restraint of competition which is prohibited if it is the result of behaviour falling under Art 85 [now 81], cannot be permissible by the fact that such behaviour succeeds under the influence of a dominant undertaking and results in the merger of the undertakings concerned. In the absence of explicit provisions one cannot assume that the Treaty, which prohibits in Art 85 [now 81] certain decisions of ordinary associations of undertakings restricting competition without eliminating it, permits in Art 86 [now 82] that undertakings after merging into an organic unit, should reach such a dominant position that any serious chance of competition is practically rendered impossible. Such diverse legal treatment would make a breach in the entire competition law which could jeopardise the proper functioning of the Common Market'.

Thus firms could avoid Art 81 (ex 85) by establishing close connections which did not constitute full merger and so be caught by Art 82 (ex 86). This would allow market partition and a defeat of the aims of the Community.

In any case Arts 81 and 82 (ex 85 and 86) cannot be interpreted in such a way that they contradict each other, because they serve to achieve the same aim. So, depending on the circumstances, it would be wise to consider the possibility of the application of both Arts 81 and 82 (ex 85 and 86). Following the *Continental Can* case, the Community realised that a new approach was required to tackle the problems of concentrations and, after some delay, a Mergers Regulation (4064/89) was enacted. This now has even been considered by the ECJ as applicable to situations of collective dominance rather than Art 82 (ex 86). See the cases of *France* v *Commission*

(C-68/94) and *Société Commerciale des Potasses et de l'Azote (SCPA)* v *Commission* (C-30/95). Therefore under certain circumstances it might also be necessary to consider the application of the Mergers Regulation as well. Recent case law also demonstrates a link between the two main competition law articles in that the ECJ has held that an agreement within the meaning of Art 85 (now 81)(1) between legally separate undertakings may nevertheless result in undertakings being so linked that they become and act as a collective entity as far as their competitors and customers are concerned. As such then it can lead to a position of collective dominance which is then capable of being abused. See *Compagnie Maritime Belge Transports* (C-395 & 396P/96). Some activities clearly need to be considered in the light of both Arts 81 and 82 (ex 85 & 86) and the Mergers Regulation.

9 Sex Discrimination

INTRODUCTION

The topic of sex discrimination or equal rights in the EC, within the European Community's social policy generally, may not be covered in all EC law courses, but it is a topic which has given rise to quite a considerable number of cases, some of which have become leading cases on general principles of EC law; see, for example, the cases of *Marshall* (152/84) and *von Colson* (14/83), amongst others. It may be surprising that the topic has given rise to so many cases as there is only very narrow Treaty provision for it and, certainly at first, little secondary legislation. On the other hand, it might be concluded that it is exactly because there is little statutory provision that equal rights have had to be fought for in the courts. Furthermore, the range of rights provided by Community legislation in this area is contained within a quite narrow band and is concerned largely with the employment context. As the Community makes further legislative moves into the area of social policy, further opportunities for equal rights legislation will no doubt arise.

To some extent the questions on the topic of sex discrimination which are considered on EC courses reflect this narrow band of issues, and questions are likely to focus on issues concerned with equal pay and equal treatment, especially in matters relating to retirement and dismissal.

To a more limited extent there may be questions on social security aspects of equal treatment but as this is a developing area of Community law, which still has a long way to go, there is less scope for questions.

The questions in this chapter have been divided into a general question on the inclusion of sex discrimination in the first place, problem questions on aspects of equal pay and equal treatment and an essay question on a specific development in this area of law which considers the overlapping area of pay and pensions.

QUESTION 1

How can the appearance of rights for women in the EC Treaty be explained, when the Community seems to be a vehicle for economic integration rather than a champion for women's rights.

Commentary

This is a general question aimed to address the reason for the inclusion of Articles concerned with the prohibition of sex discrimination in the EC Treaty.

The first part requires you to consider the original aims of the Community and the reason for the inclusion of social rights and, in particular, rights concerned with equality. The second part requires you to consider the development of the Community and the development of those rights. Thus, the aspects of this question which need to be addressed are: the actual provision of rights in the Treaty; the suggestion that the Community is essentially an economic Community; the limited place that social concern had or has in its development; and what the position is now, following the legislative and judicial developments in the area. The eventual provision of rights is best discussed in the light of the attitude displayed by the Court of Justice in case law.

Suggested Answer

The area of sex discrimination law or rights for women in Community law is a later developer than the other areas of law because of the less extensive provision for it in the Treaty than for other policy areas, the delays by the Community and, in particular, the Commission in introducing secondary legislation and the delays by the Member States in implementing the principles of equal pay from Art 119 (now 141) of the Treaty, and equal pay and equal treatment from the secondary legislation. Article 119 (now 141) was the sole original Treaty provision for the European Community to concern itself with sex discrimination.

Given that the EEC was, at least originally, of limited scope, it was clear that the main aim of the Community was undoubtedly the harmonisation of specific aspects of the Member States' economies and principally, at first, the creation of the common or single market. Social policy was, at first (and still by some) not regarded as greatly assisting the achievement of this result. However, it is also suggested that the original reason for including Art 119 (now 141) in the EEC Treaty when drafted was not for reasons of social justice, but out of economic considerations. The Article was allegedly included more at the request of the French, whose legislation purported to provide for equality between male and female workers. It was feared that French industry would be at a disadvantage if equal pay were not a principle enforced in the other Member States. Thus the aim was to ensure that similar economic conditions applied in all the Member States. A consideration which supports this view is the fact that Art 119 (now 141) originally applied only to equal pay and not to all discrimination on the grounds of sex, although the ECJ has since then considerably expanded its scope in a number of judgments. The objective to achieve an economic equality between Member States is acknowledged by the ECJ in the second *Defrenne* case (43/75). Additionally, however, in that case, the ECJ went on to declare that Art 119 (now 141) also forms part of the social objectives of the Community and therefore emphasised that the Community was not merely an economic union. The Court of Justice considered that it was at the same time intended, by common action, to ensure social progress and to seek the constant improvement of the living and working conditions of their peoples, as could be observed by considering the Preamble to the Treaty. It concluded that the double aim, which is at once economic and social, shows that the principle of equal pay forms part of the foundations of the Community. This has been followed up more recently in the case of *Deutsche Telekom* v *Vick* (C-324 & 5/96) in which the ECJ pronounced the social aims of Art 119 (now 141) prevail over those of the economic aims.

Therefore, whilst the initial concern may have been for economic reasons and originally the economic goals of the Community were undoubtedly paramount, if not exclusive, continuing concern is arguably more genuinely concerned with social rights and rights of equality in themselves, as demonstrated by developments to date, including the Directives on equal treatment and the considerable body of Community law on the subject. These developments might lead to an amended conclusion to the question. This developing concern was prompted by a desire by the Member States in the European Summit meetings in 1972–3 to demonstrate that the Community was also concerned about social needs and equal rights and the view, adopted by the original Member States, was that it was necessary to get their act together before the new Member States joined in 1973. Requiring greater legislative changes by the new states should have worked to the advantage of the existing Member States who had, at least on paper, more time to make the necessary adjustments. The reality of this was somewhat different as can be observed by some of the case law on the matter.

Consequently, therefore, the Commission was encouraged to produce proposals for a Social Action Programme. After some considerable delay and somewhat watered down in their final form, an almost inevitable result of the Community legislative process, the following Directives were adopted: Council Directive 75/117, the Equal Pay Directive 1975; Council Directive 76/207, the Equal Treatment Directive; and Directive 79/7, the Social Security Directive. Much later, Directive 86/378 on equal treatment in occupational pensions, Directive 86/613 concerning equal treatment of the self-employed and Directive 92/85 on pregnancy and maternity were adopted. To these can now be added the Parental Leave Directive (96/34), the Burden of Proof in Sex discrimination cases Directive (97/80) and the Part-time workers Directive (97/81), although this latter Directive is not directly aimed to address sex discrimination, it will have this effect as it aims to reduce the inequality between full-time workers and part-time workers, the majority of which are women.

However, Community law is characteristically framed in broad general terms and concepts which seemed unsuitable for the provision of individual rights. Community legislation was criticised because of its formality, limited accessibility and distance from those who needed the effective application and enforcement of the provisions, i.e., women at work. The effect was, at first, that very little knowledge of European Community equal rights law was disseminated beyond the small number of people in direct contact with these laws, except where there was substantial media publicity after the event, as in the leading cases such as the *Marshall* case (152/84), the *Pickstone v Freemans* case ([1988] 3 CMLR 221), the *Drake* case (150/85) and the *Webb v EMO* case (C-32/93). Community law has, however, provided a considerable source of legislative impetus for women's rights in employment in the Member States.

Community law provisions have been largely dependent on individual enforcement for effectiveness. This is because governments have failed to take appropriate measures to implement them, or enforce them if implemented, and the European Commission has not taken enforcement actions against the recalcitrant governments. It has largely been on the individual level that these rights have been successfully established as positive rights for women.

Notable successes are cases such as the *Defrenne* litigation (80/70, 43/75 and 149/77), involving a Belgian air stewardess, whose action, albeit after a lengthy process, gave the European Court of Justice the opportunity to interpret Art 119 (now 141) to include indirect and more subtle forms of discrimination. Another prime example of individual action required to force change is the *Marshall* case.

These cases alone would appear to create more interest in the creation, the enforcement and the development of women's rights than the efforts of many national groups. However, the backing of national agencies to promote equal rights has been fundamental in promoting women's rights, particularly in Belgium and the UK.

An additional very important factor which has helped promote and develop these rights is that the EC legal provisions can be and have been subject to very liberal interpretations by the European Court of Justice, far beyond a literal reading of the Articles; see, for example, the wide interpretation of Art 141 (ex 119), including the concept of pay, the *Garland* case (12/81), and the concept of indirect discrimination in the *Jenkins* v *Kingsgate* (96/80) and *Bilka-Kaufhaus* (170/84) cases. The Equal Treatment Directives have also been interpreted generously in cases such as *Marshall* (152/84) and *Barber* (C-262/88). The Court has even advanced the cause of equal rights through procedural means so that an effective remedy should be given by the Member States in cases where rights have been breached, see the *von Colson* case (14/83) and *Johnston* v *RUC* (222/84).

Although sex discrimination rights, of course, apply equally to men and women they have been regarded as more beneficial, for the most part, for women who were generally discriminated against more. However, the body of case law involving claims by men is increasing.

Women's rights in the Community have been considerably strengthened by changes introduced by the Treaty of Amsterdam. The Treaty has introduced as one of the goals outlined in Art 2 EC 'equality between men and women' and has added a new final sentence to Art 3 EC which reads: 'In all the activities referred to in this Article, the Community shall aim to eliminated inequalities, and to promote equality, between men and women'. Furthermore a new enabling power has been introduced in new Art 13 EC which provides that the Council, acting unanimously, and in consultation with the EP, may take appropriate action to combat discrimination based on sex or sexual orientation, amongst others. Finally the Treaty has amended and added two sentences to Art 141 (old 119) which locate within a Treaty base the principles of equal pay for work of equal value and positive discrimination previously contained in Directives only. Being contained in the latter meant that they could not give rise to direct effects against other individuals (no horizontal direct effects of Directives — *Marshall*).

Measures of positive discrimination have, however, been given a mixed reception by the ECJ and rules of positive discrimination which try to promote the appointment of women to achieve more substantive rather than just formal equality have been subject to exacting criteria to ensure that men are not men discriminated against. See the case of *Marshall* (C-409/95).

In summary, although Art 141 (ex 119) provided the only specific mention of equal treatment in the EC Treaty, it has formed the basis upon which the principle has been expanded into areas beyond equal pay, and has become a fundamental social principle of the Treaty. Whilst the amount of legislation is limited, it has been subject to very liberal interpretations by the Court of Justice, far beyond a literal reading of the Articles, in cases more often brought by individuals than the Commission in Art 226 (ex 169) actions; see the *Garland, Defrenne* (80/70, 43/75 and 149/77) and *Marshall* cases.

According to your own view on what the Court of Justice has done, or what it should do, your conclusion may range from considering that the Community and, in particular, the Court of Justice, have contributed significantly in promoting and enforcing equal treatment rights for women, to the view that it has only done what was to be expected, or maybe has not done enough so far.

QUESTION 2

Meg and Nicola work part-time for the Telephone Call centre of the 'Chaste Direct Bank'. They discover that even though they were working what they considered to be anti-social hours (from 6.00 pm until 12.00 midnight), they were receiving less per hour than their full-time colleagues working during daylight hours. There are 18 female and two male part-time evening workers. The day time staff are evenly divided between male and female workers. Meg complains to her boss, Mr. Branston, that this appears to be discrimination. He explains that it is far easier to get staff for evening work because they are able to fit this in with family commitments and, in particular, women find this a very suitable way of combining their commitment to a family and being able to earn money. He has very many applicants for the part-time evening work but in contrast far less for the day time work. Soon after, Meg is dismissed on the grounds of displaying a poor attitude. She has found it difficult to obtain alternative employment as Mr. Branston has failed to respond to enquiries for a reference for Meg.

Nicola became pregnant but suffered ill health as a result of the pregnancy. She was forced to take time off during the early part of the pregnancy but, after a successful birth, she returned to work at the end of her 14 weeks maternity leave. Her rights to the Sports and Social Club were suspended during her maternity leave. However, ever since the birth of her baby, the health problems which had first manifested themselves during pregnancy flared up again and, combined with the depression from which Nicola also suffers, has meant she has been absent for 25 days in 12 weeks. She was dismissed because she exceeded the number of days off which could be taken on the grounds of ill health.

The Call Centre has advertised for a new manager. The shortlist for applications consists of two equally qualified persons only. George is an internal candidate who already works for the company and Posy is an external applicant. 'Chaste Direct' stated its positive discrimination policy for filling job vacancies in the advertisement and as a result has appointed Posy as the new manager. George has protested that he has been discriminated against by the company and threatens to take the matter to court. In response the company issue him with a formal warning that he will be dismissed if he causes any more difficulty. Shortly afterwards another management position is advertised and George applies again but under the name Georgina. Appearing at the interview, George/Georgina states that he intends to undergo a sex change operation. This time there was no equally or better qualified female applicant. George/Georgina, however, was dismissed.

Meg, Nicola and George seek your advice as to their rights, if any, under EC law.

Commentary

This is quite a complex and involved question with a number of points to be addressed. It would probably be regarded as on the demanding side of undergraduate examination questions. As a general introduction to this problem on discrimination you could state the narrow Treaty base for Community law, but that a number of Directives have now been issued and that the Court interprets these rights liberally, to give the maximum protection to the rights provided. Given that this is such a long question, any general treatment must be brief to give you time to deal with the many substantive issues arising.

You must identify the issues which start with part-time pay, an old favourite but nevertheless still frequently appearing in exam questions. This may be an equal pay claim or possibly equal pay for work of equal value. There is a possible objective justification which needs to be discussed. Then, the dismissal of Meg and the failure to give a reference, Nicola's treatment during pregnancy and dismissal afterwards and finally the issues affecting George. These are the failure to be appointed which includes an aspect of positive discrimination and the dismissal. For the purposes of answering the question, at least, you will have to assume that the stated intention of George is genuine. Then with reference to the appropriate statutory provisions first, and case law where relevant, you should suggest the outcome of these issues.

Additionally, you should consider the right to pursue these claims before the national tribunals. It is to be noted that this last issue is particularly important because they are employed by a private employer, which may affect their rights to remedy in the national courts if they are dependent on the direct effects of Directives. However, unless you are advised on a particular course that a full discussion of the procedural aspects of the case must be given, a brief statement of the problems and possible solutions should complete an answer in a question which essentially concerns sex discrimination.

Suggested Answer

The area of law applicable to the factual situation in this problem stems originally from a very narrow legislative base in the EC Treaty. This is Art 119 (now 141) which was the sole primary legislative provision for the European Community to concern itself with sex discrimination. It is concerned predominantly with equal pay but also following the Treaty of Amsterdam with positive discrimination. There also exists a growing body of Community law on the subject following the enactment of a number of Directives, on matters of equality between men and women. Case law on these, as with the original Treaty provision, has extended the scope of protection further.

The factual circumstances in this question give rise to a number of issues to be resolved. They are: part-time pay, the possible objective justification, the dismissal of Meg and the failure to give a reference, Nicola's treatment during pregnancy and dismissal afterwards and, finally, the failure to appoint George and his dismissal.

The part-time staff, who are predominantly women, receive less pay per hour than the full-timers. Meg is claiming that she has been indirectly discriminated against compared to full-time workers and despite the fact they are paid the same as male part-time workers, of which there are only two out of 20. It is well established law that the prohibition of discrimination in pay under Art 141 (ex 119) applies not only to direct but also to indirect discrimination. The cases of *Jenkins* v *Kingsgate* (96/80) and *Bilka-Kaufhaus* v *Weber* (170/84) confirm that this situation will be regarded as indirect discrimination, when a disadvantage falls on a category which is predominantly female, unless it can be justified objectively. The *Bilka-Kaufhaus* case also provides three guidelines to determine whether a difference in pay is objectively justified. The measure employed must correspond to a real need on the part of the undertaking, be appropriate to achieve the objective and be necessary for that objective. It is in the end a question of fact to be decided by the national court but the ECJ has further held in the case of *Dansk* v *Danfoss* (109/88) that the burden is to be placed on the employer to prove that the difference is justified and that this should be transparent. The reasons put forward in the present case appear to be an objective justification because there is no shortage of applicants for part-time positions compared with full-time day time positions. However, it is combined with references to marital and family status, which is expressly provided for in Art 2 of the Equal Treatment Directive (76/207) that there shall be no discrimination whatsoever on grounds of sex either directly or indirectly by reference in particular to family or marital status. This would appear to be unlawful indirect discrimination but if there is a doubt given the applicants for the positions, a reference under Art 234 (ex 177) to the ECJ may be necessary to decide the point. There may also be an argument here that Meg has a claim for equal pay for work of equal value. The Treaty now includes the words 'equal pay for work of equal value', previously restricted to Directive 75/117. In the present case, Meg is comparing her wages with a male worker whose work is arguably of equal or lesser value because it is day time work and she is working anti-social hours but receives lower wages. She could ask for a job-evaluation scheme and should the company refuse to carry out a job evaluation scheme to test this, it can be imposed on them through court proceedings: *Commission* v *UK* (61/81). Following the *Murphy* v *Irish Telecom* case (157/86) and the *Enderby* v *Frenchay* (C-127/92) case, in which the ECJ held that Art 119 (now 141) could be used to make a comparison of work of equal value, this claim has a good chance of success.

Meg was then dismissed, which appears to be a reaction to her making a complaint and this is specifically covered by Art 5 of Directive 75/117 which serves to protect complainants from unfair dismissal on the grounds that they have complained. The procedural difficulty that this is a private employer will be considered at the end of this answer.

Finally concerning Meg is the refusal to give a reference. This point is covered by the case of *Coote v Granada* (C-185/97) which holds that a refusal to provide a reference would undermine Art 6 of Directive 76/207 (the equal treatment Directive) under which Member States should take measures to achieve the aims of the Directive and must ensure the rights can be enforced by an individual before the national courts. The ECJ held that Art 6 of the Directive also covers measures an employer might take as a reaction against legal proceedings of a former employee outside of dismissal.

Turning to Nicola, the suspension of rights during 14 weeks would appear to be a straightforward breach of Art 11 of Directive 92/85 which serves to protect employment rights during pregnancy and maternity (see *Susanne Lewen v Lothar Denda* (C-333/97)). If there was any doubt about this, a reference to the ECJ would be necessary. However, the dismissal for absence outside of the 14 week protected period due to ill health arising from pregnancy would appear to be lawful according to the case law of the ECJ and not protected by either Directive 76/207 or 92/85. See *Larsson v Dansk Handel & Service* (C-400/95) in which the ECJ confirmed that Directive 76/207 does not prevent dismissals for absences due to illness attributable to pregnancy even where the illness arose during pregnancy and continued during and after maternity. Directive 92/85 does not help as this also only protects an individual from dismissal from the beginning of pregnancy to the end of maternity leave as confirmed in *Brown v Rentokil* (C-394/96) where it was held that absences due to illnesses thereafter are treated in the same way as any other illness and may constitute grounds for dismissal according to provisions of national law. Hence then the dismissal appears to be lawful.

George was not appointed and suspects the stance made by Margaret under positive discrimination has actually discriminated against him. Positive discrimination is now located in Art 141(4) of the Treaty although the first cases arose under Directive 76/207 Art 2(4). In the case of *Hellmut Marschall v Land Nordrhein-Westfalen* (C-409/95), the ECJ held that clauses favouring women applicants would only be acceptable if they contained a 'saving clause' which provides that if a particular male candidate has grounds which tilt the balance in his favour, women are not to be given priority. Further, such clauses are acceptable provided the candidates are objectively assessed to determine whether there are any factors tilting the balance in favour of a male candidate but that such criteria employed do not themselves discriminate against women. This position is now supported by the *Badeck* case (C-158/97) which is based on Art 141(4). The facts reveal no such clause in the present case, and unless there is such a clause, it is unlikely that the positive discrimination policy of the bank conforms with EC law.

George was dismissed after stating that he was to undergo a sex change operation. These facts fit within the case of *P* v *S and Cornwall County Council* (C-13/94) which involved a male-to-female transsexual who was dismissed from employment in an educational establishment after informing the employers he was going to undergo gender reassignment. The ECJ held that this was unlawful discrimination on the grounds of sex because it was 'based, essentially if not exclusively on the sex of the person concerned'. The dismissal would be contrary to Art 6 of Directive 76/207 which provides that Member States must introduce into their own legal systems such measures as are necessary to enable all persons who consider themselves wronged to pursue their claims by judicial process.

The final aspect concerns the difficulties which might arise in respect of pursuit of the claims in the national tribunals. Any claims made under Art 141 (old 119) will be safe in all circumstances because this was held to be directly effective in *Defrenne (No. 2)* (43/75), both vertically against the state and horizontally against other individuals. If the Member State has accurately implemented the Directives, then applicants can invoke national law before the national court. However, if they have not been implemented or correctly implemented, the claimants will be unable to rely directly on the Directives because a private employer is involved and there are no horizontal direct effects; see the *Marshall* case (152/84). The result in such a circumstance would depend on whether the national court could interpret any national law in compliance with Community law, thus following the *von Colson* (14/83) and *Marleasing* cases (C-106/89). If this is not the case, a further possibility exists in that a claim may be made against the state, in accordance with the *Francovich* case (C-6/90), for a failure to implement the Directive with the result that the claimant has suffered damage.

QUESTION 3

In 1985, Margaret set up a Ladies Hairdressing Salon called 'Thatcher's Cuts'. Her cuts were cheap and popular because her wage costs were kept low by the employment of a large proportion of part-time staff who were paid a third less than full-time employees. All except one of the part-time employees were female. When asked by Sharon and Tracey why this was, Margaret explained that she wanted to attract more male full-time hairdressers. She considered that they were more popular with her clients and higher salaries were needed to fill the posts advertised. She also regarded this as justified to redress the balance positively in favour of men in a profession largely dominated by female hairdressers. Margaret, who was an advocate of private pensions, additionally established a redundancy scheme and an 'opted-out' pension scheme for her employees.

Tracey, a female part-timer, who wanted to work full-time, was unable to obtain a position which was advertised but filled by a man with the same qualifications. In January 1990, Tracey, who had read in a Women's magazine that she had rights to equal treatment under European law, mentioned this to Margaret. Margaret, who disliked Europe, dismissed her for impertinence. Tracey went to a solicitor who filed a claim on her behalf in respect of both pay and, in case it was relevant, pensions.

Margaret fell on hard times and, in November 1990, had to shut up shop. She closed the salon and made the staff redundant. The amount of the redundancy payments and pensions made were based pro-rata on earnings so that full-time ex-employees received 50% higher payments than part-timers. Sharon was made redundant at this time.

Advise Tracey and Sharon as to their rights under Community law, if any, including any procedural difficulties which they may face.

Commentary

This is also a challenging question. It involves questions of indirect discrimination of part-time workers and a possible objective justification for this. It also includes a policy of positive discrimination which has to be considered to see whether this offends Community law. The most difficult part of this question is that dealing with the redundancy payments and pensions, particularly as claims for equal pensions are subject to a time bar introduced by the *Barber* case (C-262/88).

The answer should be started with a brief statement on the community legal regime, list the issues which need to be considered and suggest possible solutions based on the legislative provision and case law of the ECJ. The lack of horizontal direct effects of Directives should also be mentioned if only in brief.

Suggested Answer

The area of law applicable to this question stems originally from a very narrow legislative base in the EC Treaty. This is Art 141 (ex 119) which remains the sole primary legislative provision for the European Community to concern itself with sex discrimination. It is concerned predominantly with equal pay but also following the Treaty of Amsterdam with positive discrimination. There also exists a growing body of Community law on the subject following the enactment of a number of Directives, on matters of equality between men and women. Case law on these, as with the original Treaty provision, has extended the scope of protection further.

The factual circumstances in this question give rise to a number of issues to be resolved. They are: part-time pay, the possible objective justification, positive discrimination, the dismissal of Tracey and the redundancy payments and pensions for both Tracey and Sharon.

The part-time staff, who are predominantly women, receive less pay per hour than the full-timers. Sharon and Tracey are concerned that they are suffering discrimination on the grounds of sex contrary to Art 141 (ex 119) of the Treaty. It appears as if they have been indirectly discriminated against compared to full-time workers and despite the fact they are paid the same as male part-time workers, of which there is only one. It is well established law that the prohibition of discrimination in pay under Art 141 (ex 119) applies not only to direct but also to indirect discrimination. The cases of *Jenkins* v *Kingsgate* (96/80) and *Bilka-Kaufhaus* v *Weber* (170/84) confirm that this situation will be regarded as indirect discrimination, when a disadvantage falls on a category which is predominantly female, unless it can be justified objectively. The *Bilka-Kaufhaus* case also provides three guidelines to determine whether a difference in pay is objectively justified. The measure employed must correspond to a real need on the part of the undertaking, be appropriate to achieve the objective and be necessary for that objective. It is in the end a question of fact to be decided by the national court but the ECJ has further held in the case of *Dansk* v *Danfoss* (109/88) that the burden is to be placed on the employer to prove that the difference is justified and that this should be transparent. The reasons put forward in the present case are the policy to attract more full-time workers and to carry out a policy of positive discrimination in favour of men. Would these justify the discrimination? Clearly favouring men above women would not be justified as the discrimination is based expressly on sex. How does the positive discrimination policy affect this? Originally only contained in Art 2(4) of Directive

76/207, positive discrimination is now located in Art 141(4) of the Treaty although the first cases arose under the Directive. In the case of *Hellmut Marschall* v *Land Nordrhein-Westfalen* (C-409/95), the ECJ held that clauses favouring women applicants would only be acceptable if they contained a 'saving clause' which provides that if a particular male candidate has grounds which tilt the balance in his favour, women are not to be given priority. Further, such clauses are acceptable provided the candidates are objectively assessed to determine whether there are any factors tilting the balance in favour of a male candidate but that such criteria employed do not themselves discriminate against women. This position is now supported by the *Badeck* case (C-158/97) which is based on Art 141(4). The facts reveal no such clause in the present case, therefore it is unlikely that the positive discrimination policy conforms with EC law. If there is any doubt that this judgment could not be applied in the same manner to determine whether positive discrimination in favour of men offends Community law, then a reference to the ECJ would be needed. It is unlikely that the higher payments would be lawful discrimination and unless there was sufficient safeguards in the system of positive discrimination, this would also be unlikely to satisfy Community law requirements.

Tracey has not been accepted for the full-time position. This aspect would also be covered by Art 3(1) of Directive 76/207 which provides that there shall be no discrimination whatsoever on the grounds of sex in the conditions, including selection criteria, for access to all jobs or posts, whatever the sector or branch or activity and to all levels of the occupational hierarchy. If the positive discrimination policy offends Community law then Art 3(1) will also have been breached.

Tracey was then dismissed, which appears to be a reaction to her making a complaint and this is specifically covered by Art 6 of Directive 76/207 which provides that Member States must introduce into their own legal systems such measures as are necessary to enable all persons who consider themselves wronged to pursue their claims by judicial process and thus serves to protect complainants from unfair dismissal on the grounds that they have complained. The procedural difficulty that this is a private employer will be considered at the end of this answer.

Turning now to the redundancy payments and pensions which were 50% higher for full-time staff than for the predominantly female part-time workers. Again, unlawful indirect discrimination appears to be present here. Dealing first with the redundancy payments, it has been confirmed in *Barber* v *GRE* (C-262/88) that payments in connection with redundancy are to be considered a part of the concept of pay under Art 141 (ex 119). As a consequence, there will be no difficulty with direct effects, if this aspect of the claim becomes material. As pay, therefore, the amount should be equal and, if not, this is a clear breach of Art 141 (ex 119). Sharon would be unlawfully discriminated against.

Any claims in respect of pensions are more problematic because it was originally considered that pensions were so linked to personable age that they would be exempted from the equal treatment regime of the EC by virtue of Art 7 of Directive 79/7. However, the case of *Barber* held that pensions were 'pay' within Art 141 (ex 119) because they were a part of the employment relationship. The pensions provided by Margaret were opted out from the state scheme hence then clearly pay according to the ECJ for the purposes of Art 141 (ex 119). As such then a difference in payment for the part-time workers who were predominantly female would unlawfully discriminate against them contrary to Art 141 (ex 119).

An additional aspect here is the procedural difficulty of any claim for equal rights in pensions. The *Barber* decision caused severe problems as it was not expected that pensions should be pay because they were linked to retirement and this had been different for men and women as most schemes were set up on the basis that women would retire earlier. Actuaries knew they would live longer so they were necessarily different, i.e., there would be differences based on the different ages in the schemes. As a result of the *Barber* judgment, this would mean that there would be unlawful discrimination not previously thought to be the case, for which huge amounts of compensation, not previously contemplated, would be payable. This would not have been taken account of in the actuarial schemes and the pension schemes would have had severe difficulties in making payments not previously foreseen. Hence then ECJ declared Art 141 (old 119) to be directly effective for pensions only from the date of judgment, i.e. 17 May 1990.

Hence then the date of the pension claim is important in respect of the *Barber* case. Tracey has put a claim in before the date of judgment, so her claim will be accepted but Sharon was only able to claim after she was made redundant which is after the date of judgment in the *Barber* case and her claim will be time barred. The Member States also introduced Protocol II to the Maastricht Treaty when it was negotiated confirming and clarifying the *Barber* judgment that only payments attributable to periods of service after the date of judgment would count for pay under Art 141 (ex 119). Hence then for Sharon only the period from 17 May to her redundancy in November 1990.

The final aspect concerns the difficulties which might arise in respect of pursuit of the claims in the national tribunals. Any claims made under Art 141 (old 119) will be safe in all circumstances because this was held to be directly effective in *Defrenne (No. 2)* (43/75) both vertically and horizontally. If the Member State has accurately implemented the Directives, then applicants can invoke national law before the national court. However, if they have not been implemented or correctly implemented, the claimants will be unable to rely directly on the Directives because a private employer is involved and there are no horizontal direct effects: see the *Marshall* case (152/84). The result in such a circumstance would depend on whether the national court could interpret any national law in compliance with Community law, thus following the *von Colson* (14/83) and *Marleasing* cases (C-106/89). If this is not the case, a further possibility exists in that a claim may be made against the state, in accordance with the *Francovich* case (C-6/90), for a failure to implement the Directive with the result that the claimant has suffered damage.

QUESTION 4

Whilst the case of *Barber* (C-262/88) may have finally decided that benefits paid in connection with redundancy were to be considered pay within the meaning of Article 141 of the EC Treaty, the precise effect of the judgment was far from clear. Discuss the difficulties raised by this judgment and the solution found to overcome them.

Commentary

This essay type question concentrates on a particular difficulty which has developed in the case law of the Court of Justice. This is the interpretation which should be given in respect of payments made in connection with redundancies and whether such payments should be considered as pay within the scope of Art 141 (ex 119) EC. The problem had arisen from the fact that redundancy payments and pension payments have been regarded as connected with state pensions and thus a part of the social policy reserved to the Member States, outside the jurisdiction of the Community. The *Barber* case has now upset this previous position.

In answering this question you need to set out in some detail the facts and decision in the case of *Barber* as the basis to your answer. The words 'finally

208 — header test

decided' in the first sentence suggest that there had been previous cases which had considered this but without coming to the conclusions reached in the *Barber* case. You should, therefore, at least summarise the earlier case law development. The statement then suggests in the words 'the precise effect of the judgment was far from clear' that there is some uncertainty about the decision. You should identify the difficulties which have been noted in respect of this judgment and the ensuing problems and the steps that have been taken to overcome them.

Suggested Answer

The case of *Barber* v *Guardian Royal Exchange Assurance Group* (C-262/88) concerned the provision of a non-state pension scheme, known as a contracted-out scheme, as a part of the contract of employment. The contract also stated that the normal pension ages were 65 for men and 60 for women. Early retirement with immediate pension could be made at any time within 10 years of pensionable age. Barber was made redundant at the age of 52. The severance terms required that men must be 55 and women 50 to obtain immediate pensions. Ineligible for this, Barber was granted instead a deferred pension and a severance payment. He claimed that because the scheme involved an age differential as to when men and women were able to obtain redundancy pensions (50 for women 55 for men), it was discrimination contrary to Community law.

Essentially, the Court of Justice held that benefits paid in connection with redundancy, even though compulsory and even though they reflected considerations of a Member State's social security policy, were a form of payment made after the termination of the contract of employment and therefore covered by Art 119 (now 141). Article 141 (ex 119) applies to any consideration, immediate or future, and whether received indirectly as a result of a contract of employment with an employer. This conclusion was reached even though the UK argued that the payments reflected considerations of a Member State's social security policy and should be assessed under Art 118 (now 140) and were not within the scope of Art 119 (now 141). The ECJ held that they were a part of the employment relationship and that redundancy benefits were to be regarded as pay regardless of whether they were a part of the contract of employment, or compulsory under national legislation, or paid voluntarily by the employer.

The case follows a number of previous cases considered by the Court of Justice concerning the complicated relationships between pay and contributions to state pensions, state redundancy payment schemes and non-state pensions schemes. In *Defrenne (No. 1)* (80/70) the ECJ held that contributions made to a state social security scheme were not pay because they were the result of legal requirements imposed by the state. The decisive criterion in that case was the fact that the pension rights in question related wholly to a state social security scheme. In *Barber* the Court of Justice held that, contracted out pensions schemes were not covered by the rule in *Defrenne* and they should be considered under Art 119 (now 141), even if they were a substitute for part of the state scheme.

In *Worringham and Humphreys* v *Lloyds Bank* (69/80), the Court of Justice ruled that a contribution to a retirement benefit scheme, which is paid by employer on the employee's behalf by means of an addition to gross salary, was pay within the meaning of Art 119 (now 141), and that amounts which determine other benefits linked to salary were also part of the pay of the employee within the second paragraph of Art 119 (now 141) even if they were deducted at source by the employer and paid into a pension fund on behalf of the employee.

In *Bilka-Kaufhaus* v *Karin Weber von Harz* (170/84), it was held that where payments are made in respect of a non-contributory occupational pensions scheme established under contract with the employer, they constitute pay under Art 119 (now 141).

In *Liefting* v *University of Amsterdam* (22/83), a Dutch statutory social security scheme for civil servants meant that lower employer contributions were paid by the employer to women than men with the consequence that if the women were to make this up themselves, their take home pay was less. It was argued on the basis of *Defrenne* that social security was not pay and therefore was excluded from the scope of Art 119 (now 141) and the jurisdiction of the Community. The Court of Justice held that the sums provided by the employer become pay if they form part of the gross pay calculation for other benefits and if these are not the same for males and females they will breach Art 119 (now 141).

However, the case of *Newstead* v *Department of Transport* (192/85) concerned the question of whether a compulsory deduction from the gross pay of male unmarried civil servants towards a widow's pension amounted to a breach of Art 141 (ex 119) and Directives 75/117 and 76/207. The Court of Justice ruled that the requirement to pay was neither a benefit paid to workers nor a contribution paid by the employer to a pension scheme on behalf of the employee. It fell, therefore, within the scope of Art 118 (now 140) not Art 119 (now 141) because it was argued that it affected net and not gross pay, thus distinguishing itself from *Liefting*. This case would now seem to be overruled by the *Barber* case.

Therefore, having decided in the *Barber* case that the pension was pay, the age difference causing deferred pension rights for males was a form of unlawful discrimination.

The deciding factor in the light of these cases is whether the rules of the specific scheme are a part of the employment relationship. Schemes which are entirely compulsory state security schemes are not considered to be a part of the employment relationship and so are not subject to Art 141 (ex 119).

The immediate consequence of the *Barber* judgment was that the employer in the case was required to pay out pensions to men earlier than was previously thought necessary. However, the most difficult aspect of the case is the further consequence for all other employers and the calculation for pension schemes which were based on different retirement ages according to the previous legal position. The judgment of the Court reflects that and the ECJ held that because of the confusion over the exact scope of Art 119 (now 141), the Member States could not previously have planned on the correct basis as decided in this case, so the judgment could not be retroactive. Retroactivity would cause too many complications for pension schemes because employers could not have foreseen that Art 119 (now 141) was applicable to contracted out pension schemes. Therefore, the Court of Justice held that Art 119 (now 141) could not be relied on to claim an entitlement to a pension prior to the date of judgment of 17 May 1990, except where claims were already in the pipeline.

A controversy then arose as to the precise meaning and effect of this ruling. It was uncertain whether it referred to benefits or pensions received from the date of judgment, or whether it referred to benefits to be received in respect of periods of employment, i.e., earnings, from the date of judgment. The latter is less onerous on employers than the former.

The matter appeared temporarily to be resolved by the issue of a Protocol at Maastricht which stated that the benefits arising from occupational social security schemes were not to be considered as remuneration in respect of periods of employment prior to 17 May 1990 with the exception of those who had instigated proceedings prior to that date. This overcame the damaging economic effect on employers which would have resulted from a retroactive application of the ruling of the Court of Justice in *Barber.*

It was not, however, the end of the story. *Barber* sparked off many more cases seeking to establish its exact meaning and consequences, so that the whole area became even more complex and confusing and another legislative intervention was considered necessary to resolve the matter. The ECJ confirmed in the *Ten Oever* (C-109/91) and *Coloroll* cases (C-200/91) that pension equality is guaranteed only to awards arising from employment after 17/5/1990, however, in *Vroege* v *NCIV Instituut* (C-57/93) and *Fisscher* v *Voorhuis Hengelo BV* (C-128/93) it held the time limit in *Barber* and Protocol 2 does not apply to discrimination in relation to the right to join, i.e. gain access to, an occupational pension scheme, which is governed by the previous judgment in *Bilka Kaufhaus* (C-170/84) a well known case, of which employers should have been aware. Additionally in *Coloroll*, the ECJ ruled that additional benefits stemming from contributions paid by employees on a purely voluntary basis are not covered by Article 119 (now 141) of the Treaty. In *Neath* v *Hugh Steeper* (C-152/91) different lump sum pension payments for men and women which were the conversion of a periodic pension payments were held to be valid. Whilst benefits and payments must be equal this is not the case for the employers' contributions as other factors other than a simple difference in sex are involved. The amount needed for the lump sum is determined by actuaries who base their figures on the fact that women live longer after retirement so greater contributions are needed. This becomes a larger lump sum when converted. The ECJ held that the inequality in employers contributions arising from actuarial factors such as life expectancy, which differed according to sex was not to be caught by Article 119 (now 141).

In view of the *Barber* case law developments, the Council decided it was necessary to amend the provisions of Directive 86/378 which had been affected by Directive 96/97. Without going into fine detail this confirms that Directive 86/378 does not apply to occupational schemes where the benefits are financed by contributions paid by workers on a voluntary basis, that pension supplements to bridge the age between the occupational pension age and the statutory pension age are acceptable, where the aim is to make equal or more nearly equal the overall amount of benefit paid to these persons compared to payments to the other sex in the same situation. The *Neath* judgment was also incorporated and the claim by men and women for a flexible pensionable age under the same conditions would not be incompatible with the Directive. It remains, however, a complex area of law with many more cases in the pipeline.

10 Mixed Subject Questions

INTRODUCTION

The questions in this chapter involve a consideration of more than one topic. They may take the form of a combination of procedural actions or a mix of a substantive law topics with a procedural action before the Court of Justice. It may well be that questions you will face will be formed in such a way. Inevitably, the mixed question will mean that there is less time that can be spent on each of the possible actions and the answers will reflect this.

QUESTION 1

Whilst the doctrine of the supremacy of Community law is a logical if not necessary inference from the Community Treaties, the same cannot be said of the doctrine of direct effects of Community law.

Discuss.

Commentary

This is a combined topic question which concerns the now well established doctrines of the supremacy of EC law and direct effects. First of all, both of these legal concepts need to be defined. So you need to state clearly and concisely what you understand by the phrases 'the doctrine of the supremacy of Community Law' and 'the doctrine of direct effects'. Both of these concepts are ones developed by the Court of Justice in leading cases of Community law, including the notable cases of *Van Gend en Loos* (26/62) and *Costa* v *ENEL* (6/64).

You are first asked whether it is the case that it is 'a logical if not necessary inference' and you have to determine exactly what this cryptic part of the question is demanding for an answer. It suggests that the supremacy of Community law is logical, but that it is not a necessary inference from the Treaties. You must address both these contentions. Although the word 'logical' appears first, you would be advised to address the part about the necessary inference first, because this refers you to the Treaty provisions. It is arguable that it makes sense to consider whether the Treaties do provide for supremacy before having to consider the logic of whether Community law is supreme. Finally, you must decide whether and if so, how, the Treaties logically provide for supremacy. Do this by reference to any help from the Treaty Articles and the ECJ view of them in case law.

This particular question is a variation on the question in chapter 4 on the supremacy of Community law, with a twist in the tail, because in contrast to the position on supremacy, the converse is expressed to be the case with direct effects, i.e., it cannot be said that the doctrine of direct effects is a logical if not necessary inference. You therefore need to consider whether it means it is either logical or necessary.

Suggested Answer

The doctrine of the supremacy of Community law will be considered first. The doctrine of the supremacy of Community law is one which has been developed by the Court of Justice in a series of cases, the most notable of which are *Van Gend en Loos* (26/62), *Costa* v *ENEL* (6/64) and the *Simmenthal* (106/77) case.

The question has already hinted that the Treaties do not expressly provide for supremacy, i.e., there is no Article which clearly states that Community law is supreme and by a direct reading of the Treaty you might not necessarily infer that Community law is supreme. However, whilst there is no express statement of supremacy in the Treaty, it can be argued that some of the Articles of the EC Treaty impliedly or logically require supremacy.

Thus, a conclusion as to whether Community law supremacy is a conclusion to be drawn from the Treaty depends upon a consideration of some of its provisions. For example, Art 10 (ex 5), the good faith or fidelity clause; Art 12 (ex 6), the general prohibition of discrimination on the grounds of nationality; Art 249 (ex 189) in respect of the direct applicability of Regulations; Art 292 (ex 219), the obligation of Member States to submit only to Treaty dispute resolution and, Art 228 (ex 171), the requirement to comply with rulings of the Court of Justice. So this could lead to the conclusion that Community law requires supremacy, but it cannot be stated that the Treaty expressly or categorically imposes it.

The Court of Justice in the cases of *Van Gend en Loos, Costa* v *ENEL* and *Simmenthal*, amongst others, has held that Community law supremacy is a logical conclusion to reach. Community law should be supreme because of the transfer of powers from the Member States and, because it has its own law making machinery, it must have precedence if the Community is going to work.

In the *Van Gend en Loos* case, the Court of Justice held that the Community constitutes a new legal order of international law for the benefit of which the States have limited their sovereign rights. Further elaboration of the new legal order in *Van Gend en Loos* was given in the case of *Costa* v *ENEL*. The Court of Justice stressed the autonomous legal order of Community law in contrast with ordinary international treaties. It held that the EEC Treaty has created its own legal system which became an integral part of the legal systems of the Member States and which their courts are bound to apply. Thus, by creating a Community of unlimited duration which has its own institutions, its own personality, its own legal capacity and more particularly real powers stemming from a limitation of sovereignty or a transfer of powers from the states to the Community, the Member States have limited their sovereign rights and have created a body of law to bind their nationals and themselves. It is impossible, in the light of this, for the states to accord precedence to a unilateral and subsequent measure over a legal system accepted by them. The Court summed up its position 'It follows . . . that the law stemming from the treaty, an independent source of law, could not because of its special and original nature, be overridden by domestic legal provisions, however framed, without being deprived of its character as Community law and without the legal basis of the Community itself being called into question'. Therefore Community Law is to be supreme over subsequent national law.

The case of *Simmenthal* (106/77) arises from a conflict between the Italian constitution and Community law. A lower court was faced with inconsistency between a Community law provision and a national provision, but was aware that a reference to the Italian constitutional court would have the effect of subrogating Community law to national law and that would have been inconsistent with existent Community case law on the matter in the *Costa* v *ENEL* case (6/64). However, disregarding the national law was contrary to constitutional requirements. The Italian magistrate made a reference to the ECJ and asked whether subsequent national measures which conflict with Community law must be disregarded without waiting until those measures are formally repealed or declared unconstitutional. The ECJ firstly declared that the doctrine of direct effects of Community legislation was not dependent on any national constitutional provisions but a source of rights in themselves. Therefore, national courts which are called upon to apply provisions of Community law are under a duty to give full effect to those provisions, including a refusal to apply conflicting national legislation, even if adopted subsequently. The ECJ also ruled that directly effective provisions of Community law also preclude the valid adoption of new legislative measures to the extent that they would be incompatible with Community provisions and that any inconsistent national legislation recognised by national legislatures as having legal effect would deny the effectiveness of the obligations undertaken by the Member State and imperil the existence of the Community.

Hence, the Court of Justice in the cases of *Van Gend en Loos* (26/62), *Costa* v *ENEL* and *Simmenthal,* amongst others, has held that Community law supremacy is a logical inference to make from the Treaties.

The second part of the question requires a consideration of whether the doctrine of direct effects of Community law is a logical conclusion or a necessary inference.

Direct effects is the term given to judicial enforcement of rights arising from provisions of Community law which can be upheld in favour of individuals in the courts of the Member States. It describes the right to rely directly on Community law in the absence of national law or in the face of conflicting national law. Direct effects can apply to Articles of the Treaty, Regulations, Directives and Decisions, in fact any binding law in terms of Art 249 (ex 189) EC and, in some circumstances, outside Art 249 (ex 189) as with international agreements. Certain criteria have to be fulfilled before the ECJ can declare a particular Community law provision to give rise to direct effects. These were determined by the ECJ in a series of cases commencing with the leading Community law case of *Van Gend en Loos* (26/62). In *Van Gend en Loos*, a private legal individual company challenged a new import duty imposed by the Dutch authorities and claimed it was contrary to Arts 12 and 13 (now 25) of the EEC Treaty. The Dutch authorities in their defence claimed that the obligation was one imposed by the Treaty on the Dutch state alone and could not be invoked by an individual of that state. The Court of Justice held that the institutions of the Community are endowed with sovereign rights the exercise of which affects not only Member States but also their citizens and that Community law was capable of conferring rights on individuals which become part of their legal heritage. The provision must, however, be clear, precise, require no further implementation on the part of the Member State and must be complete.

There is nothing in the Community Treaties from which it could be logically concluded or inferred that provisions of Community law could be held to have direct effects in certain circumstances. Whilst Treaty Articles and Regulations are directly applicable, this does not mean to say that they can be invoked by individuals, and Directives are in any case addressed to the Member States. The criteria by which direct effects may be established are entirely a judicial creation of the Court of Justice. However, it may be stated that direct effects are a logical and necessary inference from the supremacy of Community law. If a Community provision is supreme over inconsistent national law, to deny direct effects, where appropriate, would be illogical. Directly effective law is therefore logically and necessarily supreme over national law.

QUESTION 2

How and to what extent are the rights of individuals protected in the Community legal order?

Commentary

This is a general overview question on the range of actions which are available to individuals to protect their rights in Community law. An underlying aspect of the question is that there are many new laws which have been created by the European Community directly affecting individuals, both by bestowing advantages on them but also by imposing duties and sometime infringing their rights. The scope of these laws can be discovered from a review of the Treaties and Community legislation. Yet, the means by which individuals can protect their rights are less obvious. It would be useful to preface your answer with this concern.

In answering the question, you should broadly identify the range of legal activities encompassed by the Community. This can be done by briefly outlining the major areas of Community law included in the Treaty and secondary legislation which may affect individual rights.

Secondly, you should outline the procedures by which these rights can be protected in the Community legal order and where these rights can be protected, i.e., in which legal forums.

Finally a qualitative element is introduced by the term 'to what extent' which requires you to consider how well or how effectively these rights are protected in reality.

Suggested Answer

The European Community or Union now covers vast tracts of the economic sphere and, increasingly, the social sphere of the Member States' national jurisdictions. The Treaties and secondary law established under the Treaties straddle many areas of law and impose very many duties and rights. Individuals in the Community are subject to a multitude of new laws which have emerged from both the Council and the Commission in Brussels, and to an increasing extent today have been subject to the influence of the European Parliament in the legislative process. They have created a new source of law, which is external to the Member States' own laws and established protection of individual rights. Since the establishment of the EC, Community individuals have become subject to the legislative, executive and judicial authority of the Community. Concerns have quite rightly been raised about the protection that individuals have in the face of this new legal source of authority, particularly as the democratic protection in the EC from the

European Parliament is not as strong at the Community level as national parliaments and political answerability in the Member States.

Thus it is necessary first to define how the Community affects the individual and then to outline the legal protections available. The term 'individuals' is taken to mean both natural and legal persons in the Community who are concerned in some way with the substantive and procedural law of the Community.

Essentially, three different aspects need to be considered. First, the substantive rights under the various chapters of the Treaty; secondly, the procedural rights, i.e., the various actions that can be pursued in the Community courts and, thirdly, a set of general fundamental rights.

The impact of the Community on individuals will be considered first of all. Individuals are affected by a vast range of substantive laws enacted by the Community. Legislation enacted in any of the areas of Community law can affect the rights of individuals. Legislation can be enacted to regulate agricultural activities, to ensure or standardise product or trading rules, to ensure the free movement of goods, to ensure that competition in the Community is being maintained, or to provide for the free movement of persons, to give just a few examples of the range of areas covered by the Community. The full scope can be determined by looking at Art 3 of the Treaty. This legislation can either promote or infringe individual rights. Whilst for the most part these laws impose duties on the Member States, they can also give rise to corresponding rights of individuals; see as a classic example the *Van Gend en Loos* case (26/62) and the establishment of the doctrine of direct effects by the Court of Justice.

Individuals may, as a result, consider their rights have been infringed by the institutions of the Community in enacting these rules. Sometimes they can also be affected by the national implementation of Community law by Member States. Thus, individuals may need to be protected against the acts of the Community institutions and the Member States, or to challenge Member States where they have failed to implement Community law. Protection needs to be considered in the actions both against the Community and the Member States.

The difficulties experienced in pursuing these actions or, in terms of the question posed, the *extent of the protection*, will be considered at the same time.

The main forms of protection are provided by the EC treaty which outlines a number of actions which, in varying circumstances and subject to differing criteria, may aid an individual in the protection of rights. Actions against the Community can be made under a number of Treaty provisions.

Article 230 (ex 173) allows a direct challenge against legislative acts of the institutions where they are unlawful and the infringement can be classified under one of the four grounds listed in the Article itself. This action, however, can only be used by individuals in limited circumstances. It cannot be used to challenge Regulations and can only be employed to challenge Decisions which are of direct and individual concern. There is a time limit of two months in which actions can be brought following the 15th day after publication in the Official Journal.

Article 232 (ex 175) provides an action against the institutions of the EC for a failure to act but this can only be employed by the potential addressee of the legal act, or those in view of more recent case laws are in an analogous position as applicants under Art 230 (ex 173) in that they are directly and individually concerned with a potential act. Articles 230 and 232 (ex 173 and 175) are regarded as particularly difficult actions for individuals, who are unlikely to succeed in them. They seem more designed for use by the Member States and the institutions of the Community.

An indirect challenge to Community Regulations can be made under Art 241 (ex 184) but this is only available providing a related matter of Community law is already being adjudicated in the Court of Justice and, again, is of limited use to individuals.

Of more use and more likely to be successful to assist individuals, is an action for damages where loss has been suffered as a result of the action or act of the Community, which can be made under Art 288 (ex 215) (2). However, where legislative acts are concerned, the damage must be the result of a sufficiently serious breach of a superior rule of law for the protection of an individual, something which has been demonstrated in the case law of the Court of Justice to be extremely difficult to prove.

All of the above actions take place before the Court of Justice.

As far as the Member States and the national courts are concerned, individuals can defend their rights arising from Community law generally in the national courts against the inconsistent legislation of the Member States and where Member States have failed to implement EC law and seek to prosecute individuals for breaches of national law; see the *Van Gend en Loos* (26/62), *Ratti* (148/78), *Francovich* (C-6 & 9/90) and *Factortame* (C-213/89 and C-46 & 48/93) cases. The latter cases highlight the developments by which an individual can sue a Member State where he or she has suffered damage which was the result of the Member State's breach of Community law.

Individuals can also defend rights against Community law provisions if these unlawfully affect individual rights by infringing fundamental rights of the individual. Fundamental rights for the protection of individuals can be brought into play in the course of any of the procedural actions to enforce individual rights in substantive areas of Community law. These have been recognised by the Court of Justice because they are contained in many of the Member States' constitutions, and the European Convention for the Protection of Human and Fundamental Rights has also been held by the Court of Justice to apply in the Community legal order and Art 6(2) (ex F2) of the Treaty on European Union now obliges the Community to conform to it. The intergovernmental conference in 2000 considered but postponed the decision to include a Community catalogue of human rights for the next revision of the Treaties, therefore the rights protection for individuals may be increased in the future.

In support of all of these actions and before the national courts individuals may, if necessary, request that a reference to the Court of Justice be made using the preliminary ruling procedure of Art 234 (ex 177) of the EC Treaty. It is through this that leading principles of Community law have been developed by the ECJ and which have greatly enhanced the protection of individual rights in the Community. One only has to consider the cases of *van Gend en Loos* (26/62) or *Francovich* (C-6 & 9/90) to see how the ECJ has secured the rights of individuals.

In conclusion the development of direct effects in actions before the national courts may be regarded as far more successful than the use of direct actions before the Court of Justice and potentially more useful, in respect of Member State's breaches, is the action to claim damages from the Member State for loss under the *Francovich*-type actions.

QUESTION 3

On 1 May 1996 the Council adopted a Directive concerned with the protection of young persons in employment. The Directive, inter alia, provides that no person under 18 years old shall be required to work at night, and that any such person who is dismissed by his/her employer for refusing to work at night when requested to do so shall be entitled to 'an appropriate remedy from a national court or tribunal, which may include compensation'. Member States were given one year in which to implement the Directive.

The British government was opposed to the Directive on ideological grounds and actually voted against its adoption in the Council, where the Directive, in accordance with the Treaty provision on which it was based, was adopted by a qualified majority vote. For this reason, and because it is concerned by the possibly adverse economic consequences of the Directive for employers, the British government has not yet taken any steps to implement the Directive.

Jake, who is 17 years old, has been employed in a Ministry of Defence munitions factory for 12 months. As a consequence of the need to reduce the size of the manufacturing facility and economise on production, Jake has been asked to work at night on the newly established night shift. Not wishing to ruin a happy social life, Jake has refused to do so. As a result he has been threatened with dismissal unless he complies.

Advise:

(a)   The Commission of what steps it can take against the United Kingdom to ensure that the Directive is implemented.

(b)   Jake as to whether he can take legal proceedings to uphold his legal position and obtain compensation if dismissed.

Would your advice to Jake differ if the factory where he worked was in private ownership?

For the purposes of this question, you should ignore actual Directive 94/33!

Commentary

This problem question requires you to consider two main judicial procedures. The first one involves a consideration of an Art 226 (ex 169) action by the Commission against the Member State for a failure to implement the Directive. The second one concentrates on Jake's ability to take action in the national courts using an Art 234 (ex 177) reference to the ECJ if necessary.

Apart from a brief discussion of the procedure involved in the two particular actions, the substantive issues which arise in the problem must also be considered.

First, it is necessary to determine whether there has been a breach by the UK or whether they can rely on any defence for their lack of action. Secondly, it must be determined whether Jake can rely on the direct effects of the Directive and whether there is a remedy he can seek, both to defend himself against the threatened dismissal or to obtain damages from the employer, if dismissed.

You are also asked to consider the situation where the employer is a private employer and this requires a discussion of horizontal direct effects and the consequences for employees of private employers. You should then follow this with suggestions of how these difficulties may be overcome by Jake.

Suggested Answer

The UK government was given, along with the other Member States, one year to implement the Directive. That year expired on 1 May 1997. In the circumstances, the Commission would be entitled to commence a formal Article 226 (ex 169) action, if behind the scenes persuasion failed to convince the UK that it should implement the Directive in full. Article 226 (ex 169) states: 'If the Commission considers that a Member State has failed to fulfil an obligation under this Treaty, it shall deliver a reasoned opinion on the matter'. The Commission will inform the state and give the state the opportunity to answer the allegation or correct its action or inaction before the Art 226 (ex 169) action continues. Following the reply from the Member State or after a reasonable time where no reply is received, the Commission will then deliver a reasoned opinion which records the reasons for the failure of the Member State. If the state should then fail to comply with the reasoned opinion of the Commission within a reasonable time, the Commission has the discretionary right to bring the matter before the Court of Justice. The judgment of the Court of Justice is merely declaratory but the Member State is required under Art 228 (ex 171) to take the necessary measures to comply with the judgment.

There would appear to be no defence that could be raised by the UK that would justify its non-compliance, as Art 10 (ex 5) EC requires Member States to fulfil all Community law obligations and Art 292 (ex 219) obliges Member States not to seek other solutions to disputes. The UK should therefore comply and implement the Directive.

If it does not do this, a further action may lie against the UK, by the Commission under Art 226 (ex 169), for a breach of Art 228 (ex 171). Following the coming into force of the Treaty on European Union, Arts 228 and 229 (ex 171 and 172) provide that sanctions can be requested by the Commission in an action to establish that the Member States have failed to comply with a previous judgment of the Court of Justice. Thus, if the UK has still failed to implement the Directive and the further action to establish that it also failed to comply with the Court of Justice has taken place, the UK may be fined by the Court of Justice. It is, however, extremely unlikely that the matter would go so far and it is more likely that the UK will have complied either before the first action or, at the latest, after the judgment of the Court of Justice in the first action.

Turning to Jake, he is advised either to seek an action in the UK industrial tribunal to prevent the employer from dismissing him, basing his right to refuse to work nights on the EC Directive, or to commence an action for compensation for unfair dismissal in the event of his dismissal. In order, however, to rely on Community law, it must either have been implemented in the UK, which it has not been, or give rise to direct effects.

Directives can give rise to direct effects providing they satisfy the criteria as laid down in *Van Gend* (26/62) and subsequent cases. The criteria are that in order for a particular provision of Community law to be upheld before a national court in the face of non-implementation, or incorrect implementation of national law, the provisions have to be clear, precise, they should leave no discretion to the authorities of the Member State, they must be unconditional and require no further implementation by either the Community or the Member State. The special concerns of Directives and the time limits given for their implementation were considered in *Pubblico Ministero* v *Ratti* (148/78) which concerned the prosecution by the Italian authorities for breaches of national law concerning product labelling. Ratti had complied with two Community Directives the expiry period for implementation of one of which had not expired. The Court held that he could rely on the one for which the time period had expired provided it satisfied the other requirements, but not for the Directive whose implementation period had not expired. So, when the time period for implementation has expired an individual can rely on a Directive providing it fulfils the other criteria.

In the present case, the obligation states quite clearly that no person under 18 years shall be required to work at night and the time period of one year for implementation has expired, therefore the Directive has direct effects which can be relied on by Jake to avoid dismissal. If, however, he has been dismissed, the Directive provides that an appropriate remedy must be provided. Whilst not as clear as the first part, it has been held in *von Colson* (14/83) and the second *Marshall* ([1988] 3 CMLR 389) cases that the Member States' courts are required to ensure that an adequate remedy, in this case compensation, must be awarded. Jake will thus be entitled to receive adequate damages.

The advice to Jake would differ if the factory where he worked was in private ownership, because in the case of *Marshall* (152/84), the ECJ held that Directives could not be enforced against other individuals but could only be enforced vertically against the state to whom they were addressed, i.e., there are no horizontal direct effects stemming from the Directive. Jake would have to try pleading the principle under *von Colson*. The ECJ held in *von Colson* that, although a Directive may not be horizontally directly effective, the Member States' courts should take the provisions of the Directive into account when applying national law. However, as there are no rights in national law, a national court cannot interpret according to EC law. In these circumstances, the *Marleasing* (C-106/89) and *Kolpinghuis* (80/86) cases should be applied which state that there are general obligations under Arts 10 and 249 (ex 5 and 189) of the Treaty for the Member States to ensure compliance with Community law. But if the UK court was unable or unwilling to rely on national legislation to interpret, Jake might have to attempt suing the state to obtain damages under the principle established in the *Francovich* case (C-6 & 9/90) for liability arising from the failure to implement a Directive. If an individual suffers damage as a result of the failure of a Member State to implement a Directive, the Member State may be liable to pay damages, providing the Directive itself defined and conferred a right on individuals, the content of which was clear.

This principle appears to be satisfied in the present case. Furthermore, the court held in *Brasserie du Pêcheur* (C-46 & 48/93) that all manner of breaches of Community law by all three arms of state could lead to liability to individuals. Thus it expands the circumstances which might give rise to liability in cases where otherwise there would be no enforceable rights because there is either no horizontal direct effect or even no direct effect at all. But the focus has been moved to the seriousness of the breach. *Factortame III* (C-46 and 48/93) introduced the revised criteria that the breach must be analogous to that applied to liability of the EC institutions under Art 288 (old 215) (2). This is known as the Shöppenstedt Formula and in order for liability to arise on the part of the Member State, there must have been a sufficiently serious breach of a superior rule of law designed for the protection of individuals. This has provoked further case law to help decide how serious a breach is required for Member States to incur liability. *British Telecom* (C-392/93) takes a generous view of what constitutes a breach but this can be contrasted with the *Hedley Lomas* case (C-5/94) where a mere infringement will invoke potential liability. Thus, if there is a breach, Member States must compensate according to the principles established in *Francovich*. Finally, damages must be adequate to reflect the loss suffered. It may be concluded that there appears to be sufficient alternative possibilities for Jake to receive some form of compensation against a private employer for the unlawful dismissal.

QUESTION 4

On 20 October 1999, the Council adopted a Regulation, to take effect on 1 January 2000, under which the sales of sugar beet to food and drinks manufacturers were to be subsidised in order to reduce the Community's sugar mountain. Sweetness Ltd is an aspartamine (an artificial sweetener) manufacturer and fears that the business will suffer as a result of this subsidy.

On 10 November 1999, Sweetness Ltd wrote to the Council asking it to withdraw the Regulation on the ground that in adopting the Regulation, the Council had failed to observe the principle of non-discrimination in Art 34(2) of the EC Treaty.

On 5 January 2000 the Council replied to Sweetness Ltd saying it understood why Sweetness Ltd was aggrieved but considered there was no alternative but to adopt the Regulation.

The next day Sweetness Ltd wrote to the Commission asking it to bring an action against the Council under Art 230. Two weeks later the Commission replied to Sweetness Ltd saying that it did not consider the Council to be in breach of the EC Treaty.

What actions, if any, can Sweetness Ltd take against either the Commission or the Council before the Court of Justice?

Commentary

This question requires you to consider the possible actions which may be attempted by the applicant arising from the factual circumstances. The problem which can be identified and which has caused Sweetness Ltd to take action is the passing of a Community Regulation which provides subsidies for sugar sales. Thus you need to outline the problem and the possible remedies which may be available and then go through those possible actions in turn, commenting on the chances that the individual may have under each one. In the light of the fact that there is very limited factual information supplied, many of the courses of action will be somewhat speculative, however you should still give at least an outline of them and the problems arising and reasons why the action is likely to be unsuccessful.

Suggested Answer

The problem, as far as Sweetness Ltd is concerned, is that a Community Regulation has been passed which provides subsidies for the sale of sugar. The effect will be to reduce the price of sugar and thus increase its competitiveness, particularly in relation to manufacturers of artificial sweeteners who will probably lose sales and profits as a result. The informal moves Sweetness has made have been of no success, therefore the possibilities of the following formal actions must be considered.

Before the Court of Justice the possible actions are: a direct challenge to the Regulation as an act of the institutions under Art 230 (ex 173) or a challenge to the letters written by the Council and Commission; an action under Art 232 (ex 175) requiring the Council to remove the Regulation; an action under Art 232 (ex 175) requiring the Commission to take action against the Council; an action under Art 241 (ex 184), the indirect challenge to Community Regulations; and an action for damages under Art 288 (ex 215) (2).

(a)   The action under 230 (ex 173) to challenge the Regulation.

Overcoming the admissibility hurdle in respect of time limits and *locus standi* are the biggest stumbling blocks with this action. Art 230 (ex 173) imposes a two month time limit in which actions should be taken. The Regulation was passed on 20 October and the earliest date that a possible legal challenge by Sweetness Ltd could be made is 20 January given that the letter to the Commission was written on 6 January and the reply was written two weeks later. This is three months after the Regulation was enacted and thus outside the time limit. Even with the allowance of the Court of Justice from its rules of procedure of a further 15 days, it will still be too late. An action under Art 230 (ex 173) will therefore be inadmissible without the need to discuss the difficulties of individuals challenging Regulations.

Sweetness would not be able to challenge the letters written by the Commission and Council under Art 230 (ex 173) as they are not reviewable acts within the meaning of Art 230 (ex 173) unless they can be shown to alter the legal position of the company; see the *Noordwijks Cement Accord* case (8–11/66). On the facts, there is no alteration of the company's legal position which remains the same.

(b)   An action under Art 232 (ex 175) requiring the Council to remove the Regulation.

This is also doomed to failure because of the strict *locus standi* requirements imposed by the Treaty. Individuals can only challenge acts which could and should have been addressed to them. As Regulations are normative acts they cannot be addressed to individuals; see *Lord Bethell* v *Commission* (246/81) and *Holtz* v *Council* (134/73). Trying to plead that the matter is nevertheless of direct and individual concern will only help if it can be shown that the Regulation would have directly and individually concerned the applicant (*T. Port* C-68/95). Regulations do not directly and individually concern individuals. Furthermore, where the Council has written and advised that it has decided to do nothing, this definition of position by the Council would satisfy the terms of Art 232 (ex 175) even if an action by the individual were admissible and the action would be consequently dismissed.

(c)   An action under Art 232 (ex 175) requiring the Commission to take action.

An individual cannot force the Commission to take Art 230 (ex 173) proceedings as the Commission has a discretion under the terms of the Article. Again the action would fail because Sweetness would be seeking the adoption of an act which it was not entitled to claim; see *Mackprang* v *Commission* (15/71). Even if the action were admissible, the Commission has defined its position and thus brought an end to the proceedings; see *Lütticke* (48/65).

(d)   A challenge under Art 241 (ex 184) to Community Regulations.

This would also be rejected by the Court if it was made directly and not in the course of some other proceedings before the Court of Justice (see *Wöhrmann* v *Commission* (31 & 33/62). It might be done in the course of the final possible action against the Council or Commission for damages.

(e)   An action for damages under Art 288 (ex 215) (2).

The Court of Justice is given jurisdiction under Art 235 (ex 178) to consider actions for damages brought by individuals under Art 288 (ex 215) (2). However, in order to be successful a number of criteria have been identified which must be fulfilled. These are that an act or omission on the part of the institutions must be shown to have caused damage to the applicants. Furthermore in cases which involve a legislative act, necessarily involving a choice of economic policy on the part of the Community, a sufficiently serious breach of a superior rule of law for the protection of individuals must be shown; see the *Schöppenstedt* case (5/71).

In the present case the superior rule of law for the protection of individuals is the principle of non-discrimination and there is even a Treaty Article which requires that there be no discrimination between suppliers, *viz.*, Art 34(2) (ex 40(3)) which has been pleaded by the applicants. In the *Gritz* and *Quellmehl (Dumortier Frères)* cases (64 and 113/76), the ending of the subsidy was held to be a breach of the principle of non-discrimination because it was retained on starch which was in direct competition.

The next requirement to ascertain whether the breach is sufficiently serious. Sufficiently serious has been defined as 'manifest and grave' (*HNL* case (83/76)), and further as 'verging on the arbitrary' (*KSH Isoglucose* case (143/77)). A breach of the rule on its own is not enough. In order to determine whether the breach was sufficiently serious a number of criteria must be considered. Things to look at are the nature and the effect of the breach. For example, in the *Gritz* and *Quellmehl* cases the Court looked at the numbers affected, and the extent of the loss suffered and the seriousness of the damage caused, i.e., is it far beyond the risks normally associated with business? However, in *Mulder* (C-104/89 & 37/90) the presence of a large group of claimants did not defeat a claim, although it still had to be demonstrated that there was a serious breach and that there was no higher public interest of the Community.

In the *HNL* case, which concerned the requirement to buy milk products rather than soya products, the increase in production costs was limited. The Court of Justice considered whether the company could pass on the increases with little loss of profit. If the company was not able to do so, this suggested that the breach was serious, but if it could pass on the increase then the breach was not sufficiently serious. The damage must go beyond the risks normally associated with business, but in the *KSH Isoglucose* case (143/77) although the damage was beyond normal, including causing the liquidation of some of the companies involved, the breach was not flagrant and therefore not verging on the arbitrary. The damage sustained must also be a direct consequence of an action or omission of the Community.

In the *Sofrimport* case (C-152/88) involving the import of Chilean apples which were on the high seas when the Regulation took effect, the Court of Justice held that it would look at the number of people affected, the degree of loss and, most importantly, whether there was a Community interest involved. The *Sofrimport* case was held to involve a closed group because no other could be similarly affected after the date of the Regulation.

In this case it is unlikely that the breach will go beyond that which is considered to be an inherent business risk, in the light of the judgment in the *KSH Isoglucose* case. In this case the Community interest in reducing the sugar mountain may be considered to outweigh the losses caused.

The action may give an opportunity to challenge the Regulation indirectly, outside the time limits under Art 241 (ex 184), because it has breached the principle of non-discrimination under Art 34(2) (ex 40(3)), which would satisfy the requirements of Art 241 (ex 184). The substantive grounds from Art 230 (ex 173) are employed. If the Court of Justice, despite the previously expressed view of the Commission, held it to be in breach of the Treaty, it will hold the Regulation to be voidable and inapplicable in the case. So, despite the fact that the Regulation may be held inapplicable, damages may still not be payable as the breach may still not satisfy the test of being sufficiently serious; see *HNL* v *Council and Commission* (83/76).

The final possibility is that, if there is a national element to the case and an action is taking place in the national courts, the company may raise the possibility of the Regulation being unlawful and ask for a reference to be made from the national court to the Court of Justice under Art 234 (ex 177) to question the validity of the Regulation. However, it is still up to the Court of Justice to decide whether the Regulation has breached Art 34 (ex 40) and the same considerations as have already been noted will apply.

QUESTION 5

Prior to the General Election and in view of increasing concern about the numbers of migrant workers taking up employment in the UK, the Government introduced an Act of Parliament under which it temporarily suspended the right of foreign workers to enter the UK to take up employment. The Act says that it applies regardless of any provision of the European Communities

Act 1972. Arturo, an Italian, was appointed to a post in a hospital just before the Act came into force. He was refused entry to the UK to take up his post. He applies to the High Court for a declaration that he is entitled to enter the UK and that the UK legislation is incompatible with EC law. He also complains to the Commission, who notify the UK Government that they consider them to be in breach by having introduced their law in contravention of Art 39 of the Treaty. The Commission has received many complaints from others in the same situation as Arturo, who have now been told that unless they can take up employment within two weeks their jobs will be re-advertised.

Comment on the following issues:

(a)   What is necessary on the part of the Commission to bring an action under Art 226 to an effective conclusion in securing the UK Government's compliance with EC law?

(b)   What arguments in defence can be advanced by the UK Government?

(c)   What remedies are available to Arturo and how effective are they likely to be in securing his rights?

(d)   What additional measures could be requested in the course of proceedings by the Commission and Arturo?

(e)   Would your answers to (a) and (c) differ if the UK Government had already been declared to be in breach following Art 226 proceedings in respect of the new UK law?

Commentary

This is a slightly tricky question in that it is a hybrid question consisting of a problem to be solved but set in a series of questions. As with other questions in this chapter it also covers a number of the judicial actions in the Community legal order. The question also includes the supremacy of EC law in the UK legal order. Due to these aspects, the structure you need to have for your answer has been pretty much set by the question itself.

You should start with a brief overview of the factual issues arising from the text of the question which need to be addressed and then in turn each of the questions posed should be answered. Inevitably, as you are being asked to provide information on a number of topics your answers will be brief, for the most part. Thus, the Commission enforcement action should be outlined, followed by the possible defences of the UK Government. Arturo's own possible remedies should then be outlined and a view taken on each of the above as to how effective you think the various actions and remedies are. Point (d) asks you to suggest additional measures. This implies interim measures. Finally, you are asked to address a slight alternative whereby the Commission has already been successful in obtaining a declaration from the ECJ that the UK is in breach of its Treaty obligation. You are asked to consider whether this would make a difference to either the Commission or Arturo.

Suggested Answer

There is a UK national statute stating that no more foreign workers will be accepted into the UK which appears to be in breach of the UK Community law obligation of Art 39 (ex 48) EC. It also states that it applies regardless of the ECA 1972, which then is seeking to protect itself from interpretation or construction by the ECA 1972. Arturo has been appointed to a position before the Act came into force but was refused entry to the UK. He has applied to a national court for a declaration that the UK is in breach of EC law and has complained to the Commission to encourage them to take action.

(a) The Art 226 (ex 169) action by the Commission

The Commission as a part of its duties under Art 211 (ex 155) should guard the Treaty. There would certainly be an Art 226 (ex 169) action open to the Commission against the UK for failing to comply with its Community law obligations under Arts 10 (ex 5) and 39 (ex 48).

Basically there are four stages of an Art 226 (ex 169) action:

1.   Suspicion of the infringement and informal proceedings by the Commission.

2.   Informing the Member State by formal notice and asking it to submit its observations.

3.   The formal issue of a reasoned opinion containing legal arguments, after the Commission has considered there is a breach.

4.   If the Commission considers that the member state is not in compliance the matter would be submitted to the ECJ which would eventually be concluded by a judgment of the ECJ.

In view of the serious and blatant nature of the breach by the UK in this case, it is all but certain that the ECJ would declare a breach of EC law by the UK (see *Commission v UK (Re: Nationality of Fishermen)* (C-246/89)). A Member State is under a duty under Art 228 (ex 171) to comply with the judgment of the ECJ but if the Member State fails to comply and breaches this duty, it can only be remedied by another Art 226 (ex 169) action to try to get the Member State to comply.

The drawbacks of such action are that an Art 226 (ex 169) process from start of judicial proceedings before the ECJ to judgment can take anything from 18 months to two or three years or longer depending on the outcome and how quickly the Member State responds and reacts to the various stages of the procedure or the judgment. In total with both actions, it could take five years and potentially longer. However, at the end of this process this time, the Member State can be fined under Art 229 (ex 172) by the ECJ for a breach of its obligations. The Commission action under Art 226 (ex 169) will be effective in the long run, if not in the short term, as most Member States do comply with judgment of the ECJ and so far fines have been needed to be levied only once in *Commission v Greece* (C-387/97). So the action is ultimately likely to secure compliance with Community law.

(b)   Arguments of UK Government

Under the EC Treaty, as amended by the Treaty of Amsterdam, there are no specific rules which could be seized on by the UK and only general arguments to defend an alleged breach of a Community law obligation. These have been comprehensively rebutted by the ECJ in its case law. All sorts of argument have been put forward in the past. Few seem particularly relevant here. Perhaps, a defence from international law of economic necessity but this was rejected in *Commission v Italy* (Art Treasures case) (48/71). The only real defence to succeed is that there was no breach on the facts or where the defence fits into exemptions allowed in the Treaty, e.g., Art 39 (ex 48) (3) or (4). This does not appear to be the case here.

(c)   What remedies are available to Arturo?

He may notify the Commission in the hope that they take action, which he has already done but, possibly more effective, are actions he can take on his own behalf.

First of all, he can seek to rely on the direct effects of Art 39 (ex 48), which we know previously from the *Van Duyn* case (41/74) does give rise to direct effects.

Arturo has already commenced an action in the UK courts by an application to the High Court in which he has challenged the UK rules. If the UK court is reluctant to recognise the direct effects, he should request a reference to the ECJ under Art 234 (ex 177). However, both the attempt to rely on direct effects and getting a reference to the ECJ depends on the cooperation of the High Court in recognising the supremacy of EC law over UK and applying it in the face of the UK Act which states it is not subject to the ECA interpretation. The question here would be whether the UK court would follow EC law or national law. If the Court follows the lead of the House of Lords in *Factortame* ([1991] 1 AC 603) the answer should be yes, in which case direct effects would be recognised and Arturo would be able to rely on them to secure entry to the UK and his post in the UK. If the court is not prepared to follow EC law and acts in accordance with the obiter dicta of Lord Denning in the case of *MacCarthys* v *Smith* ([1979] ICR 785), then Arturo will have trouble. In this case, Lord Denning considered that with regard to an express or intentional repudiation of the Treaty or expressly acting inconsistently, the courts would be bound to follow the express and clear intent of Parliament to repudiate the Treaty or a section of it by the subsequent Act. In which case, Arturo would be obliged to request that national law be interpreted according to EC law along *von Colson* (14/83) guidelines and, if this is also refused, he should request for an Art 234 (ex 177) reference. However, the reality would be that if the court was inclined to apply UK law in preference to EC law, then it would not be likely to want to make an Art 234 (ex 177) reference and the matter ends there for Arturo. It would really be down to the judges' views in the UK court and, as this has not yet been tested in a UK Court, it would be pure speculation.

If direct effects were not recognised and upheld, Arturo is likely to loose his job and would thus be put in a position of having suffered loss. There would then be the question of whether Arturo and other persons in a similar position to him could recover damages from the UK authorities. The case of *Francovich* (C-6 & 9/90) would be then applicable here. This referred to the failure to implement a Directive which gave rise to liability to give damages. But a difference here exists in that it is not the absence of any implementing measures but that national law is in conflict. Does *Francovich* apply to such situations? Yes, and it is arguably a stronger case where there has been a breach of a Treaty Article, as confirmed by the *Brasserie du Pecheur* and

Factortame III cases (C-46 & 48/93) that an action for damages lies against all breaches by a state of community law obligations but subject to further criteria. The breach must be analogous to that applied to liability of the EC institutions under Art 288 (old 215) (2). This is known as the Shöppenstedt Formula and in order for liability to arise on the part of the Member State there must have been a sufficiently serious breach of a superior rule of law designed for the protection of individuals. In our case, the breach is quite blatant and it is argued that all the criteria are satisfied here. The breach would seem to be sufficiently serious (see the *Hedley Lomas* case C-5/94).

But at the end of the day what does this secure for Arturo? The national courts must entertain this action or make a reference to the ECJ if in doubt. Certainly the new Act does not preclude the national courts from following EC law with regard to a *Francovich* action and it is likely therefore that Arturo would be successful in obtaining compensation, but not the job.

The Community law answer would be that the UK court should disapply the application of the UK law, with or without an interim order from the ECJ, whilst the substantive action is going on, to determine whether the UK law is contrary to EC law. This would of course be answered that it is not.

(d)   Additional measures

Interim measures could be asked for by the Commission in this action under Art 243 (ex 186). The ECJ may prescribe any necessary interim measures in any case before it. They have been used in Art 226 (ex 169) actions in the past. See in particular *Commission* v *UK (Re: Nationality of Fishermen) (Factortame)* (246/89R). The interim measures then would be the order to suspend the national legislation in doubt.

The same would count in Arturo's case. If a reference was being made to the Court of Justice, then interim measures, i.e., an injunction to suspend the allegedly unlawful measures by the UK Government, could be requested.

(e)   Prior Article 226 proceedings

If there had already been a successful Art 226 (ex 169) action by the Commission then the subsequent Commission action to secure compliance would certainly be at least two years further ahead so it would speed up the eventual compliance by the UK. It would not affect the inevitable result, however.

Again, whilst probably not affecting the result, from the EC point of view with Arturo, it would certainly make clear to the national courts what the outcome should be.

The final conclusion is that both actions are likely to be effective but that the national court action and Art 234 (ex 177) reference are potentially quicker, unless there is outright intransigence on the part of the UK judiciary and they refuse to either apply EC law or make a reference to the ECJ. Thus far, however, the UK judges have not been given the opportunity to do this.

Bibliography

A limited and selective list only of standard texts on EC law is provided here. For more extensive reading, consult the texts listed.

Craig and de Búrca, *EC Law: Text, Cases and Materials* 2nd ed. (Oxford: Oxford University Press, 1998).

Ellis and Tridimas, *Public Law of the European Community: Text, Materials and Commentary* (London: Sweet & Maxwell, 1995).

Foster (ed.), *EC Legislation*, 11th ed. (London: Blackstone Press, 2000).

Foster, *EC Law (SWOT)*, 3rd ed. (London: Blackstone Press, 2000).

Hartley, *The Foundations of European Community Law*, 4th ed. (Oxford: Clarendon Press, 1998).

Kapteyn and van Themaat (Gormley, ed.) *Introduction to the Law of the European Communities*, 3rd ed. (Deventer: Kluwer, 1998).

Kennedy, *Learning European Law* (London: Sweet & Maxwell, 1998).

Korah, *EC Competition Law and Practice*, 6th ed. (Oxford: Hart Publishing, 1997).

Lasok and Bridge, *Law and Institutions of the European Communities*, 7th ed. (London: Butterworths, 1994).

Nielsen and Szyszczak, *The Social Dimension of the European Community*, 3rd ed. (Copenhagen: Handelshojskolens Forlag, 1997).

Rudden and Phelan, *Basic Community Cases*, 2nd ed. (Oxford: Oxford University Press, 1997).

Steiner and Woods, *Textbook on EC Law*, 7th ed. (London: Blackstone Press, 2000).

Tillotson, *European Union Law: Text, Cases and Materials*, 3rd ed. (London: Cavendish Publishing Limited, 2000).

Ward, *A Critical Introduction to European Law* (London: Butterworths, 1996).

Weatherill, *Cases and Materials on EC Law*, 5th ed. (London: Blackstone Press, 2000).

Weatherill, *Law and Integration in the European Union* (Oxford: Clarendon Press, 1995).

Weatherill and Beaumont, *EC Law*, 3rd ed. (London: Penguin Books, 1999).

Wyatt & Dashwood, *European Union Law*, 4th ed. (London: Sweet & Maxwell, 2000).

Index

Abuse of dominant position   173, 174, 175, 179, 180–2, 186–90
Acquisitions *see* Concentrations
Actions
  admissibility
    challenging decisions or Regulations
      (Art.230)   87–8, 91–5, 226–7
    damages actions (Art.235)   96
  Art.226 *see* failure to comply with
    obligations (Art.226)
  Art.228 sanction request   79–80
  Art.229 sanction request   79
  Art.230 *see* challenging decisions or
    Regulations (Art.230)
  Art.232 *see* failure to act (Art.232)
  Art.234 *see* referrals (Art.234)
  Art.235 *see* damages actions (Art.235)
  Art.241 *see* plea of illegality (Art.241)
  Art.244 interim measures   80
  Art.288 *see* wrongful adoption of acts
    (Art.288)
  challenging decisions or Regulations
    (Art.230)   86–91
    admissibility   87–8, 91–5, 226–7
    direct and individual concern tests
      93–4
    locus standi   226–7
    merits or substance of action   88, 89,
      94
    Regulations   87–8, 91–5, 219, 225–9
    time limits   92–3, 226
  commencement of procedure   77–8
  Court refusal to accept reference   103–7
  damages actions (Art.235)   95–9

Actions – *continued*
  admissibility   96
  ascertainability of damage   98–9
  dependent actions   96
  locus standi   96
  manifest and grave   98
  seriousness of breach   97–8
  severity of damage   98
  superior rule of law   97
  time limits   96
  damages actions (Art.288)   227–9
    comparisons with Art.235   95–9
    locus standi   100
    manifest and grave   228
    seriousness of breach   101–2, 103,
      228–9
    superior rule of law   101, 102–3
  ensuring compliance (Art 169)   77–81
    effectiveness   79–80
  failure to act (Art.232)   111–14, 219
    definition of position   113, 114
    duty to act   112
    explanation of refusal to act   113
    individuals   112
    invitation to act   113
    locus standi   112, 226–7
    time limits   113
  failure to comply with Directive
    arguments of state   232
    Commission action   231–2
    delays   232, 235
    interim measures   234
    prior Art 226 proceedings   234–5
    remedies   232–4

Actions – *continued*
  failure to comply with obligations
      (Art.226)
    defences from member states   81–6
    ensuring compliance   77–81
    individuals   80, 84–6, 221–3
    reasoned opinions   78
    time limits   223
    see also failure to comply with
        Directive; failure to implement
        Directive
  failure to implement Directive   221–3,
      231–5
    compensation   233–4
    conditions for state liability   231–2
  individuals, actions of   84–6, 216–20
    failure to act (Art.232)   112–13
    in national courts   80, 219–20, 223–5
  interim measures (Art.244)   80
  jurisdiction   75–117
  locus standi
    challenging decisions or Regulations
        (Art.230)   86–95, 226–7
    damages actions (Art.235)   96
    failure to act (Art.232)   112, 226–7
    plea of illegality (Art.241)   116
    wrongful adoption of acts damages
        (Art.288)   100
  national courts   80, 219–20, 223–5
  migrant workers   231–5
  non-privileged applicants   86, 92
  penalty payments   79–80
  plea of illegality (Art.241)   115–17, 227
    locus standi   116
    time limits   116–17, 229
  preliminary ruling procedure
      (Art.234)   103–7
  reasoned opinions, failure to comply
      with   78
  referrals (Art.234)   107–11
    obligation or discretion to refer   110
    recognition of court   108
    refusal to accept   103–7
  requests for sanctions   79–80
  seriousness of breach   97–8, 228–9
  superior rule of law
    damages actions (Art.235)   97
    wrongful adoption of acts
        (Art.288)   101
  time limits
    challenging decisions or Regulations
        92–3, 226
    damages actions   96
    failure to act   113

Actions – *continued*
  failure to comply with obligations
      223
    plea of illegality   116–17, 229
    refusal to accept reference   105–6
  wrongful adoption of acts (Art.288)
      99–103, 227–9
    breach of duty   100
    breach of superior rule   101, 102–3
    choice of court   100–1
    damages
      comparisons with Art.235   95–9
      locus standi   100
      manifest and grave   228
      seriousness of breach   101–2, 103,
          228–9
    locus standi requirements   100
    manifest and grave   101
    numbers of people affected   102
    seriousness of breach   101–2, 103,
        228–9
    superior rule of law   101, 102–3
    see also Defences
Acts, wrongful adoption *see* Actions,
    wrongful adoption of actions (Art.288)
Administrative tribunals   108–10
Admissibility
  challenging decisions or Regulations
      (Art.230)   87–8, 91–5, 226–7
  damages actions (Art.235)   96
Advertising
  government sponsored   124
  national rules   124
Advocates General
  law-making   26–31
  nationality   34
  numbers   27
  reasoned opinions   27–8, 78
  role   27, 28
  see also Court of Justice
Agreements
  competition law *see* Competition law
  international *see* International agreements
Arbitration tribunal   108–10
Architects, *see also* Professionals
Assembly *see* Parliament

Belgium Bar, admission to   161
Belgium courts, supremacy and   71
Block exemptions   169, 170–1, 187
Budgetary procedure
  contributions   8–9
  Council role   19–20
  Parliament role   19–20, 21

Cassis de Dijon case   118, 119, 122, 128,
       129, 132, 134–40
Challenging decisions or Regulations
       (Art.230)   86–91
    admissibility   87–8, 91–5, 226–7
    direct and individual concern tests   93–4
    locus standi   226–7
    merits or substance of action   88, 89, 94
    Regulations   87–8, 91–5, 219, 225–9
    time limits   92–3, 226
Co-decision procedure   17, 18, 19, 21–2
Cohabitees of workers   145, 149, 157–8
Commercial property exception   121, 137
Commission   13
    actions for failure to act (Art.232)
       111–14
    competition law investigation   182–6
    legal base   23
    legislation proposals   16
    membership   16
Committee of the Regions   23
Common Agricultural Policy   9, 20
Common customs tariff   120
Commonwealth ties   7, 8
Community law
    compliance with *see* Actions
    direct effects *see* Direct effects
    public sector and   44–6
    sources *see* Sources of law
    supremacy *see* Supremacy of Community
       law
Companionship right (social advantage)
       145, 149, 150, 157–8
Competition law   13, 164–90
    activities of business undertakings   167
    activities of States   167
    agreements between parties   172, 173,
       179, 186–90
    antidumping measures   167
    application of rules   167
    artificial barriers   167
    associated undertakings   172, 173, 179,
       186–90
    basis   165–6
    block exemptions   169, 170–1, 187
    branches of non-EC companies   172–7
    complaints   184
    concerted practices   170, 172, 173, 174,
       179, 180, 187
    dominant position abuse   174, 175, 179,
       180–2, 186–90
    exclusive distribution agreement
       168–72
    geographic market   175, 181

Competition law – *continued*
    internal market and   166
    interpretation   167
    investigations   182–6
       complaints   184
       disclosure of informants   184–6
       duty to assist   185
       failure to comply   185
       information requests   184
       notification of agreements   184
       powers and duties of Commission
          183, 184
       professional privilege   185–6
       right of entry   184–5
    mergers   173, 176–82, 188–90
    notification of agreements   184
    overview   165–8
    pricing agreements   171, 176, 177–82
    reasons for   166
    restrictive practices   173, 187
    selective distribution agreement   171–2
    vertical distribution agreements   179–80
Compliance
    Art.226 defences   81–6
    Art.226 procedure   77–81
    Art.228 sanction request   79–80
    Art.229 sanction request   79
    Art.244 interim measures   80
    defences *see* Defences
    penalty payments   79–80
Concentrations   173, 176–82, 188–90
Concerted practices   170, 172, 173, 174,
       179, 180, 187
Conciliation procedure   17, 18–19, 23–4
Confidentiality, competition investigations
       185–6
Conseil D'Etat   74
Consultation process   16–17, 18, 23–4
Consumer protection   20
    free movement of goods exception
       128–30
Cooperation procedure   6–7, 17, 18, 24
Council of Europe   7
Council of Ministers   13
    actions for failure to act (Art.232)
       111–14
    budget procedures   19–20
    complaint by Parliament (Art.232)   114
    democracy   21–2, 26
    duties   15
    efficiency   20–1
    federal institution   14–17
    legal base   23, 24–5
    legislation role   15, 18

Council of Ministers – *continued*
  main tasks 15
  membership 15
Cour de Cassation 73
Court of Justice 13
  democratic process 26
  general function 27–8
  House of Lords and 68–70
  individuals and 89, 90–1
  interpretation 28, 103–6, 144, 196
  jurisdiction 75–117
  law-making role 29–31
  legal bases 25–6
  membership 27
  new legal order 54, 57–8, 60–1, 66
  precedent 29
  preliminary ruling procedure 103–7
  reasoned opinions 27–8, 78
  referrals 54, 80–1, 107–11, 220
    acceptable reference 109
    obligation or discretion to refer 110
    recognition of referring court 108
    see also refusal to accept reference
  refusal to accept reference
    abuse of procedure 105, 106
    exceeding jurisdiction 105–6
    guidelines for national courts 106
    no genuine dispute 105
    preliminary ruling procedure 103–7
    time limit expired 105–6
    see also referrals
  sex discrimination interpretation 196
  single judgment only given 29
  source of law 35–6
  supremacy doctrine and 54–61, 62
  see also Advocates General
Criminal convictions 146, 149, 152, 154
Customs union 120, 125

Damages actions (Art.235) 95–9
  admissibility 96
  ascertainability of damage 98–9
  dependent actions 96
  locus standi 96
  manifest and grave 98
  seriousness of breach 97–8
  severity of damage 98
  superior rule of law 97
  time limits 96
Damages actions (Art.288) 227–9
  comparisons with Art.235 95–9
  locus standi 100
  manifest and grave 228

Damages actions – *continued*
  seriousness of breach 101–2, 103, 228–9
  superior rule of law 101, 102–3
De Gaulle, President Charles 8
Defences
  ensuring compliance with Art.226 81–6
  force majeure 83
  no legal interest remained 83
  overriding necessity 83
  reciprocity 83
Democracy 21–2, 26
Deportation 147–8, 151–5
  grounds 149–50
  mental health 150
  personal conduct 159
  previous convictions 146, 149, 154
  stay for month 148, 153, 156
Direct effects 38, 39–42, 60
  Directives 40–2, 44–50, 223
    non-implementation 46–7, 231–5
  horizontal 40, 43–7
  Regulations 39–42
  supremacy and 56, 57, 213–16
  vertical 43–7
Directives 41
  direct effects 40–2, 44–50, 223, 231–5
  implementation requirement 41
  individuals and 44–6
  non-implementation 46–7, 231–5
  public and private employment 44–6, 51
  sex discrimination 195
  see also Failure to comply with Directive; Failure to implement Directive
Directly applicable 37–9
Discrimination
  family status 200
  marital status 200
  positive 196, 199, 201–2, 204–5
  refusal to give reference 201
  sexual orientation 197
  transsexuals 202
  unfair dismissal of complainant 201, 205
  see also Sex discrimination
Distribution agreements
  exclusive 168–72
  selective 171–2
  vertical 179–80
Doctrine of direct effects *see* Direct effects
Doctrine of parliamentary sovereignty *see* Parliamentary sovereignty

Doctrine of supremacy *see* Supremacy of
  Community law
Dominant position abuse 173, 174, 175,
  179, 180–2, 186–90
Dualism 59, 60

Economic and monetary union 10, 12–13
Economic and Social Committee 23
Efficiency 20–1
Environmental protection, free movement of
  goods 131–2, 133–4, 135
Equal pay 194, 197–202
  pension payments as pay 206–7
  redundancy money counted as pay
    207–11
  work of equal value 200
Equal rights *see* Equal pay: Sex
  discrimination
Equivalence principle 137, 139–40
Establishment rights 142–3, 145
  establishment definition 148–9
  lawyers 161, 162, 163
  permanence 162–3
  professionals 150–1, 159–63
  qualification recognition 161
  self-employed persons 148–9
  service provision distinguished 161–3
European Atomic Community 8
European Coal and Steel Community
  (ECSC) 7
European Commission *see* Commission
European Communities Act 1972 63–4,
  65
  new legal order and 66
European Community
  federalism 12–13, 14–17
  historical analysis 6–9
  institutions *see individual institutions eg*
    Commission: Parliament
  integration *see* Integration
  meaning 2
  political motivation for setting up
    11–12
European Court of Human Rights, source of
  law 34
European Court of Justice *see* Court of
  Justice
European Economic Community 8
European Federal State 12–13
European Free Trade Area (EFTA) 8
European Parliament *see* Parliament
European Road Transport Agreement 33
European Union (EU), meaning 2
Exclusive distribution agreement 168–72

Failure to act (Art.232) 111–14, 219
  definition of position 113, 114
  duty to act 112
  explanation of refusal to act 113
  individuals 112
  invitation to act 113
  locus standi 112, 226–7
  time limits 113
Failure to comply with Directive
  arguments of state 232
  Commission action 231–2
  delays 232, 235
  interim measures 234
  prior Art 226 proceedings 234–5
  remedies 232–4
Failure to comply with obligations (Art.226)
  defences from member states 81–6
  ensuring compliance 77–81
  individuals 80, 84–6, 221–3
  reasoned opinions 78
  time limits 223
  see also Failure to comply with Directive;
    Failure to implement Directive
Failure to implement Directive
  compensation 233–4
  conditions for state liability 231–2
Federalism 12–13
  Council of Ministers as federal institution
    14–17
  meaning of federal 15
Floodgates argument 90
Food additives 124, 128
Force majeure defence 83
Free movement of goods 118–40
  bans on imports 123–4, 128, 131–5
  Cassis de Dijon case 118, 119, 122,
    128–9, 132, 134–40
  challenging Regulation against 225–9
  common customs tariff 120, 125
  consumer protection exception 128–30
  customs duties and charges 120, 125–6
  customs union 120, 125
  domestic products, equal treatment 122,
    124–5, 133–4, 137, 139–40
  environment protection 131–2, 133–4,
    135
  equivalence principle 122, 124–5, 134,
    137, 139–40
  exceptions 121–2, 128–30, 131, 136–7
  food additives 124, 128
  government assistance 125
  government sponsored advertising 124
  health protection restrictions 121, 124,
    125, 131, 133–4, 136

Free movement of goods – *continued*
  industrial and commercial property 121,
    137
  inspection charges 126–7, 130, 131
  internal market 119
  internal taxation measures 126, 128,
    130–1
  measures having equivalent effect
    120–1, 123–31, 136
  national marketing rules 124
  national treasure protection 121, 137
  parking fees 131
  Pharmaceutical Society rules 124
  physical trade barriers 125
  preservatives ban 129
  public health exception 121, 122,
    128–30, 131, 133–4, 136
  public interest 134
  public morality exception 121, 122, 136
  quantitative restrictions 120, 123–31,
    136
  quotas 123–4
  rule of reason 138, 139–40
  security exception 121, 122, 136
  'spot checks' for health reasons 125,
    126–7, 130, 131
  Sunday trading 138
Free movement of persons 141–63
  benefit claims 150, 151–3, 156, 158
  co-habitees 145, 149, 157–8
  companionship 145, 149
  criminal convictions 146, 149, 152,
    154
  dependants 155–9
  deportations *see* Deportation
  establishment 142–3, 145
    definition 149
    lawyers 161, 162, 163
    professionals 150–1, 159–63
    qualification recognition 161
    self-employed persons 148–9,
      153–63
  ex-spouses 152, 154
  family members 145, 146–7, 150,
    155–9
  internal market and 143
  job seekers 143, 144, 149, 157, 158
  liberal interpretation 144
  meaning of worker 148, 153
  mental health 150
  previous convictions 152, 154
  professionals 150–1, 159–63
  public or private employer 153
  public service provision 144

Free movement of persons – *continued*
  self-employed persons 143, 148–9,
    159–63
  service provision 142, 143, 145, 150,
    160
    establishment distinguished 161–3
    permanence 162–3
  social advantage 149, 150, 157–8
  spouses 145
  students 145
  teleological approach 144
  unemployed 143, 144
  vocational training courses 145
  workers 13, 142–59, 231–5
Freedom of establishment *see* Establishment
  rights
Freedom of movement of goods *see* Free
  movement of goods
Freedom of movement of persons *see* Free
  movement of persons
French courts, supremacy and 73–4

GATT agreements 33, 35
German courts, supremacy and 71–2
Goods, free movement *see* Free movement
  of goods

Health protection
  free movement of goods exception 121,
    124, 125, 130, 131, 133–4, 136
  spot checks 125, 126–7, 130, 131
Heath, Edward 8
Holiday entitlement 50, 51
House of Lords 68–70
Human rights, sources of law 34, 36

Illegality plea (Art.241) *see* Plea of illegality
  (Art.241)
Individuals, actions taken by 84–6,
  216–20
  Court of Justice and 89, 90–1
  failure to act (Art.232) 112–13
  failure to comply with obligations
    (Art.226) 80–1, 84–6, 221–3
  impact of Community on 218–19
  infringement of fundamental rights 220
  in national courts 80, 219–20, 223–5
Industrial property exception 121, 137
Inland Revenue, public-private status 51
Inspection charges 126–7, 130, 131
Institutions 13
  see also individual institutions eg Court
    of Justice: Parliament
Integration 10–14

Integration – *continued*
  functional 12
  political motivation 11–12
Internal market
  aims 119
  competition and 166
  definition 119
  free movement of workers and 142, 143
International agreements
  European Road Transport Agreement 33
  GATT 33, 35
  Lomé Conventions 33
  North Atlantic Fisheries Convention 33
  sources of law 33–6
  trade associations 33
  Yaoundé Convention 35
Interpretation 28
  referral to Court of Justice 103–7
  sex discrimination 196
  teleological 28–9, 144
Investigations (competition law) 182–6
  complaints 184
  disclosure of informants 184–6
  duty to assist 185
  failure to comply 185
  information requests 184
  notification of agreements 184
  powers and duties of Commission 183, 184
  professional privilege 185–6
  right of entry 184–5
Italian courts, supremacy and 72–3

Job seekers 143, 144, 149, 157, 158
Jurisdiction of Court of Justice 75–117
  see also Actions: Defences

Labour, as commodity 143
  see also Workers, free movement
Law making *see* Legislation
Lawyers
  freedom of establishment 161, 162, 163
  see also Professionals
Legal bases 22–6
  disputes 24–5
  qualified majority voting 24–5
Legal order 29–30
  new 54, 57–8, 60–1, 66
Legal professional privilege 185–6
Legislation
  co-decision procedure 17, 18, 19, 21–2
  common position 19
  conciliation procedure 17, 18–19, 23–4
  consultation process 16–17, 18, 23–4

Legislation – *continued*
  cooperation procedure 17, 18, 24
  Council of Ministers 15, 18
  Court of Justice law-making role 29–31
  legal base 22–6
  Parliament role 16–17, 18–19, 21–2
  procedures 18–19
  retroactive 90
  two-reading co-operation procedure 19
Legitimate expectation 95, 97
Locus standi
  challenging decisions or Regulations
    (Art.230) 86–95, 226–7
  damages actions (Art.235) 96
  damages actions (Art.288) 100
  failure to act (Art.232) 112, 226–7
  plea of illegality (Art.241) 116
  wrongful adoption of acts (Art.288) 100
  wrongful adoption of acts damages
    (Art.288) 100
Lomé Conventions 33

Maastricht negotiations 10, 11, 14
Macmillan, Harold 8
Marital status discrimination 200
Maternity discrimination 201
Maudling, Reginald 8
Mental disability, free movement of persons
  150
Mergers 173, 176–82, 188–90
Merits of actions 88, 89, 94
Migrant workers 231–5
Monism 59, 60

National courts
  actions by individuals in 80, 219–20,
    221–5
  guidelines for referrals to Court of Justice
    106
  migrant workers 231–5
  sex discrimination claims 202, 207
National treasures exception 121, 137
New legal order 54, 57–8, 60–1, 66
Nice 2000 conference 22
Non-discrimination 36
Non-privileged applicants 86, 92
North Atlantic Fisheries Convention 33
North Atlantic Treaty Organisation
  (NATO) 7

Opt-outs 10
Organisation for European Economic
  Cooperation (OEEC) 7
Overriding necessity defence 83

Parental leave   195
Parking fees   131
Parliament   13, 16
  Art.232 complaint against Council   114
  budget procedures   19–20, 21
  consultation process   16–17, 18, 23–4
  democracy   21–2, 26
  efficiency   20–1
  elections   16
  legal base   23–4, 25–6
  legislative role   16–17, 18–19, 21–2
  membership   16
  powers   16–17
  sovereignty see Parliamentary
    sovereignty
  veto power   21
Parliamentary sovereignty
  European Communities Act 1972   63–4,
    65
  limitations to   63
  meaning   63
  supremacy and   61–5, 66–8, 70
Part time work
  redundancies   205–6
  sex discrimination   197–201, 204–7
Pay
  holiday entitlement as   50, 51
  pensions payment as   206–7
Penalty payments   79–80
Pensions
  equal treatment   44–5, 47–51
  free movement of persons and   150
  payments as pay   206–7
  retroactivity   210–11
  sex discrimination   206–7
  Social Security payments   207–11
Persons, free movement see Free movement
  of persons
Pharmaceutical Society, rules against
  product substitution   124
Plea of illegality (Art.241)   115–17, 227
  locus standi   116
  time limits   116–17, 229
Political motivation
  conversion into integration   13
  for setting up Community   11–12
Precedent   29
Pregnancy discrimination   201
Previous convictions   146, 149, 152, 154
Pricing agreements   171, 176, 177–82
Privilege   185–6
Professional privilege   185–6
Professionals   150–1, 159–63
  lawyers   161, 162, 163

Professionals – continued
  qualification recognition   161
Public health exception, free movement of
  goods   121, 122, 128–30, 131, 133–4,
    136
Public morals, free movement of goods
  exception   121, 136
Public sector   44–6, 51
Public security, free movement of goods
  exception   121, 122

Qualification recognition   161
Qualified majority voting   24–5

Reason, rule of   138, 139–40
Reasoned opinions   27–8, 78
Reciprocity   83
Redundancies
  part time work   205–6
  redundancy money counted as pay
    207–11
Reference to Court of Justice see Court of
  Justice
Referendum   8
Referrals (Art.234)   107–11
  obligation or discretion to refer   110
  recognition of court   108
  refusal to accept   103–7
Regulations
  challenging   86–95, 219, 225–9
  direct effect   38, 39–42
  directly applicable   37–9
  meaning   40–1
  plea of illegality (Art.241)   115–17
  publication   41
  self-executing   37
  see also Challenging decisions or
    Regulations (Art.230)
Retirement
  age discrimination   68, 195, 211
  equal treatment   44–5, 47–51
  pension rights   206
Retroactive legislation   90
Rule of reason   138, 139–40

Schuman, Robert   7
Schuman Plan   7
Security, free movement of goods exception
  121, 122, 136
Selective distribution agreement   171–2
Service provision freedom   142, 143, 145,
  150, 160
  establishment distinguished   161–3
Sex discrimination   191–211

Sex discrimination – *continued*
  Amsterdam Treaty and 196–7, 199, 204
  Court of Justice case law 207–11
  Directives 195
  equal pay 194, 197–202
  indirect discrimination 196, 198, 200, 204
  individual enforcement 195–6
  interpretation by Court of Justice 196
  job evaluation scheme 200
  justification 200, 205
  national agencies 196
  national tribunal claims 202, 207
  parental leave 195
  part time work 197–201, 204–7
  pensions and retirement 44–5, 47–51, 68, 195, 206, 207
  positive 196, 199, 201–2, 204–5
  pregnancy and maternity 201
  reasons for inclusion in Treaty 193–7
  redundancies
    part time work 205–6
    pay 207–11
  refusal to give reference 201
  retirement *see* pensions and retirement
  'saving' clause 205
  selection procedure 205
  sexual orientation 197
  transsexuals 202
  unfair dismissal of complainant 201, 205
Sexual orientation discrimination 197
Single European Act 15, 16–17
Single European Treaty 11
Social Action Programme 195
Social Policy 10, 13
Social rights
  reasons for inclusion in Treaty 193–7
  see also Sex discrimination
Social Security
  free movement and benefit claims 150, 151–3, 156, 158
  pension payments 207–11
Sources of law
  common law 34
  constitutions of States 34
  Court of Justice 35–6
  EEC-Portugal association agreement 35
  European Court of Human Rights 34
  fundamental rights 34
  general principles 34
  human rights 34, 36
  international agreements 33–6
  natural law principles 34

Sources of law – *continued*
  secondary sources 40–1
    see also Directives: Regulations
  third country agreements 35
Spaak Report 8
Spouses of workers 145
  ex-spouses 152, 154
Students 145
Substance of action 88, 89, 94
Sunday trading 138
Supremacy of Community law
  Court of Justice and 54–61, 62
  direct effects 56, 57, 213–16
  European Communities Act 1972 63–4, 65
  inference from treaties 53–7, 62
  national constitutions 55–6
  national law
    incompatible 56
    prior 54
    subsequent 55, 58–9, 60–1
  parliamentary sovereignty and 61–5, 66–8, 70

Thatcher, Margaret 9
Time limits
  challenging decisions or Regulations 92–3, 226
  damages actions 96
  failure to act 113
  failure to comply with obligations 223
  plea of illegality 116–17, 229
  refusal to accept reference 105–6
Transsexuals, discrimination against 202
Treaties
  renumbering 3
  supremacy of law inferred from 53–7, 62

Voting, qualified majority 24–5

Wilson, Harold 8
Wrongful adoption of acts (Art.288) 99–103, 227–9
  breach of duty 100
  breach of superior rule 101, 102–3
  choice of court 100–1
  damages
    comparisons with Art.235 95–9
    locus standi 100
    manifest and grave 228
    seriousness of breach 101–2, 103, 228–9
  locus standi requirements 100

Wrongful adoption of acts (Art. 288)
  – *continued*
  manifest and grave   101
  numbers of people affected   102

Wrongful adoption of acts (Art. 288)
  – *continued*
  seriousness of breach   101–2, 103,
    228–9
  superior rule of law   101, 102–3